D0983002

TOWARD AN ANTHROPOLOGY
OF THE WILL

TOWARD AN ANTHROPOLOGY OF THE WILL

Edited by Keith M. Murphy

and C. Jason Throop

Stanford University Press
Stanford, California

Stanford University Press
Stanford, California

Library of Congress Cataloging-in-Publication Data
Toward an anthropology of the will / edited by Keith M. Murphy and C. Jason
Throop.
       p.   cm.
   Includes bibliographical references and index.
   ISBN 978-0-8047-6887-0 (cloth : alk. paper)
   1. Will—Anthropological aspects.   2. Act (Philosophy)   3. Cognition
and culture.   4. Personality and culture.   5. Ethnopsychology.   I. Murphy,
Keith M.   II. Throop, C. Jason.
   BF611.T69 2010
   302′.1—dc22

                                                              2009025678

Typeset by Motto Publishing Services in 10.5/15 Adobe Garamond

CONTENTS

TOWARD AN ANTHROPOLOGY
OF THE WILL

CHAPTER I

WILLING CONTOURS

Locating Volition in
Anthropological Theory
Keith M. Murphy and C. Jason Throop

T HERE IS A LONGSTANDING TRADITION
in Americanist anthropology to engage in psychologi-
cally oriented research in efforts to expand our understanding of the cultural and personal patterning of subjective experience. From dreaming to
reasoning, desiring to thinking, motivation to internalization, psychological
anthropologists have interrogated the nuanced nature of subjective life as a
means for destabilizing many taken-for-granted assumptions about what it
means to experience the world as social actors. At the core of this enterprise
sits a motivated interest to question what psychologists, philosophers, and
other human scientists view to be the basic faculties, processes, and contents
of subjective life (cf. Biehl, Good, and Kleinman 2007). Somewhat paradoxically, however, when engaging the problem of culture and subjective life, it
is still largely the case that psychological anthropology, and the discipline

of anthropology more generally, has often relied (at least tacitly) upon an analytical model, inherited from philosophy, that partitions human behavior into three main categories: cognition (which encompasses knowledge), emotion (which includes feelings, moods, and affects), and volition (including desires, choices, and proclivities to act—cf. D'Andrade 1987).

Also quite perplexing is the fact that although most anthropologists are comfortable discussing the relationship between culture and cognition and culture and emotion (in the various ways these aspects of subjective experience are understood), it seems that we have not yet explicitly and systematically set our sights (or our sites) on how culture and volition are, broadly speaking, interconnected. The impetus for this volume thus stems directly from what we perceive as a need to better foreground and engage a comparatively under-examined aspect of subjective life in cultural context, what we in Anglophone academic traditions label the "will."

To be sure, in highlighting the fact that volition has not yet been singled out for *explicit* and *systematic* discussion by psychological anthropologists does not mean to imply that psychological anthropology, nor anthropology more broadly, has entirely ignored the topic. Perhaps anthropologists and other social scientists have indeed concerned themselves with volition all along—even if only tangentially—describing both the most fundamental and most esoteric qualities of human will, but using a different vocabulary. When psychological anthropologists discuss subjectivity, desire, motivation, action, consciousness, and self; when linguistic anthropologists talk about agency and intentionality; and even in some cases when sociocultural anthropologists discuss embodiment, power, resistance, and struggle, we are all probably indirectly touching upon, or even outright addressing, the act and experience of willing—perhaps without characterizing it as such. Indeed, within the anthropological literature a significant web of inquiry seems to surround the will, its constituents, and its effects that is translucent enough to see something caught inside, but still too opaque to sharply reveal its formal contours.[1]

Most anthropological research that has addressed topics related to volition can fit into one of two broad categories. The first approach can be called "culture as a barrier to volition." According to this perspective, culture—in the form of cultural models, norms, values, and crucially, language and linguistic structure—is, in a sense, imposed on the free will of individuals, constraining not necessarily the topics they choose to talk about, think about, and care about, but certainly the ways in which those topics are able to infiltrate everyday actions. Just as speakers are largely restricted to expressing themselves via the grammatical structures implicit in a shared language, so too can individuals only act within culturally sanctioned parameters. In other words, like language, culture is impervious to the will of ordinary people—and, it follows, will is always tethered to culture.

The second, more flexible approach, what William James would term "soft determinism," can be called the "culture as a sculptor of volition" perspective. Adherents to this point of view treat culture as *influencing* or *facilitating* how we think about, and more important for the current discussion, how we actually behave toward the world around us. Individuals are not necessarily limited by cultural structures, but instead operate most comfortably within them in a largely taken-for-granted manner. Culture gives us some of the categories with which we make sense of our environments, and we tend to behave primarily, but not necessarily exclusively, according to them.

However, what we offer with this volume is something different. All of the authors have abandoned—or at least bracketed off—exploring volition strictly within such traditional frameworks. Instead, most of the authors have refocused their studies on how culturally specific understandings of will interact with, and are often constituted by, a range of other phenomena that, though they may be universally or near-universally present, all accrue their own culturally relevant elaborations. What has emerged from these studies is an emphasis not on how volition relates broadly to culture (and its general tendency to restrict or otherwise impinge upon courses of action in everyday life), but instead on how volition is inextricably linked to local understandings of such categories as *temporality*, *narrative*, and *responsibility*. Moreover, several cases presented in this volume highlight the significance of will for individuals navigating between the world of everyday social relations and space- and time-shifted states of *irrealis*, such as imagination and dreaming.

Our goals for this volume are modest. We are pushing for a closer examination of the concept of will within a specifically anthropological framework. We urge more explicitness with terminology. Perhaps *agency* and *intentionality* do the work of *will* well enough, and we are squeezing into an already over-crowded field. However, what we are attempting to do here is test whether more rigorous forays into theorizing the will can benefit our anthropological endeavors. The chapters in this volume all approach the will in different ways with very different kinds of data and questions. What emerges from all of them, however, is a series of challenging questions for all of us to consider: Is the will a useful anthropological concept? What forms does it take? Can it be said to be a universal? Where is it located? How is willing experienced? How does it relate to emotion and cognition? How is imagination implicated in acts of willing? What is the connection between morality, virtue, and willing? Can there be specified pathologies of the will?

Before we proceed in attempting to answer these questions, however, we would like to take some time to explore more thoroughly the ways in which social science—and anthropology specifically—has teased out the "culture as barrier to" and "culture as sculptor of" positions on volition. However, what follows in this introduction is not intended to be an exhaustive archaeology of all the work that has gone into analyzing the form, function, and overall nature of the will or volition in anthropology or the social sciences more generally. It is more moderately intended to open a generative space for future dialogue about the will from an anthropological frame. That said, any dialogue concerning the development of an anthropology of the will cannot be properly undertaken without some shared understanding of the historical and contextual basis for current discussions of will in the social sciences and elsewhere. It is thus toward this goal that we will first turn.

Our first step is to lay out a brief analysis of the etymology of the English term *will* as a way to highlight possible sedimented assumptions about its meaning in English-speaking North American and European academic communities. Following this we highlight briefly two basic philosophical approaches to the will before examining the will in early modern social theory. We then shift to anthropology proper to explore what we regard to be two of the most generative approaches to willing in contemporary culture theory, namely, practice theoretical and psychocultural variants of anthropology. This chapter then concludes by discussing the contributors' chapters in terms of four recurring themes that are raised throughout the volume.

ACTION AND VOLITION IN HISTORICAL PERSPECTIVE

The Semantic View of Will

The concept of the will is implicated in topics that run the gamut from explorations of subjective experience, desire, and choice to the examination of power, social structure, and resistance. This broad topical range is at least partially attributable to the term's concomitant range of diverse denotative and connotative associations. It may not be too much of a stretch to think that the various everyday definitional associations of *will* in the English language can be at least partially credited for diluting the development of a concerted focus upon the phenomenon of willing by anthropologists writing and working in English-speaking European and North American contexts.[2]

The noun form of the English word *will* traces back to at least the Old English form *willa*, and means, according to the Oxford English Dictionary, a "desire, wish, longing; liking, inclination, [or] disposition (to do something)," with the additional sense of an "action of willing or choosing to do something; the movement or attitude of the mind which is directed with conscious intention to (and, normally, issues immediately in) some action, physical or mental." A long list representing graded shades of this general definition is also attached to the noun *will*, but it seems simple enough to acknowledge that the boundaries of its semantic domain are clear, if perforated.

The verb form, however, is more complicated. While the modern English verb "to will" means to "desire, wish for, have a mind to, 'want' (something)," its more common usage is as a simple auxiliary verb used to express the future tense. In both senses there is a certain directedness toward the future, either as a directedness toward acquiring some thing or state of affairs or as an explicit grammatical marker of the future tense. The related Old English verb form is *wille*, and the tendency for *will* to serve syntactically as an auxiliary verb (though not necessarily always marking future tense) has been around at least since Anglo-Saxon times and persists in other Germanic languages, such as modern Swedish and German. The difference, however, is the degree to which these languages typically encode "desire" and futurity in the word. Swedish *vilja*, for example (expressed as *vill* in the present tense) and German *wollen* (expressed as an inflected *will* in the present tense) both have a meaning of "to want" that is more strictly bounded than in English. Much like English, however, these forms have migrated to auxiliary verb status. Although in Swedish and German the semantics of these terms retains an element of directedness in the intentionality inherent in the act of desiring something, in English the unmarked form of *will* has come to mark mere futurity.

In these other languages, and less commonly in English, future tense is encoded with a different auxiliary verb, variants of the English *shall* (Old English *sceal*). Unlike *will*, which has historically implied an individual's inborn desire to act in the world, *shall*, until relatively recently, has signaled almost the complete opposite, a sense of assurance that some set of events will take place beyond the control of the speaker. This sense remains in Swedish, for instance, where a future tense shaded in certainty is expressed with *skall* (*ska* in everyday speech), and the simple future is generally expressed with the present tense (the same is common in German as well). Note that while this is still possible with the present progressive aspect in English (e.g., "I'm playing baseball tomorrow afternoon"), the strict division of the future tense into different degrees of certainty and control over the outcomes of action was once a much more common element of the language.

Two last points. In other Germanic languages *will* is related to words for choosing and choice, for instance *välja*, "to choose" in modern Swedish, and *wählen*, "to choose" in modern German. Additionally, *will* also most likely shares a common root with the English "well" (*väl* in modern Swedish), whose earliest meanings implied a sense of morally correct behavior (cf. Good, Garro, this volume).

What emerges from this constellation of features drawn from the linguistic biography of the word *will* is a tumultuous path—largely unreckoned by contemporary speakers—of semantic and syntactic shifts that obscure potentially helpful facts that might aid us in understanding the utility of "the will" as a philosophical and anthropological concept. Historically the lexical form *will* implies choice, it implies an inborn ability to act in the world—as opposed to the lexical form *shall*, which implies external influences on action—and early on it may also have encoded a feeling that one's voluntary actions are morally weighted. Embedded in these various meanings are notions of futurity, desire, obligation, morality, control, and differing degrees of certainty regarding one's ability to engage in and accomplish a particular act.

This rich semantic field thus includes connotations ranging from inner subjective life to external social dictates. Such various definitions and uses of *will* in English are certainly suggestive of why the term has proven to hold such a precarious place in contemporary culture theory. That said, even despite this conceptual complexity, there is one dimension of willing suggested in this etymological examination that has proven to captivate the imaginations of anthropologists and other social scientists, namely, past and ongoing debates over personal choice and external determinacy in human action.

The Argument from Philosophy

The development of modern social scientific approaches to subjectivity that touch upon some concept of willing follow a similar trajectory to what philosophers have been debating for centuries. In general terms, philosophers have understood the will to refer to the "faculty, or set of abilities, that yields the mental events involved in volition," where volition is understood to be "a mental event involved with the initiation of action" (Brand 1995, 843). As a faculty responsible for generating mental events embedded in the initiation of action, philosophical accounts of willing have often focused on examining processes that potentially impact the translation of such subjective states into expressive forms.

To this end, philosophers have traditionally distinguished between two main points of view on willing that pivot precisely on the relative freedom or determinacy of human action, namely *compatibilism* and *incompatibilism* (see Tomberlin 2001). Those who subscribe to *incompatibilism*—the philosopher's equivalent to culture as a barrier to volition—believe that determinism, whether stemming from divine, biological, or social sources, and free will cannot work together. For instance, if all human action is stimulated by prior events in the world, then truly free will cannot exist (cf. Van Inwagen 1983). Incompatiblism can thus lead to hard determinist claims that, for example, even such seemingly trivial behaviors as scratching my nose or winking my eye (or, for that matter, sending a conspiratorial signal to a friend) are not performed because I *choose* to, but rather because the series of events in which I have found myself over time have left these actions as the only possible ones I can take. Note, however, that supporters of hard determinism and radical free will are both considered to be incompatibilists since, despite their having diametrically opposing views on the efficacy and ontological status of the will, they both equally share in the view that determinism and free will are mutually exclusive existential possibilities.

Compatibilists, on the other hand, argue that notions of free will and determinism are not necessarily irreconcilable and that there is possibility for both constraint and flexibility in human action (cf. Ricoeur 1966). They argue that behavior must be at least partially determined, for if it were not, and total free will prevailed, we would all, analysts and our informants alike, lose the power to gauge and understand with some degree of certainty the actions of those around us. Similarly, this position maintains that there must be some modicum of free will in the midst of determining conditions. Otherwise all human behavior would be completely predictable given adequate access to the causal circumstances surrounding it. As a means of compromise, compatibilists argue that individuals are presented with a finite number of predetermined alternatives from which they have the ability to choose a next course of action.

Both positions concern issues of reason and causation. Incompatibilism situates causation either completely within or completely beyond the power of the individual. Depending on whether or not an individual supports a notion of radical free will or hard determinism, the role of rational thought becomes rendered either a definitive human capacity or little more than a byproduct of how social life is structured. Compatibilism, however, actually requires some understanding, however mitigated, of rational human beings. Without the capacity to think about the justifications for and consequences of a decided-upon course of action, compatibilists argue that there would be no reason to postulate something more than determining circumstances. Therefore willing as such would not need to exist.

Hard distinctions between compatibilist and incompatibilist positions are not always fully representative of a particular philosopher's approaches to willing, however. For instance while both Karl Marx (1990) and Jean-Paul Sartre (1984) can be viewed as supporting their own version of compatibilist philosophies that take individuals to be simultaneously determined and

determining social actors, there are particular aspects of their respective positions that at times reveal incompatibilist hues. For instance, Marxian *false
consciousness* highlights the extent to which perceived willful action is instead
determined by social dictates. In contrast, Sartrean *bad faith* takes the opposite tack in emphasizing the degree to which social actors misrecognize the
freedom and efficacy of their will in light of putatively determining social
contexts. Both thinkers thus situate incompatiblist claims in the midst of a
historically dynamic understanding of human action.

The same argument holds true in the social sciences, where scholars have
long debated the extent and degree to which social structure impinges on the
actions of individuals. While anthropological discussions, like their philosophical counterparts, tend to hinge on the tension between freedom and
determinacy, they are seldom couched within the rhetorical calculus used in
philosophy. Instead, this dichotomy subsists within broader discourses fundamental to anthropological endeavors. For instance, those concerning the
role of the individual in society, culture and the patterning of thought and
action, and even those attempting to parse out what is "natural" from what
is "cultural" in human behavior. Despite these numerous discussions of the
relative freedom and determinacy of human action, however, and countless
others, *willing as an experience of acting subjects* has yet to emerge as an explicit target of investigation for many anthropologists.

Volition in Early Modern Social Theory

The position of volition in modern social theory has largely pivoted on a
struggle to articulate the place of individual subjectivity in relation to
broader social, economic, and political forces. One of the most influential
accounts of willing in this regard, an account that was deeply influenced by
Arthur Schopenhauer's (1958) philosophy of the will and of representation,
is found in Sigmund Freud's attempts to de-center the subject of experience.
Freud (1989) accomplishes such a decentering of the subject, and thus of the
will, through his development of a metapsychology that postulates an always
antagonistic relationship between individual and society. More specifically,
Freud argues that there exist multiple forms of subjection and violence that
are brought to bear in the formation of a subject who becomes internally di-

vided against him- or herself. In this view, cultural life is held to be a form of social suffering that emplaces the individual between the dangers of nature, sickness, and death on the one hand, and the dangers of an individual's "situation among his fellow men," on the other (Ricoeur 1970, 250; Freud 1989). In Freud's theories of subjectivity, desire, and the unconscious, what we are incapable of saying, of knowing about ourselves, is ironically most intimately tied to what drives our actions. That which we can say, what we do know of ourselves, is most distant from it.

The interplay between the various psychic structures postulated in Freud's metapsychology is further implicated in problematizing the act of willing (Freud 1960, 2000). Anything that might otherwise be recognized as an observable volitional act on the part of a given social actor is realized in the midst of a complex and ambivalent set of negotiations, Freud argues. This includes negotiations and conflicts between the ego in its role as representative of the external world; the id as motivated by desire, narcissism, and pleasure; and the internalizing of the social surround through the moral imperatives of the superego. It is, accordingly, the experience of being internally divided according to multiple registers of experience, one of signification, one of moral imperatives, and one of desire, that Freud most potently displaces possibilities for conscious volitional acts.

Similarly influenced by Schopenhaur's philosophy, Emile Durkheim's (1979, 1984) early work on collective representations, collective consciousness, and social facts set out to establish both the analytic autonomy and constitutive impact of social forms on individual consciousness. Durkheim subsequently shifted attention in his later writings to the potential complexities entailed in such articulations by arguing that human beings are fundamentally constituted as *Homo duplex*, or "double" (1995, 15–16). Simply put, Durkheim suggested that the individual consists of two parts: (1) an impersonal (social, moral) principle that is collectively shared and tied to the functioning of the intellect as mediated through collective representations; and (2) an individuating principle tied to the immediate experiences of the senses, the emotions, and the body (cf. Freud 1989). While he never explicitly examined how such a duality of consciousness may directly impact social action and the individual's will, he did admit that social forms are always mediated through "bodies . . . [that are] distinct and occupy a specific position in time/space—each is a special milieu in which the collective represen-tations are gradually refracted and colored differently" (Durkheim 1995, 273), a strong note in support of an early, body-based concept of the will.

The complexities inherent in Freud's and Durkheim's social theories are, as noted above, also evident in Marx (1990). On the one hand, Marx's dis-cussion of false consciousness holds that individual actors are fundamentally blind to the ways in which their putatively willful action is in fact the result of broader social and economic forces. On the other hand, his emancipatory and utopian views of the resolution and effacement of class conflict attempts to establish a correspondence between individual will and social will. For Marx, the rise of class consciousness—made possible through the inequi-ties inherent in capitalist modes of production—leads to the potential rev-olutionary processes ideally returning efficacy to concrete embodied social actors who are no longer falsely alienating their own will to abstract politi-cal ends.

In dialogue with both Durkheimian and Marxist accounts of social ac-tion, Max Weber approached the question of willing in his account of the role of choice in relationship to rational action (cf. Schutz 1967; Throop, Chap-ter 2). For Weber, individual motivation to engage in a particular course of action is necessarily rooted in a complex of subjective meanings "which seem to the actor himself or to an observer an adequate ground for the conduct in question" (Weber 1978, 11). What exactly is entailed in choosing to engage in a particular act is thus rooted for Weber in cultural meanings and values that are subjectively taken up by actors as resources for interpreting their given social situation and the possible actions that are afforded by them. In distin-guishing between four ideal types of social action, Weber proceeds to point out the differing ways that the will may be oriented to specific courses of action. In *instrumental rational action*, an actor's will is determined by expec-tations concerning the appropriate means and conditions for attaining "the actor's own rationally pursued and calculated ends" (1978, 24). *Value-rational action*, in contrast, is structured such that the will is oriented to a value "for its own sake of some ethical, aesthetic, religious, or other form of behavior, independently of its prospects of success" (1978, 25). Finally, in *affective action* and *traditional action*, the will is determined by an actor's feeling states and "ingrained habits" respectively (1978, 25).

Anthropology and Agency

Contemporary anthropology's relationship to volition is arguably built more on flirtation than commitment, though a flirtation all too often left largely unexplored.[3] Psychological anthropology, linguistic anthropology, and sociocultural anthropology have, in their own ways, theorized around the topic of volition without explicitly categorizing the work as such. Whether it is in terms of examining differing cultural perspectives on "intentions," "motives," and "internal states" in relationship to social action (e.g., Rosen 1995; Shweder 1984; White and Kirkpatrick 1985), exploring "intentionality" and "agency" in talk and interaction (e.g., Ahearn 2001; Duranti 1988, 1993a, 1993b, 2006; Kockelman 2007; Ochs and Schieffelin 1984), discussing extended, mitigated, or disavowed agency in the context of divination, spirit possession, or exchange (e.g., DuBois 1987; Lambek 1981, 1993, 2003; Munn 1986; Strathern 1988), or those few existing explicit discussions of cultural configurations of will (e.g., Lohmann 2003; Robbins 2004), anthropologists have certainly made some important contributions to narrowing in on a nuanced cultural understanding of volition.

But perhaps the closest we get to an actual rigorous engagement with volition is in two contemporary sources: the North American versions of practice theory as exemplified in the work of Sherry Ortner (1984), Jean Comaroff (1985), Jean and John Comaroff (1992), William Hanks (1990), and Marshall Sahlins (1981, 1985, 1995), among others, and in psychocultural anthropology, in the work of Roy D'Andrade (1987), Melford Spiro (1997), Claudia Strauss (1992), Dorothy Holland (1992), again, among others. It is thus to practice theoretical and psychological anthropological perspectives on the will that we now turn.

Practice, Action, and Volition. Examining everyday life through the lens of praxis is, at its core, an attempt to integrate macro-level social theory with a close examination of *in situ* activities and behaviors without falling prey to the pernicious solipsism that sometimes accompanies analyses of individual experience. Pierre Bourdieu (1977, 2000), taking his inspiration in no small part from Marx, Levi-Strauss, and the phenomenologists (see Throop and Murphy 2002; Throop, Chapter 2), has arguably been the most widely influential source of practice theory for American anthropology. Other French scholars, notably Foucault, DeCerteau, and Lefebvre—often interpreted as devout compatibilists—have also left their marks on the field. In all, practice theorists have largely sought out an understanding of will from the stand-point of the dialectic of internalized and externalized structures that are em-bodied as perduring predispositions to act, think, appreciate, judge, feel, and desire in socially particular ways.

For Pierre Bourdieu (1977) the question of volition is embedded in his understanding of the interrelationship between everyday practices, pre-given social structures and the generative internalized tendencies to engage in culturally expected forms of social action. In advancing the concept of *habitus*—the so-called structured structure that is a structuring structure—Bourdieu attempts to account for the ways in which human agents actively constitute and reconstitute social structure through practice.

Although many have characterized Bourdieu as an "agency theorist," the role of the will in Bourdieu's understanding of human agency, in as much as it exists at all, is forcefully framed in deterministic terms (c.f. Throop and Murphy 2002; Throop Chapter 2). Indeed, Bourdieu is highly critical of so-cial theories that attempt to portray social actors as engaged in conscious forms of decision-making that are explicitly oriented to social rules. Bourdieu views such a characterization of social action as a mistaken attribution of the perspective of a social theorist, who is attempting to understand social action from their third-person perspective, for the first-person lived experience of social actors who are enmeshed in ongoing social action (cf. Schutz 1967). According to Bourdieu the "choice" to act in a particular way, in particu-lar circumstances, in particular "social fields," is tied to the correspondences between the affordances enabled by such constraints and the structure of the individual's habitual ways of perceiving, appreciating, evaluating, and feeling that have themselves been informed by the social structures within which they are enacted.

Very much in line with Bourdieu's perspective, Marshal Sahlins's (1981, 1985, 1995) theory of practice views social action as significantly dictated by, and at the mercy of, pre-existing cultural categories and not as a product of an individual's free will. Indeed, it is only in the intersubjective constitu-tion of events, the different social positions of various actors, the multiplex meaning-structures utilized in the interpretation of experience, and the unintended consequences of intended action that Sahlins is able to account for change in the unfolding of an event. Influenced by French structuralism, both Saussurean and Levi-Straussian varieties, Sahlins (1981) argues for the generative influence of "structures of conjuncture" as a means to account for change in historical processes that are significantly canalized by the pregiven cultural categories informing individual choice, interpretation, and action.[4]

While it seems that the will is, in a generous reading, difficult to locate in the writings of Bourdieu and Sahlins, as Sherry Ortner (2006) has suggested, such perspectives arose precisely as a means to counter what were three prevalent "theories of constraint" evidenced in the culture theory of the 1970s: Geertzian symbolic anthropology, Marxist political economy, and Levi-Straussian structuralism. In each of these perspectives, it was held that human action is "shaped, molded, ordered, and defined by external social and cultural forces and formations: by culture, by mental structures, by capitalism" (Ortner 2006, 2). And it was largely to correct this striking absence of "agency" that Bourdieu's and Sahlins's versions of practice theory putatively first arose.

One notable counterpoint in which some of these practice theoretical arguments have been extended to an explicit discussion of willing in anthropology can be found in the work of Joel Robbins (2004). Working with Sahlins's distinction between prescriptive and performative structures—the former referring to indigenous models of social life that see social forms generating appropriate forms of action, the latter referring to those in which "appropriate kinds of action create social forms" (Robbins 2004, 189)—Robbins suggests societies subscribing to one or another of these orientations to social life may have very different understandings of social action.

According to Robbins, societies that are oriented to prescriptive structures will have highly detailed elaborations of the structures of social life (e.g., elaborate kinship systems, laws, regulations, etc). Those that are oriented to performative structures, on the other hand, "will generally also possess very complex ideas about action: what motivates it, how it is carried out, and so on" (2004, 190). For some societies this complexity is rendered in terms of a language of mental acts in the form of "love," "will," "desire," or "conscience." For others, it is evident in the language of "substances" in the form of "food," "blood," or "semen" that are exchanged in the service of creating and maintaining social relationships. In the case of the Urap-min, with whom Robbins conducted his field work, the foundations of social thinking are rooted in the idea that "social life is created by people acting out of their willful desires while taking into account the way these desires are constrained by the lawful expectations that inhere in already accomplished social relations" (2004, 190).

Psychological Anthropology and Willing. Alongside practice theory, con-temporary psychocultural anthropological research and theorizing provides some of the most explicit accounts of the will to have been addressed from an anthropological perspective. This is perhaps not surprising given that it is most often psychological anthropologists who wish to critique what Ort-ner has characterized as the relative "thinness" of both cultural and practice theoretical approaches to social action that tend to "slight the question of subjectivity, that is, the view of the subject as existentially complex, a being who feels and thinks and reflects, who makes and seeks meaning" (Ortner 2006, 110). For psychological anthropologists who have engaged the topic of willing (both implicitly and explicitly), however, it is often the case that ex-periences associated with willing are reduced to more primal determinants: internal drives, needs, inclinations, and wants on the one hand, and cognitive models, cultural frames, and shared meanings on the other (see D'Andrade and Strauss 1992).

Roy D'Andrade (1987) has offered what is perhaps one of the most ex-plicit treatments of willing in psychological anthropology. According to D'Andrade, the North American folk model of the mind is comprised of a number of different mental processes and states, including: perceptions; beliefs/knowledge; feelings/emotions; desires/wishes; intentions; and resolu-tion, will, or self control. D'Andrade's account of these differing states is a complex one, so we will confine ourselves to merely outlining some of the basic distinctions that most pertain to the topic at hand, namely, distinc-tions between desires, intentions, and resolutions. D'Andrade defines in-tentional states as those states in which an individual anticipates a future state of affairs in light of some goal. In contrast, he characterizes desires as affective responses to intentional states. Desires can thus be distinguished from both wishes, which are conceptual responses to intentional states, and needs, which are the pregiven physical or emotional drives to fulfill certain intentions.

In the folk model, then, desires and intentions are different sorts of phenomena, since "one can have desires about which one intends to do nothing" (D'Andrade 1987, 121) and one can do something intentionally without understanding what their motives or desires are for acting in such a way in the first place (1987, 120). According to D'Andrade, intentions are not qualitatively different from resolutions, given that both causally arise within the mind, assume the self as a necessary agent of action, are controllable mental events, may be multiple, and are oriented to future states of affairs and goals. The difference between them lies in the fact that "resolutions are second-order intentions—intentions to keep certain other intentions despite difficulty and opposing desires" (1987, 117). Notable here is the specificity of D'Andrade's account of willing and the extent to which it is markedly different from previous debates over the relative freedom and determinacy of human action.

Another significant contribution to psychological anthropological accounts of the will is found in the psychoanalytically inspired work of Melford Spiro, who argues that volitional action is that which is "motivated by the desire to express a sentiment or to fill a need" (1997, 80). To arrive at this definition, Spiro, much like D'Andrade, distinguishes between a number of different mental states, including needs, sentiments, aims, wishes, goals, and desires. Where "needs" refer to "any event, condition, or state of affairs that an actor feels necessary for personal physical or psychological well-being" (1997, 74), "sentiments" are tied to a combination of emotions and the relevant objects toward which particular emotions are oriented (1997, 75).

Individual actors may entertain competing needs and sentiments that may arouse the desire to realize such needs and sentiments in differing acts, Spiro explains. For this reason, the ability to choose between possible competing acts is what is meant by the term "aim" (1997, 79). "Wishes" refer to mental states that are aroused by needs and sentiments but are implicated in the desire to "achieve not just any kind of event, condition, or state of affairs but a particular kind" (1997, 79–80). Simply put, both aims and wishes are varieties of desire. Whereas a desire to *achieve* something is a wish, the desire to *do* something is an aim, with "the latter being a function of the former" (1997, 84).

According to this view, similar needs and sentiments can arouse a variety of wishes, which complicates the connection between possible aims directed toward differing courses of action. The choice between specific aims is, in Spiro's view, motivated by the expectations that certain aims will better fulfill particular wishes. The way particular wishes are translated into goals—that is, the way wishes are imagined to be fulfilled by specific aims and the acts toward with such aims intend—may be informed by both culturally constituted and privately constructed schemas, Spiro maintains (1997, 82).

Of particular interest for a theory of willing (cf. Groark, Chapter 5; Mageo, Chapter 6), however, is the psychoanalytically informed contention that psychologically threatening forms of desire may be actively repressed and thus rendered unconscious. That unconscious desires directly affect the course of otherwise volitional acts is at the basis for Spiro's further development of what Groark (Chapter 5), following April Leininger (2002) has termed "cultural psychodynamics."

Advancing a neo-Vygotskian developmental approach to the question of the motivational force of cultural meanings, Dorothy Holland (1992) provides us with yet another important example of how the will is handled from a psychological anthropological perspective. According to Holland, one of the key questions that must be addressed by culture theorists is how it is that "meaning systems 'become a desire' or, more mundanely put, that a cultural system directs or motivates people to action" (1992, 62).

Viewing her approach as a third alternative to the cultural constructivist view of cultural models directly shaping human desires and needs, and the psychodynamic view of culture providing post hoc evaluations and labels for underlying "deep-seated human needs," Holland attempts to demonstrate how "thought and feelings, will and motivation, are formed as the individual develops" through particular social encounters (Holland 1992, 63). For instance, by examining North American women's differing levels of involvement and interest in romantic relationships, Holland suggests that any given individual's emotional and motivational commitment and identification with the world of romance "comes only after a certain degree of competence is reached and that this degree of emotional involvement is necessary for further mastery" (1992, 82). Here then, aspects of what we might recognize as willing are tied not to an individual's conscious choice to act in particular ways but to the extent to which their engagement in particular practices engenders learned competencies in those practices and corresponding emotional and motivational investments in continuing one's participation in such practices.

NEW PERSPECTIVES ON VOLITION

Rethinking Will

Although all of the authors in this volume use their own specific understanding of the will to guide the arguments they make, some are more explicit than others in trying to lay down specific and operational terminology such as we have encountered in the practice theoretical and psychological anthropological approaches to the will reviewed above. Throop (Chapter 2), for instance, using phenomenologists like Edmund Husserl and Alfred Schutz alongside philosophers Henri Bergson and Paul Ricoeur, devises a potent and portable model that offers a rich description of what the deep structures of willing might look like. He proposes three experiential correlates of willing that may be variously selected, emphasized, and/or elaborated within particular personal, cultural, and social contexts: (1) a sense of own-ness, (2) anticipation/goal directedness, and (3) effortful-ness. According to Throop, a sense of own-ness is tied to the experience of authoring an act. Anticipation/goal directedness entails the imaginal previewing of an act prior to its unfolding, or the carrying out of an act in the service of an intended object, goal, project, or end. Finally, effortful-ness is the experience of the "inner push," sense of effort, or what Ricoeur characterizes as the "thrust" of consciousness that serves to "pro-ject" a project into a given field of action. For Throop this model is the first step toward understanding the experiential basis for willing in an anthropological context.

Stewart and Strathern (Chapter 7) take a somewhat different approach in offering an elaboration of the will. Establishing the very basic question, "Is there such an entity as 'free will'?" (p. 142), they proceed to explore what an anthropological perspective on volition might look like, starting with the assertion that doing so involves "identifying how constructs of ideological thought worlds constrain 'will' and how 'will' (individual and notionally group) reshapes ideological thought worlds through changing practices" (p. 143). The authors' ultimate point is that will as a desire to act in the world and effect a particular outcome necessarily involves an acute use of the imagination to bridge the gap—and any possible blockades—between the current state of affairs and an intended outcome. While purposeful imagining in this sense would most obviously be carried out by the willful actor herself, in the case of ghosts in Donegal, as well as with Duna suicide, the imaginations of those who witness or experience the volition of the deceased also work hard to establish that not even the seeming finality of death can stanch the expression of will. Stewart and Strathern conclude by placing issues of will squarely within "the general domain of choice and intentionality in human action," while highlighting the special role played by responsibility and morality in will.

Finally, several of the authors see willing as a sort of buffer between an individual and the group to which she belongs. Garro (Chapter 4) exemplifies this position, explaining that for the Canadian Anishinaabe, "bad medicine" can account for many sorts of disruptions in social expectations, and is seen as an attempt by particular, interested individuals to control social circumstances in their favor. It can be directed at certain people, though it is not always obvious who summons the "bad medicine" in the first place. Such practices divest an afflicted individual from responsibility for his or her own behavior because it is the will of the "bad medicine's" conjurer that is expressed. In this case, then, willing can be said to emerge precisely when individuals flow above the collective ebb by acting in unorthodox and self-interested ways—even if their authorship is not readily apparent. Compare this with *ondjine*, bad things happening "for a reason," a sickness said to afflict people because of their own past, often overly willful behavior. Situating will in such highly charged and afflicting cultural concepts demonstrates, as Garro points out, that in social contexts like that of the Anishinaabe, "there are moral limits to what should be willed" (p. 94). Moreover, the evocation of the potentially harmful influence of past willful action upon present circumstances brings to light the significance of temporality for understanding willing in Anishinaabe communities, temporality being a second key theme taken up by a number of our contributors.

Will and Time

The influence of temporality in matters of the will is a continuous theme in the following pages. Although the authors treat time differently according to the scale at which their analyses operate—for instance at the various levels of history discussed by Stewart and Strathern (Chapter 7), Mageo (Chapter 6), and Good (Chapter 8), and at the experiential level revealed by Throop and Mattingly in their respective chapters—all of them use time to challenge the conceptualization of will as mere choice or simple action.

A sense of the historical patterning of willing is strikingly evident in Chapter 7, by Stewart and Strathern. The authors lead us through a series of examples as varied as the representation of sacrifice in Aeschylus' *Agamemnon*, suicide among the Duna, and the appearance of the deceased in the affairs of the living in Ireland's County Donegal. What becomes apparent in their discussion of these various historical contexts within which willing is understood is that while individuals always find themselves embedded in multiple layers of social obligations and culturally shaped value systems that often impinge on the expression of inner desires, these layers are always weighted differently in different contexts. It is only by looking at practice, Stewart and Strathern argue, that we can see how these layers affect the individual and begin to understand the local meanings of will.

Mageo (Chapter 6) treats the particular history of missionization in the Pacific as central to her analysis of will. More specifically, she examines how the introduction of Christianity in Sāmoa may have radically altered native renderings of subjectivity and shifted will into a more Western form. In order to clarify how traditional conceptions of will interact with these recently introduced forms, she turns specifically to dreaming and what this side of mental life might reveal about contemporary Samoan notions of will and subjectivity.

Byron Good (Chapter 8) offers a different take on historical time and the will. After reviewing the cases that Emil Kraepelin utilizes to illustrate some of the key features of individuals who suffer from such impediments of

the will, Good examines some of the historical, political, and cultural un-
derpinnings of Kraepelin's volitionally based descriptive diagnosis of depressive states. Noting that while pathologies of the will have largely disappeared
from the great neo-Kraepelinian compendium, the *Diagnostic and Statistical
Manual of the American Psychiatric Association*, he points out that in marked
contrast to contemporary psychiatry, in nineteenth and twentieth century
neurology and neuropsychiatry, disorders of the will were prevalent diagnostic categories.

Willing can also concern shorter, more experience-based time scales.
Mattingly (Chapter 3), for instance, argues directly against a characterization of will as a "moment of choice" and instead treats willing as a processual
development. Using data collected during longitudinal studies with several
African American families, Mattingly demonstrates that willing can be seen
as a gradual shifting of orientation from one attentional target to another
rather than some sort of split-second decision. In her view, thinking of will
as a morally loaded process, achieved though thought, conversation, emotion
work, and a host of other experiences, more accurately reflects the sense of
will as struggle that characterizes many individuals' experience of volition.

Finally, focusing upon temporality and willing, Throop's contribution
(Chapter 2) is based upon an exploration of the significance of temporality in the moment-to-moment unfolding of the act, an insight developed in
the context of subjectivist philosophical writings. In his account Throop details specifically how various phases of an act understood in the context of
streaming temporality may be differentially configured according to articulated projects or may be undergone in a prereflective immersion in an activity in progress.

Will and Responsibility

While many philosophical treatments of will concentrate on the relative
freedom or determinacy of choice faced by an individual at a given moment,
many of this volume's contributors instead focus on the complex webs of
responsibility in which socially engaged individuals operate. This can mean
several different things, including a sense of moral responsibility to "act
right," or a cultural tendency to mitigate responsibility by situating will outside the acting subject.

Developing a narrative conceptualization of will, Mattingly (Chapter 3) discusses "doing the right thing" as a complex process of choices that are not always made in a particular moment, nor are they necessarily loaded with a positive moral valence. Instead choices are made gradually through a series of morally ambivalent reorientations. Moreover, she points out that will is always developed and expressed in moral environments, which include other interested individuals with their own moral orientations, that are larger than the context of a decision made in a particular moment. From this perspective willing is a process that should be read as a collection of moments rather than any one given moment. Although people may be generally aware of the difference between right and wrong, they are also acutely aware of what is right and wrong "for me," right and wrong "for my child," right and wrong "right now," right and wrong "in the long run," and so on. Such being the case, and with the weight of responsibility for making a choice often being too difficult to bear all in one go, willing becomes a long-term project of moral orienteering.

In some societies it can prove difficult to distinguish between willing and morality in contexts where expressing individuality marks one as somehow a "bad" person. Mageo (Chapter 6), for example, points out that in Sāmoa, where disagreement with a higher-ranked person is socially unacceptable, individuals are held responsible for a refusal to act. Significantly, they are seen as nonmoral persons only if the refusal is accompanied with words, vehicles for the overt expression of will. Thus morality in this context is calculated as an *absence* of verbalized will, silence in compliance, while nonverbal refusal is a morally acceptable behavior.

In some cases responsibility for willful action can be mitigated in certain culturally prescribed ways. Groark (Chapter 5; cf. Garro Chapter 4) demonstrates how by shifting a sense of volitional authority outside of the here-and-now "willful actor"—in other words, by drawing on cultural resources that facilitate the locating of responsibility elsewhere—the individual can deny both the desire and motivation underpinning certain forms of willful action (particularly those with potentially disruptive social effects linked to the adoption of prestigious social or vocational identities). For Highland Maya, according to Groark, soul beliefs allow certain forms of manifestly "willful" behavior to be projected beyond the conscious volitional control of the waking actor in everyday social life. The Tzotzil concept of self consists of three different components, each with its own physical and metaphysical contours, and each with its own sense of will. Two of these components are the consciously organized self of everyday life and the "essential soul," a quasi-autonomous transcorporeal alter that forms the vehicle for dream experience. A tension is evident in the fact that individuals are "elected" to become curers through soul-based dream encounters with powerful supernatural agents who inform them of their calling. Through these nominations, they come to stand out from the collective because of their special abilities, eventually attaining a prestigious new occupational status as professional curers. The fact that they experience this calling in dreams, however, allows them to disavow this life path choice as a product of their own will and instead attribute it to the volitional autonomy of the quasi-autonomous essential soul and the will of the deities.

Throop's contribution (Chapter 2) offers a phenomenology-based model for thinking about how willing operates and, in certain cultural contexts, becomes mitigated. The model draws on Robert Levy's (1973) notions of hypo-cognition to hypercognition in which certain concepts are made more or less salient and relevant in a given culture. Throop proposes a gradient of willing to explain how any of the three vectors of willing—a sense of own-ness, anticipation/goal directedness, and effortful-ness—can be highlighted or backgrounded in a given moment or in a given culture. According to Throop's perspective, exploring how these vectors are operationalized can lend power to understanding what the will looks like and how it works in a given culture. A culture in which will is characterized with a low sense of own-ness and effortful-ness would assign responsibility differently than one with explicitly marked senses of own-ness and effortful-ness. While this model is not the only way to start tackling the will in an ethnographic context, it does offer some concrete metrics with which to begin coming to grips with usable concept of the will in psychological anthropology.

Will and Narrative

It may be that willing is so integral an element of human experience that parsing it out as a separate and isolable component is a difficult task for both experiencer and analyst alike. When an individual reflects upon willing, as with other forms of experience, she often places it into various kinds of narrative frameworks, each with its own structural requirements and systematics for patterning content. It is perhaps not surprising that in this light several of the volume's contributor's have turned to narrative as a means for understanding some dimensions of the will. Indeed, perhaps willing only becomes apparent in a holistic context that makes sense as an entire configuration, rather than as viewing it as something independent of other variables. Stewart and Strathern (Chapter 7) make this clear by presenting their argument in the form of several compelling vignettes, each with its own internal structure that illuminates a different context-sensitive variation of willing. As these wide-ranging vignettes demonstrate, the degree to which willing is experienced as narrative or is framed as narrative after-the-fact varies. Add to that the fact that culture itself often has a strong tendency to over-elaborate whatever structuring power narrative itself provides. As a result, stories, in the form of cultural tropes, are in many cases the dominant tools by which willing becomes manifest and can be explained. The implications of this narrative approach are consequential to an anthropological understanding of the will—with this model, will is not idiosyncratic but patterned, patterns are predictable, and predictability minimizes any potential tears in the social fabric that might be caused by untamped individualism. In other words, squaring will in a narrative framework is one of the simplest means of indirect social control.

Several of the volume's authors explicitly fuse narrative theory with ethnographic particulars to show how this approach enhances the analysis of will. Mattingly (Chapter 3), for instance, argues that any "choice" can only make sense as an orientation to something within a story in which a context unfolds with a past leading up to that choice and some desired future outcome. By moving the will into a morally loaded narrative framework, she forcefully shows, using ethnographic evidence, how generally conceiving of will as some identifiable "choice" is actually fundamentally flawed.

Garro (Chapter 4), on the other hand, uses two culturally salient story structures to show how willing is controlled according to Anishinaabe culture. Certain kinds of events in Anishinaabe society are seen by some members as the result of "bad medicine," the malevolent will of another, and other events as stemming from *ondjine*, one's own will that was left unchecked at some point in the past. While these two explanations are ultimately different, both implicate specific, regular, and predictable narrative structures, which in turn people use to understand the event and explain it, and perhaps even, in the case of "bad medicine," to excuse it.

Groark (Chapter 5), illuminates similar normativizing forces among Tzotzil Maya. Tzotzil investiture dreams, in which men and women receive a calling to become a curer, follow particular regularized patterns. The Maya dreamspace exists apart from the everyday world, and as stated above, the aspect of the self that experiences dreams, the "soul," is felt by Tzotzil individuals to be both "me" and "not quite me." By narrating the dream with the soul as experiencer, and by using various grammatical and lexical features that distance the dreamer from the dream experience itself, the soul becomes objectified as a quasi-third person entity. This narrative shifting of experiential center away from the embodied dreamer and onto the soul allows the dreamer to disavow any direct role in "choosing" to become a curer—a potentially disruptive claim—since in this story the individual's own will was not involved. Social harmony is thus preserved.

Will, Imagination, and Dreaming

Finally, a number of authors bring up the significance of the imagination for understanding the will. Arguably within the realm of the imaginal, two of the chapters focus specifically on dreams as a critical locus for uncovering the textured variability of will in relation to broad sociocultural contexts. In discussing the relationship between a social actor's anticipation of future courses of events, actions, desires, wishes, and goals, many contributors evoke the imagination as implicated in the ability to forecast possible horizons of experiences (see Mattingly Chapter 3, Garro Chapter 4, Stewart and Strathern Chapter 7). That said, it is perhaps in the investigation of dream experience that the most dynamic and provocative analyses of culturally and personally constituted forms of willing in the imaginal realm are advanced. For instance, Mageo's historically based analysis of will in Sāmoa (Chapter 6) explores how the introduction of Christian ideals and practices may have impacted local understandings of subjectivity and willing. Investigating how local conceptions of will impact and are impacted by these more recently introduced forms, she looks to dreaming, which she sees as a mechanism for extracting experience from daily life and incorporating it into more abstract, experientially distant cultural schemas. Using ethnographic evidence she argues that in Sāmoa dreams are a space for playing with will and its expression. Through dreaming people are able to parse out their own desires from the restrictions that social structure places on them, to "clarify what is wish fulfillment and what is nightmare" (p. 138), and generally be free from the pressure of social expectations.

Groark (Chapter 5) likewise sees dreaming as a locus for generating social action. Because the Maya dreamspace, which is treated as real, is not directly experienced by the corporeal self there are fewer restrictions on behavior there. It is the space in which will is most freely expressed, albeit by a "not quite me" soul rather than the corporeal individual. Once the dreaming self returns to the everyday world where overly willful behavior is dispreferred, the dream experiences are often only reluctantly avowed. While the body-based self is the most experientially willful aspect of the self, it is also the most prone to social control since it subsists in the everyday world where certain behaviors are highly restricted. Thus dreaming is for the Maya one of the only options available for expressing will free from social control.

Both Groark and Mageo challenge a purely bodily basis for will, suggesting that perhaps the will may lie elsewhere in an individual's psychic intraverse. Moreover they demonstrate the power of dreams to be an equalizing force by slipping the self-evident social inequality that permeates the everyday world and entering a space where the individual's equality or inequality need not be at issue.

CONCLUSION

With this volume we do not intend merely to lay a thin veil of cultural relativism over already existing philosophical debates, nor are we trying to rehash largely dormant themes in the social sciences. We have attempted to draw together not only a complex body of research and theory on subjectivity, but also a powerful group of scholars to bring their own analytical insights to the nettlesome problem of the will. Applying anthropological reasoning and the explanatory acuity that comes from ethnographic observations of human action *in situ*, these analyses of choice and willing provide a deeper and more nuanced understanding of the relationship between individual action and sociocultural forces. As many of the volume's contributors reveal, an understanding of the constitution, efficacy, and orientation of the will is far from a simple matter of examining individual or collective agency in relation to cultural, historical, and/or social determinants.

How actors perceive, feel, think, choose, desire, remember, imagine, fantasize, and act are intimately implicated in anything that we might deem to gloss with the term of *will*. In this light, we argue that it is not enough to simply note that an individual's actions have had tangible effects upon their social world (where anthropological discussions of "agency" often begin and end), for an understanding of the very fabric of human subjectivity lies at the heart of such determinations.

Each of these chapters speaks clearly to the need for further anthropological inquiry into willing in cultural contexts. By bridging topics that range from imagination to morality, from dreams to psychopathology, we hope this volume highlights the complex and multi-faceted ways of being-in-the world that may have occasion, depending on the context, to be glossed with the term *will*. As these chapters attest, there is clearly much more to be said on the nature of willing from philosophical, historical, sociological, and anthropological perspectives. If nothing else, however, we hope that this collection has taken significant steps toward advancing a more explicit anthropology of the will through generating a modest amount of intellectual fervor around the theoretical questions that emerge when our descriptive and analytical lenses are focused upon the intersection of culture—including all of its various components—and the will.

IN THE MIDST OF ACTION
C. Jason Throop

> To be understood and rediscovered, this mystery which I am
> demands that I become one with it, that I participate in it so
> that I do not observe it as confronting me at a distance as an
> object.
>
> *Paul Ricoeur ([1950] 1966)*

PHILOSOPHERS SINCE THE TIME OF THE ancient Greeks have tended to categorize subjective experience according to three basic faculties. These include the faculty of perception (cognition, intellection, memory), the faculty of feeling (emotion, affect, sensation), and the faculty of will (volition, conation, intention). While this tripartite set has long informed philosophical and later psychological models of the fundamental structures of subjective experience, the faculty of will has remained largely under-examined in many anthropological investigations concerning the organization of cultural subjectivities (see Murphy and Throop, Chapter 1).

In this chapter, I will take some initial steps toward addressing this apparent oversight in anthropology by suggesting a phenomenologically grounded approach to willing as informed by the writings of Henri Bergson ([1889] 2001), Alfred Schutz ([1932] 1967), and Paul Ricoeur ([1950] 1966). I hold that this approach to willing can significantly inform anthropological theorizing and research because it postulates a number of distinct phenomenal aspects of willing that are differentially obfuscated and highlighted in the context of everyday experience and which may be distinctly configured in differing cultural contexts. These phenomenal aspects of willing can be understood as existential structures that are variously emphasized in competing theoretical traditions in the human sciences and in the context of the patterning of sub-jective experience cross-culturally.

THEORIZING THE ACT

Whether explicitly addressed or not, the act of "willing" is, of course, not solely the concern of philosophers. From Marx to Weber to Bourdieu to Gid-dens, social theorists have often situated their views concerning the relative dynamics of social life in theories that attempt to account for both "agency" and "structure" (see Ahearn 2001; Alexander 1988; Archer 2003; Dornan 2002; Duranti 2004; Kockelman 2007; Ortner 1984, 1996, 2006; Williams 1977). It is not my intention to provide anything approximating a compre-hensive review of social theories of agency and social action in this chapter (see Ahearn 2001; Kockelman 2007; Murphy and Throop, Chapter 1). There are, however, some key themes that evidence an incipient interest in the will that recurrently appear when problems of agency and structure are addressed from a social scientific scope of inquiry.

Indeed, in those social scientific perspectives that set out to theorize the social act, we find a number of associated tensions between a series of pu-tatively antagonistic qualities that speak, at least indirectly, to the problem of willing. Whether it is in terms of such familiar distinctions as spontane-ity versus deliberation, habit versus reflection, unconsciousness versus con-sciousness, consequence versus intention, or determinacy versus freedom, we find social theorists often struggling to articulate a portrait of the social actor as differentially impacted by, and impacting, the social world within which he or she is enmeshed.

The Problem of Willing in Bourdieu's Practice Theory

Pierre Bourdieu's writings provide an excellent illustrative example of an in-fluential social theoretical approach to agency in which a number of these key distinctions are evoked in an effort to critique the concept of the will.

In a previous work, Murphy and I (see Throop and Murphy 2002) have argued that Bourdieu's concept of *habitus*, which is positioned as a foil to both philosophical and social scientific assessments of social actors as "willful" agents, pivots on his attempts to align *habitus* with the unfolding of thoroughly determined yet spontaneous, unconscious, and unpredictable forms of action. As Bourdieu asserts, *habitus*, as a generative internalization of social structure, should be considered a "second nature" or forgotten history that operates as "a spontaneity without consciousness or will" (1990, 56).

In using the term *spontaneity*, Bourdieu is referring to a nonconscious, prereflective activity that is not predictable. To this end, he makes a clear distinction between predictability and determination (Throop and Murphy 2002). While it may certainly be true that we can never come to view practice as perfectly predictable, Bourdieu (1977, 15, 73, 116) holds that this does not mean that an individual's *habitus* is not thoroughly *determined*; a position that leads him to fault theorists who posit social actors as acting in accordance with explicit, reflexive, and goal-directed projects.

According to Bourdieu, it is important to recognize that it is not through conscious attention to predetermined "roles," "rules" or "models" that agents are able to negotiate their interactions with the social world (1990; 2000). It is instead through the unintentional triggering of strategic patterns of thought and action produced by *habitus* in its mutually informing relation to structure that they are able to do so (Bourdieu 1977, 73).[1] Here lies what Bourdieu labels the "fallacy of the rule." According to Bourdieu, "the fallacy of the rule" refers to the idea that agents are not consciously oriented to rules governing their behavior when directly engaged in activity. That is, agents are not conscious of how their practices are "objectively governed" by social expectations and conditions. They lack, Bourdieu argues, an explicit cognizance of the "mechanisms producing . . . conformity in the absence of *intention* to conform" [emphasis added] (1977, 29).

Connected to the "fallacy of the rule" is what Bourdieu labels the "finalist illusion." In Bourdieu's estimation, practices are produced by *habitus*, which serves as a generative principle allowing individuals to adjust and respond to ever-changing situations. In stressing the generative and spontaneous "strategic" functioning of *habitus,* he asserts, however, that it is a mistake to believe that these strategies are determined in accord with an actor's ex-

plicit orientation to future goals, plans, or projects. It is not conscious attention to imagined final goals or outcomes that drives action but unconscious
habituated responses to present contextual conditions.

Never explicitly distinguishing between "intention" and "will," Bourdieu
further asserts that *habitus* is transmitted without conscious intention.[2] He
stresses that *habitus* is grounded exclusively in the "intentionless invention
of regulated improvisation" in which an agent's "actions and works are the
product of a *modus operandi* of which he is not the producer and [of which
he] has no conscious mastery" (Bourdieu 1977, 79). For precisely this reason
Bourdieu criticizes researchers who attempt to work back from practice (*opus
operatum*) to motive (*modus operandi*) in their attempts to analyze human
action. Again, he argues that this underlies the perpetuation of a pernicious
view of the agent as a conscious, "intentional" and "willful" actor (Bourdieu
1977, 36). He suggests, in fact, that much of the evidence leading researchers
to believe that agents are acting in accord with "consciously felt goals" should
be understood as nothing other than attempts on the part of agents to retro-
spectively rationalize their behavior only after it has spontaneously occurred;
an issue that I will discuss in more detail. From Bourdieu's perspective then,
spontaneity, generativity, and strategy should not be conflated with willing.
The latter is an all too conscious, reflexive, and mentalistic construct that
fails, in his estimation, to account for the primacy of the structurally determined, unconscious, embodied, and yet generative structures entailed in the
habitual patterning of human action.

Social Theory and the Philosophy of the Will

One of the purposes of engaging in this all too brief discussion of Bourdieu's
practice theory is to highlight how distinctions between consciousness and
unconsciousness, spontaneity and reflection, and predictability and determination, may be variously utilized to articulate a position that critically challenges the role of willing in the enactment and orchestration of social action.
Again, it is important to recall that Bourdieu's emphasis on the spontaneous
and unpredictable nature of *habitus* does not lead him to characterize the active phases of *habitus* as comparable to an act of willing. In highlighting the
thorough lack of attention to the experience of willing in Bourdieu's theory
I also hope to show in this chapter how a more rigorous examination of the

phenomenology of willing might in fact better serve the development of culture theory than Bourdieu's outright dismissal.

It is interesting to note with Paul Ricoeur ([1950] 1966) that many classical debates in philosophy have also sought to examine the problem of deliberation in relationship to willing by employing a number of very similar distinctions in the service of very different visions of "freedom" and "choice." For instance, rationalist philosophical approaches to volition tend to characterize "freedom" of will as belonging "exclusively to rational motives sweeping away affective motives (or inclinations)" ([1950] 1966, 150). Irrationalist philosophical approaches to the will, in contrast, hold that "freedom" and willing are associated with a "surge from the deep which breaks through anonymous, dead, intellectual reasons" (ibid.).

Depending upon the philosophical tradition or social theory in question, constraint can be understood to reside either "inside" or "outside" a given social actor. There is also great debate over whether or not conscious deliberation or spontaneous activity should be held to be at the heart of freedom and choice. Overall it seems that there are very few points of clear convergence regarding what counts as an instance of willing in either social scientific or philosophical circles. While each of the distinctions discussed above have served to bolster differing visions of what constitutes willing, I hope to demonstrate how a more careful phenomenological analysis of the temporality of acts of willing might provide some much needed clarity in our understanding of the phenomena of willing and its cultural and interactional entailments.

PHENOMENOLOGY OF THE WILL:
OWN-NESS, ANTICIPATION, AND EFFORTFUL-NESS

Generally speaking, in philosophy and social theory there has been much debate over the causal efficacy of willing, whether willing should be characterized as free or determined, and whether or not the will should be construed to be a faculty of the soul or mind.[3] In taking a phenomenological approach to willing, however, I will begin by bracketing these debates and turn, as Edmund Husserl taught, to the "things themselves": the experiential correlates of willing. My present project is thus *not* to claim a position for or against the freedom, determinacy, or ontological status of the will (see Stewart and Strathern, Chapter 7). It is instead to elaborate a phenomenological basis for exploring willing and the various ways that cultural processes may inform an individual's experience and expression of willing. In so doing, I will draw from, and build upon, Paul Ricoeur's ([1950] 1966) pioneering descriptive phenomenological analysis of volition[4] (what I am currently calling "willing") in the context of his book, *Freedom and Nature*.

My overall goal in this chapter is to delimit, by means of descriptive phenomenology, those structures of experience that may be differentially foregrounded or backgrounded in the context of any given subject's experience of willing. The necessity of working to gain a phenomenologically informed discernment of what exactly it is we mean by willing is rooted in the fact that current discussions in anthropology and the social sciences concerning the will—however indirect or vague those discussions might be—are largely lacking in any definitional consensus. Indeed, terms such as *desire, emotion, motive*, and *intention* seem at first glance to have a certain family resemblance to the concept of willing. Depending on the particular theorist or ethnographer who uses these terms, however, there appears at present to be no simple means for discerning the extent to which these concepts have much, if any, bearing on the phenomenon of willing. Of course, these definitional issues are not solely of theoretical import, since practically speaking, it is only in gaining some conceptual clarity with regard to what it is we mean by the concept of willing that we will be able to begin to assess the extent to which such a concept is indeed translatable in other cultural contexts.

As Thomas Csordas (1990) has convincingly argued, a powerful aspect of phenomenological analysis lies in its ability to provide fine-grained descriptions of the cultural patterning of those subjectively and intersubjectively mediated constitutive acts underpinning the formation of objects of experience. To this end, drawing specifically from Maurice Merleau-Ponty (1962), Csordas (1990) argues for the significance of shifting our analytic gaze from pregiven objects of experience to those processes of constitution that first give rise to such objects. This, he asserts, is an important step in any cultural analysis given the fact that perception, even social scientifically mediated forms of perception (cf. Goodwin 1994; Schutz 1967), does not begin with but rather ends in objects.

Three Experiential Correlates of Willing

When examining willing phenomenologically—that is, from the perspective of an examination of phenomena as they are presented to the experiencing subject—we are confronted with at least three distinct phenomenological aspects of willing,[5] what I will call: (1) a *sense of own-ness*, (2) *anticipation/goal directedness*, and (3) *effortful-ness* or what psychologist Daniel Wegner terms "feeling of doing." (cf. Bayne and Levy 2006; Ricoeur [1950] 1966; Wegner 2002; see also Garro, Chapter 4)

Let's begin with the sense of "own-ness." This aspect of the experience of willing is tied to a recognition (implicit or explicit) that the act of willing is somehow our own. In other words, the act is understood to arise from and be initiated by an "I"; understood in the Jamesian sense of the term as that aspect of the self that serves as a locus of experience and action (James [1890] 1983). That is, the experience of willing implies that a currently unfolding act is understood to be initiated by, and is thus associated with, the self as experiencer to the exclusion of other causal agents. As such, the sense of ownness is thereby implicated in attributions of *control* and *authorship* over a particular act (see Garro, Chapter 4). It appears that for many anthropologists, psychologists, and philosophers, it has been the aspect of own-ness that has often proven to be quite controversial when discussing the will.

It is important to note with Ricoeur ([1950] 1966, 58–59), however, that this sense of own-ness need not be an explicitly reflexive act. Instead, as Ricoeur explains, "all acts carry with them a vague awareness of their subject-pole, their place of emission" ([1950] 1966, 60).[6] That said, to postulate both reflexive and prereflexive varieties of a sense of own-ness does not thus perforce entail that these should be necessarily considered two disparate ways of being-in-the-act. For there may also be a significant connection made between a prereflexive "vague awareness" of the act's "place of emission" and full fledged reflexive assessments of one's authorship of an act. As Ricoeur suggests, there is always a "prereflexive imputation of myself" in the willing of an act, which contains within itself "the germ of the possibility of reflection" ([1950] 1966, 58).

In terms of anticipation/goal directedness, I am referring to the idea that willing often implies either the pre-viewing of the act prior to its unfolding, or the carrying out of an act in the service of an intended object, goal, project, or end. Hannah Arendt recognizes the significance of this anticipatory structure of willing when she proclaims that "the Will, if it exists at all . . . is as obviously our mental organ for the future as memory is our mental organ for the past" ([1971] 1978, 13). Willing can thus be understood as a conscious feeding forward to anticipate and then realize a possible or desired future (cf. Bourdieu 1977). And it is this aspect of willing—willing as anticipatory—that is so clearly highlighted in the semantic overlap that exists between willing and intentionality, both in terms of its everyday usage as planned or deliberate action and in terms of its more rigorous phenomenological definition as consciousness directed toward an intentional object (Husserl [1931] 1962; Jacquette 2004; see also Duranti 1993a, 2001).

The third aspect, effortful-ness or feeling of doing, recognizes the fact that the act of willing is indeed experienced as an "act." That is, there may often be a perceptible force or energy to willing, what Wegner (2002) calls an "internal 'oomph.'" And it is often this effortful-ness that is held to be the catalyst that propels action forward. As Ricoeur notes, in the context of willing, the myself "commits" itself to the project of an action, such that even on a prereflexive level willing can be understood as that "which makes the leap, which pro-jects the project" ([1950] 1966, 63). To this end, effortful-ness can be understood in accord with a "commitment," a "leap," what Ricoeur also calls that "thrust" of consciousness that serves to "pro-ject" the project into a given field of action. I would suggest that it is the effortful-ness, or the inner push of willing, that is perhaps responsible for encouraging some thinkers to equate "desire" with the "will," a potentially problematic equation considering that individuals may often "desire" objects that they "willingly" abstain from obtaining.

Experiential Correlates and Phenomenological Vectors

Having outlined three experiential correlates of willing, I would like to suggest that the sense of own-ness, anticipation, and effortful-ness, can each be understood as instances of what Drew Leder has termed "phenomenological vectors" (1990). According to Leder, a phenomenological vector is "a structure of experience that makes possible and encourages the subject in certain practical or interpretive directions, while never mandating them as invariants"

(1990, 150). Significantly, Leder argues that the motivated possibilities inherent in any given phenomenological vector ensure that although there might be important commonalities potentiated by these vectors cross-culturally, their final organization and meaning will importantly depend upon the cultural field within which they present themselves. From this perspective then, a cultural model that may have been suggested by phenomenological vectors (e.g., a sense own-ness, anticipation, and effortful-ness) can recursively feed back to further highlight and elaborate those somatic and psychical experiences that most accurately correspond to the cultural model in question.

Of great significance for exploring the cultural patterning of willing is the idea that these three experiential correlates can be construed as somewhat independent from one another. For instance, there are often times—like when an individual "absent mindedly" plays with his or her hair while reading—when the individual performing an action does so without explicit anticipation of a specific goal. And yet, the actor *may* still have both a sense of own-ness and effortful-ness associated with the action. Similarly, there are cases where actors carry out action in the service of a goal, experience effortful-ness, and yet have a questionable sense of own-ness associated with the act—a classic example is that of driving a car down the freeway only to later realize that one has only a vague memory of the actual route taken. Finally, there are also cases where an actor may experience effortful-ness and no corresponding anticipation or sense of own-ness associated with his or her actions. Such an orientation to action has often been of reported in the context of some forms of spirit possession and so-called dissociative disorders (see Garro, Chapter 4; Good, Chapter 8; Mageo, Chapter 6).

Although I have set out to highlight how the experiential correlates of a sense of own-ness, anticipation, and effortful-ness can be understood as somewhat independent from one another, there are almost always possibilities for important connections between these three phenomenological vectors. For instance, anticipation is often directed toward a particular project that is also imbued with the actor's sense of own-ness. As Ricoeur makes clear, the prereflexive myself may insert "itself into the plan of action to be done; in a real sense it becomes *committed*. And, in becoming committed, it binds itself: it constrains its future appearance" ([1950] 1966, 59).

ON THE TEMPORALITY OF WILLING

Having briefly outlined these three phenomenal vectors of willing, I would now like to draw from the work of Henri Bergson, Alfred Schutz, and Paul Ricoeur in order to develop a better understanding of the dynamics of these three vectors in the context of everyday social interaction. A key insight advanced by each of these thinkers is that an adequate view of willing lies in a necessary examination of the role of temporality in the moment-to-moment unfolding of the act.

Bergson on Willing and a "Certain Misconception of Duration"

In his book *Time and Free Will* ([1889] 2001), Henri Bergson points out that a significant problem associated with long-standing debates in philosophy over the nature of the will is that these debates are grounded in a "certain misconception of duration" ([1889] 2001, 173). This misconception is rooted in what he holds to be a prevalent tendency in philosophy to imbue the flux and plurality of immediate temporality ("duration") with the static homogeneity of extensity ("space"). Bergson argues that most philosophical discussions of freedom and determinacy in relationship to willing have tended to focus on either the preformed anticipation of action or the retrospective assessment of action. As Bergson observes, both temporal orientations to willing rely upon "symbolical," "spatialized" understandings of duration in the form of the image of a completed act ([1889] 2001, 239; cf. Whorf 1956).[7] In the case of anticipation, it is reliance upon an imagined projection of the completed act as a goal toward which the individual orients her action. In the case of recollection it is reliance on a retrospective assessment of a completed act that stands out against the background of other possible, yet unrealized, completed acts.

As a result, Bergson holds that what has been ignored in previous philosophical discussions of willing is an exploration of willing in the context of the dynamic progress of lived temporality.[8] As he states, all of the various perspectives focusing on the relative freedom or determinacy of the will have relied upon an overly intellectualized schematic understanding of willed action as "a *thing* and not a *progress*; . . . [that] corresponds, in its inertness, to a kind of stereotyped memory of the whole process of deliberation and the final decision arrived at: how could . . . [this] give us the least idea of the concrete movement, the dynamic progress by which the deliberation issued in the act?" ([1889] 2001, 181). Implicit in Bergson's attempt to clarify this "misconception of duration," is thus the important insight that willing may be differentially realized temporally in different phases in the moment-to-moment unfolding of the act.

Schutz on the Progressing Phases of the Act

Drawing directly from Bergson and Edmund Husserl in the context of a critique of Max Weber's theory of meaning and social action, Alfred Schutz makes these implicit insights explicit in his book *The Phenomenology of the Social World* ([1932] 1967). Here, Schutz holds that there is an ever-present tension between "living experience within the flow of duration and reflection on the experience thus lived through" ([1932] 1967, 70; see Throop and Murphy 2002; Throop 2003a). Accordingly, he suggests "the meaning of an action is different depending on the point in time from which it is observed" ([1932] 1967, 65).[9]

Behavior as it occurs in pure duration is, Schutz observes, "prephenomenal"; without explicitly formed goals, motives, projects or recollections. In the immediacy of the "deed in the doing" there is no reflection upon the act in progress or upon the goals to which that act may be directed. In terms of the three phenomenological vectors of willing, we find that at the stage of pre-phenomenal behavior, action seems, according to Schutz's characterization at least, to be carried out either in the absence of, or with only a vague awareness of, the vector of anticipation.

While Schutz ([1932] 1967, 75) does argue that there is a "primal unity" to the stream of duration in which diverse experiences are "bound together as mine," there is further still some ambiguity as to whether or not Schutz would argue for the possibility of a sense of own-ness arising in pre-phenomenal behavior. Regardless of Schutz's position, I would like to suggest with Ricoeur (see below) that we entertain the possibility that this aspect of willing, the sense of own-ness, may or may not arise during this particular phase of the act. Likewise, the feeling of doing need not necessarily but might be potentially associated with pre-phenomenal behavior.

Schutz is careful to distinguish pre-phenomenal behavior from phenomenal action, however. In contrast to pre-phenomenal behavior, phenomenal action is behavior carried out in service of an explicitly recollected or projected act (cf. Giddens 1984). Here Schutz, following Bergson, argues that the conscious project—the span of which determines the unity of an actor's perception of what activities are to be included within the boundaries of the act—"anticipates not the action itself but the [completed] act" ([1932] 1967, 67).

One way in which the image of a completed act informs a project is through what Schutz terms an "in-order-to motive." As Schutz explains, when a project is constituted in light of an in-order-to motive a given goal is "phantasied in the future perfect tense" as already executed ([1932] 1967, 87). For instance, I have been working on this chapter in order to see it published in an edited collection on the problem of "the will" in anthropology. Here an imagined already executed act of a completed chapter is what guides my present motive to continue writing in order to accomplish this goal. This stands in contrast with reflective orientations to causally based "because-motives" that are directed to "those conscious experiences which precede (in the pluperfect tense) the actual project" as it was undertaken by the actor ([1932] 1967, 95). It could thus be said, for example, that I am writing this chapter because I have made particular choices in the past (such as applying to graduate school) that eventually led me to a career in anthropology. It is significant to note that in the case of "because motives" it is still completed acts, this time recollected and not anticipated, that define the goals and motives informing my present project.

Overall, Schutz makes clear that depending on whether or not a theorist is focusing upon the pure project stage, the action in progress, or the act as it has been already executed, there may be very different ways to interpret an agent's conscious attention to his or her motivations, intentions, plans, and goals ([1932] 1967, 64).[10] And I would also add, such different temporal orientations to the relative progress of an action might also entail very different ways for us to understand the extent to which own-ness, anticipation, and effortful-ness might be variously foregrounded or backgrounded for individual actors in the real-time unfolding of the act.

Ricoeur on Time and (In)voluntary Action

A focus on the significance of temporality for developing an understanding of how aspects of willing differentially articulate in the context of the unfolding of the act is also found in the work of Paul Ricoeur. Indeed, Ricoeur holds that "the dynamics of the act, can only be clarified in a temporal perspective" ([1950] 1966, 163). Central to Ricoeur's project is an exploration of the relation of a project to its temporally mediated execution in the context of a variable fluctuation between what he characterizes as delay, distention, or hesitation and action, contraction, or impulse ([1950] 1966, 39). Ricoeur holds that it is largely with regard to the former, wherein a "decision [is] cut off from its execution by a delay" (ibid.), that a sense of what constitutes "voluntary" action most explicitly emerges experientially. This is because the latter set of existential characteristics are entailed in "truly involuntary action, an explosive, impulsive action in which the subject cannot recognize himself and of which he says that it escaped him" (ibid.). Ricoeur, much like Bergson and Schutz, also alludes to a differential relationship between reflective action and prereflective behavior when he asserts that a social actor

who is going to act or who is acting does not normally reflect on his fundamental self; only in memory and particularly in the retrospection of remorse does there appear to him suddenly, at the same time at the center and outside of his act, a self which could and should be other ([1950] 1966, 28).

Moreover, much like Schutz, Ricoeur suggests that the voluntary and the involuntary are capable of working both in concert and in opposition. They are never to be simply considered as two necessarily opposing poles on a gradient of determinacy and freedom. As he puts it, "the initial situation revealed by description is *the reciprocity of the involuntary and the voluntary.* Need, emotion, habit, etc., acquire a complete significance only in relation to a will which they solicit, dispose, and generally affect, and which in turn determines their significance" [emphasis in the original] ([1950] 1966, 4). For Ricoeur, "willing" is thus only possible in relationship to an ongoing and active engagement, reliance upon, and ultimately some form of mastery over, "involuntary" aspects of human mentation and behavior.[11]

Finally, a key component of Ricoeur's analysis of willing and the temporal unfolding of the act lies in his recognition of the central role of attention in modifying an actor's subjective experience of willing.[12] Drawing from Husserl ([1931] 1962) and Bradley (1901a, 1901b), Ricoeur defines attention as the capacity—either passive or active—to detach an object "from the background of which it is a part" ([1950] 1966, 154). Attention is thus "an action which accentuates, yet brings out something already given" ([1950] 1966, 154). Because there is an ongoing, dynamic shifting of attention from those objects foregrounded in awareness and those residing in the background, Ricoeur reminds us that attention "is something which unfolds in time, accentuating and bringing to light various alternative 'aspects' of a disordered situation, the diverse 'value' aspects of a practical puzzle" ([1950] 1966, 157). And it is through the medium of a consciousness constituted through the dynamic shifting of attention to various aspects of perceptual, sensorial, and imaginal objects that various forms of being-in-the-act are imagined, evoked, and carried out in the context of possible and actual fields of social activity (see also Throop 2003a, 2008, forthcoming).

In variously focusing on the "myself" (i.e., "a sense of own-ness"), the "'what' of the action" (i.e., the project or goal) and the "thrust" of decision (i.e., "effortful-ness") that are framed according to that which is "to be done by me in the future," (i.e., "anticipation/goal directedness), Ricoeur argues that the functioning and resolution of attention serves a prominent role in both the organization of the project in an actor's awareness and its ultimate "launching" in the field of action ([1950] 1966, 166). In fact, it is always at least partially the case that what we call "control over process is attention in motion: choice in a sense is a fixing of attention" ([1950] 1966, 149).

A PHENOMENOLOGICAL RE-EXAMINING OF PROJECTS AND ACTS IN PROGRESS

In the work of Bergson, Schutz, and Ricoeur, we find evidence for a struggle to articulate the relationship between prereflective behavior and reflective action in the context of social activity. Such a perspective importantly pivots on the nature of the anticipatory vector of willing as directed toward a project that may be variously imagined in a retrospective or prospective, and yet still always completed, form. Recall that Bergson argues that it is the very tendency of philosophers to spatialize the project as a completed act instead of turning to attend to the act in progress that fuels ongoing debates in philosophy over the relative freedom or determinacy of the will. Similarly, Schutz holds that there is a qualitative difference between the act in progress—what he calls pre-phenomenal behavior—and those phases of the act that are organized in accordance with an imagined, completed act, as the goal—what he terms phenomenal action. Ricoeur also postulates a related distinction when he suggests that capacities for fully reflexive awareness are largely attenuated in the real-time unfolding of the act in progress.

I concur with these thinkers in recognizing how various phases of the act, when understood in the context of streaming temporality, may be differentially configured according to articulated projects or may be undergone in a pre-reflective immersion in the activity in progress. I differ from them, however, in arguing that it is *not* solely the image of a *completed act* that must always serve as the intentional object fulfilling the anticipatory vector of willing. Edward Casey's phenomenological analysis of imagination in his book *Imagining: A Phenomenological Study* (1976) is quite helpful in this regard. Casey's work is not in explicit dialogue with developing a phenomenological account of willing. It does indirectly, however, point to the fact that when we are discussing the anticipatory or goal-directed nature of willing we have to account for the various imaginative act phases that may be associated with orienting one's actions to a particular goal or project, as well as to the "central" or "peripheral placement of the imagining self" (1976, ftn. 45).

While Schutz maintains that phenomenal action is based on an orientation to the completed act, and not the act in progress, Casey's careful phenomenological investigations of the act-structure of imagination point to the possibility that phenomenal action—in the Schutzian sense of the term—may indeed be organized intentionally—in the Husserlian sense of the term—either toward the completed act or the act in progress. Moreover, Casey points to the possibility of imagining a project or goal from either the perspective of an *actor standing outside of the act* who observes it from a third-person perspective or an *actor immersed in the unfolding field of social action* who observes that action from a first-person perspective (cf. Bahktin 1990; see also Groark, Chapter 5). It is this latter point that significantly highlights the possibility for the variegated interplay of anticipation and a sense of own-ness in the progress of the unfolding act. Casey's insight into possible variations in the actor's perspective in relationship to an act can be seen as a basis for developing an understanding of the various senses of own-ness that can arise in the midst of action—variations that pivot on the placement of the self either "outside" or "inside" the imagined, projected, or recollected act (Groark, Chapter 5). Similarly, the completed act and the act in progress may be yet another dimension of variation in the organization of the project informing the anticipatory vector of willing.

Imagination, which I hold to be necessarily implicated in the anticipatory vector of willing, is understood by Casey to be operating in the guise of at least three different "act-phases." These act-phases include: (1) *imaging*—an "imaginative presentation whose content possesses a specifically sensuous . . . form" (1976, 41); (2) *imagining-that*—a sensuous or non-sensuous imagining "*that* individual objects or events together constitute a circumstance or situation: a 'state of affairs'" (1976, 42); and (3) *imagining-how*—which entails an ability to imagine "*how* to do, think, or feel certain things, as well as how to move, behave, or speak in certain ways" (1976, 44). Of these three act-phases, it is *imagining-how* that is missing from Bergson's and Schutz's analyses of the project as it is articulated in the context of reflective action.

Whereas both imaging and imagining-that correspond quite well with Bergson's and Schutz's assertions that it is the completed act and not the act in progress that arises as a content of consciousness in reflective action, imagining-how serves to situate the actor in the ongoing stream of activity; what Bergson labeled as the act's dynamic progress. As Casey explains,

To imagine-how is to imagine what it would be like *to* do, think, or feel so-and-so, or *to* move, behave, and speak in such-and-such ways. This kind of imaginative activity is not realized by projecting an unfolding scene of which the imaginer is the mere witness, but rather by entertaining an imagined state of affairs in which he (or a figure who stands proxy for him) is envisaged as *himself an active and embodied participant*. (1976, 45; emphasis in original)

Thus, to "imagine-how is to project not merely a state of affairs *simpliciter* (i.e., one in which the imaginer is not a participant) but a state of affairs into which the imaginer has also projected himself (or a surrogate) as an active being who is experiencing *how* it is to do, feel, think, move, etc. in a certain manner" (1976, 45; emphasis in original; cf. Iacoboni 2008).

What I am suggesting here is therefore an extension of Schutz's model of phenomenal action, what I prefer to call reflective action, to include the imaginal anticipation of a project in an act-phase of "imagining-how." In my estimation, this importantly complicates the various ways that willing may be impacted by both personal and cultural proclivities. Indeed, differing personal and cultural assumptions may variously configure imaginal anticipatory stances toward an act as framed according to either its projective completion or its real-time unfolding. That is, an actor's imaginal anticipation of a project, such as, for instance, the act of picking up a pencil, may be oriented to either a completed act (i.e., the pencil in hand) or an unfolding act (i.e., reaching to pick up the pencil). And these two orientations may themselves be further articulated according to the perspective of a non-participatory third person imagining-that the self is acting in the context of a particular state of affairs (i.e., observing oneself from outside the act as having already picked up the pencil or as being in the process of picking up the pencil). Finally, the same act may also be experienced according to a first person imagining-how of the self as "an active and embodied participant" (i.e., observing and feeling the pencil in one's hand or observing and feeling one's arm move to grasp the pencil and lift the pencil from the desk). The importance of this observation lies in opening a possibility for investigating the ways in which different cultures or different individuals may favor one or another form of anticipatory imaginings of the act from the perspective of these various orientations.

TEMPORALITY, ACTION, AND CULTURAL MODELS OF WILLING

In light of this discussion of the temporal and phenomenological aspects of the experience of willing it is evident that these three phenomenological vectors of willing, each being somewhat independent, can be differentially obfuscated or highlighted in the context of everyday experience. In other words, acts of willing can have varying degrees of own-ness, anticipation, and effortful-ness depending on what stage of action we are analyzing or observing. From the pure project stage to prereflective behavior to social action undertaken in accord with a conscious project—projects that may be themselves variously constituted as intentional objects—we thus see a *gradient of willing* operative in most varieties of social action. The key is temporality.

The "pure project" stage may be characterized by anticipation and a sense of own-ness. Since the act has yet to be realized, however, there may be no corresponding effortful-ness in this phase of the act. In the case of prereflective behavior—action as experienced from the perspective of pure duration—explicit anticipation may fade as a salient object of attention, while a sense of own-ness and effortful-ness may in fact remain a part of the actor's experience. From the perspective of reflective action (either in terms of anticipatory or recollected assessments of a completed act or the anticipatory or recollected assessment of an act in progress that arises in the context of "imagining-how"), we might often find anticipation, effortful-ness, and a sense of own-ness each potentially contributing to the experience of the act as willed. Here, we are thus given a glimpse as to how these three phenomenological vectors might variously interweave with the unfolding of the act in the context of everyday experience.

Moving from the phenomenology of the act to cultural models of the will, I wish to argue that these same three phenomenological vectors of willing may be variously exploited or emphasized in differing cultures in differing contexts. That is, while some cultures may emphasize that "willing" is to be understood as a combination of effortful-ness and anticipation, while backgrounding the necessity that willing entails a sense of own-ness, others may highlight a sense of own-ness and anticipation while backgrounding effortful-ness. To wit, I would like to suggest the possibility for a *gradient of willing* that ranges, to play on Robert Levy's (1973, 1984; cf. Throop 2005) terminology, from *hyper-conation* to *hypo-conation*, depending on which, and the extent to which, these differing aspects of willing are conceptually elaborated in any given culture or community.

In cultures where two or more of these vectors are backgrounded in the articulation of subjective experience it might be said that the culture in question is one that can be characterized as hypo-conative in orientation. While an explicit emphasis on two or more of these vectors could be characterized as hyper-conative. Since these phenomenological vectors of willing can, in different cultures and in different social situations, be differentially foregrounded or backgrounded as salient objects of attention for particular actors, the cultural saliency of these vectors may importantly influence not only the way that willing is conceptualized by those actors, but also the way that it is experienced by them.

Modes of Attention, Culture, and Phenomenal Correlates of Willing

I believe that the potential impact of cultural models of willing on the subjective experience of willing for any given social actor can be generatively grounded in what an increasing number of scholars have come to recognize as the cultural organization of attention. According to these scholars, the cultural organization of attention significantly affects the ways in which individuals discern, delimit, parse, monitor, and interpret their lived experience (Berger 1999; Berger and Del Negro 2002; Csordas 1993; Duranti in press; Howes 1991, 2003; Kirmayer 1984; Leder 1990; Ochs and Schieffelin 1984; Throop 2003a, 2008, forthcoming). This insight, which also plays an important role in Ricoeur's discussion of differing aspects of willing as unfolding in various phases of the act, can be traced at least to William James's observation that "in a world of objects thus individualized by our mind's selective industry, what is called our 'experience' is almost entirely determined by our habits of attention" ([1892] 1985, 39).

The significance of the role of the patterning of attention in the constitution of differing cultural models of willing and their impact on an individual's lived experience of willing in everyday interaction is certainly also supported by Levy's (1973, 1984; cf. Throop 2005) writings on hyper and hypo-cognition. Levy's understanding of the cultural and personal patterning of attention draw from Ernest Schachtel's early insights on the important connections between shared schemata, an individual's focal attention, and the process of selectively parsing the vast field of sensory experience that confronts an individual from the moment of her birth (see Chodorow 1999; Hollan 2000; Throop 2003b). Central to Schachtel's perspective is the idea that schemata—a term he borrows from Bartlett ([1932] 1995)—selectively highlight some forms of experience, while "starving" others (Schachtel 1959, 259). Accordingly, it is often the case that non-schematic experiences are difficult to incorporate and preserve in memory (1959, 295). As Schachtel puts it, "That part of experience which transcends the memory schema as performed by the culture is in danger of being lost because there exists as yet no vessel, as it were, in which to preserve it" (1959, 295).

From this perspective, cultural models of willing (cf. D'Andrade 1987; D'Andrade and Strauss 1992) that are sedimented in particular semiotic forms might be understood to serve, at least partially, to differentially schematize each of the phenomenological vectors of willing for individuals raised in differing cultures. And as such, such cultural models of willing may potentially impact the ways in which those individuals not only meaningfully express willing in interaction but also the ways in which they actually experience willing in the real-time unfolding of the act. For instance, Steven Levinson (2003) has observed a predictable relationship between the differential encoding of spatial orientation in differing languages' grammatical structures and particular forms of spatial cognition. In a similar way, it seems quite possible that cultures that evidence preferences for certain grammatical features that emphasize either passive or active voice constructions, that have tense structures elaborating particular varieties of future, present, or past orientations, or that have an aspect system that encourages individuals to habitually speak of actions as acts in progress or as completed acts (see Duranti 2004), may play a significant role in shaping an actor's habitual attention to the vectors of effort-fullness, own-ness, and anticipation.

To take one example from Alessandro Duranti's recent work on political oratory and agency in Sāmoa, it seems possible that ergative languages—languages wherein the subject of transitive clauses (clauses in which the subject affects a direct object) are marked differently from the subject of intransitive clauses (clauses in which a subject does not affect a direct object)—might serve to significantly highlight an actor's attention to the phenomenological vector of own-ness (1994, 21). Indeed, as Duranti points out, in distinguishing between those actors whose actions have direct consequences for another entity and those actors whose actions only have consequences for themselves, Samoan grammar is well suited to canalizing an actor's attention to the responsibility of an individual, group or deity for some specific act or occurrence. This is evidenced in the prevalent usages of ergative agents in those instances where individuals wish to assign blame or a negative assessment to another's comportment (1994, 25). In so doing, such linguistic practices might also importantly direct actors' attention to a sense of own-ness that is attributable to their own and others' activities.

CONCLUSION

To conclude, there is much merit to approaching the experience of willing from a culturally informed phenomenological perspective. Such an approach allows us to begin the complicated task of understanding willing as it is variously manifest in differing cultures, for differing individuals, in differing interactional contexts. What I have offered in this chapter should, accordingly, be understood as only an initial, and modest step, toward the accomplishment of a broader anthropological investigation of willing in cultural context. The approach to willing discussed in this chapter is thus *not* intended to represent a complete or a prescriptive account. Instead, I hope that the insights garnered from this examination of these three phenomenological vectors of willing is understood as a means to further generate much needed discussion, critical examination, and debate in anthropology concerning the phenomena of willing. And as such it should be construed as one possible means to begin theorizing willing in cultural contexts. With this in mind, I would like to end this chapter with a brief discussion of what, if any, contributions the particular, and certainly partial, take on willing advanced in this chapter can offer the development of cultural theories of social action.

First, I believe that in returning to examine the real-time progression of the act in the context of differing temporal orientations of social actors engaged in particular activities, what is brought into relief is not only the various ways that willing is differentially constituted in the context of different act-phases, but further how this might impact our theoretical and practical investigations into the temporally mediated organization of subjective experience more generally. As I have noted elsewhere (Throop 2003a, forthcoming), accounting for the effects of differing temporal orientations on the structure of experience necessarily complicates our understanding of the different ways that social actors can orient to being-in-the-act, while further offering new avenues for exploring the ways in which both cultural, interactional, and personal factors may play a role in shaping cultural subjectivities.

In addition to encouraging us to attend to how variations in temporal orientations in different phases of social action may affect both the articulation of experience and of willing in cultural context, I believe that this approach may further shed some light on long-standing debates over freedom and determinacy in social theory. In the spirit of Bergson, I hold that it might well be the case that many overly deterministic views of social action have their roots in inattention to the phenomenological structure of willing as a necessarily temporally mediated phenomenon. As Ricoeur has noted in the second volume of his book *Time and Narrative* (1984), assessments of freedom and determinacy may be tied to the necessity that often arises out of a retrospective glance over an already completed field of activity and the contingency that often arises from a future orientation to uncompleted acts in progress (1984, 80). Both "retroactive necessity" and "progressive contingency" might thus importantly, if only partially, be understood to arise from the temporal orientation of the subjectivities of theorists who interrogate the act from perspectives that are situated either within or outside of its progressive unfolding (cf. Schutz [1932] 1967; Bourdieu 1977, 2000).

Finally, I would like to both acknowledge and highlight the necessity of shifting from this descriptive phenomenological approach to willing to exploring how these various experiential correlates of willing may be differentially organized, affected, and expressed in the context of unfolding social interaction, personal narratives, and reflections upon past, present, and future experiences. And indeed, whenever we broach questions of the authorship of the act we are, as Ricoeur so clearly asserted, confronted with questions of ethics and responsibility (Throop forthcoming; see also Garro, Chapter 4; Mattingly, Chapter 3). Such a shift thus calls for careful and thorough ethnographic, person-centered, and linguistic anthropological explorations of the ways in which these experiential correlates of willing may be differentially sedimented in linguistic, semiotic, and symbolic forms. That is, what is now needed (and which this volume is intended to initially address) is a sustained inquiry into how it is that experiences of willing are embedded and reflected in the culturally constituted understanding of morality, subjectivity, and social action as manifest directly in the "gushing reality of life." (Ricoeur ([1950] 1966.)

CHAPTER 3

MORAL WILLING AS NARRATIVE RE-ENVISIONING

Cheryl Mattingly

I T I S N O E A S Y J O B T O S I T U A T E A D I S C U S -
sion of the will within anthropology, which is perhaps why the editors of this volume chose the title they did. It is a subject some of us might want to move toward, but there is no sense of arrival. Even the paths toward it are dauntingly elusive. One is either faced with too much relevant literature or too little. On the too little side, there has been scant explicit consideration of willing as a cultural phenomenon, in contrast to philosophy and psychology where there has been enormous interest in willing as a general human capacity. On the too much side, a consideration of willing as a cultural process invokes an ever growing anthropological literature on intentionality and social action, as well as the cultural shaping of emotions. This wealth of work is clearly relevant but generally it speaks only indirectly about willing, often treating it as part of a general argument about intentionality or emotion in theories of human agency. My solution to this dilemma is that in

setting out a notion of moral willing, I briefly refer to recent anthropological considerations of agency, intention, and emotion, especially those most relevant to the arguments I make. However, as will quickly become evident, the notion of moral willing I develop relies most heavily upon philosophy, where it has been an object of explicit attention and debate.

For some time within anthropology there has been a desire at least in some quarters, to develop and incorporate notions of personal agency into social theory. Critiques of cultural holism and the rise of alternative frames, especially the "practice turn" and the "phenomenological turn" have foregrounded the need, and offered an opportunity, to insert social actors—including individual actors and not only collectivities—within the social scene. We are confronted with specific people and their particular interests, desires, and motives. But this insertion creates new puzzles, new theoretical gaps. Even if the social predominates as anthropology's underlying analytic concern, individual subjectivity and practical reasoning cannot be unproblematically inferred by reference to some kind of collective subjectivity. As William Reddy puts it, regarding the anthropological study of emotions, "A central theoretical difficulty remains unresolved: how to conceptualize a terrain of individual autonomy without selling short the great scope of collective construction" (1999, 262).

In short, it has become clear to many of us that we need to formulate more complicated notions of what individual agents are up to when they act or experience the world, and anthropology still has some way to go in developing rich conceptions of agency. I take this book as one contribution in a very important project to consider such agentive activities as willing, desiring, intending, wishing, judging, and the like. Willing is an especially interesting phenomenon to explore since, traditionally within the western philosophical tradition and in western folk models, it has been so identified with a notion of personal agency, especially a disciplined personal agency— as when we speak of exerting "will power." If we want to move away from deterministic models of social action, if, in other words, we want to claim that social life is neither completely culturally predesigned, nor utterly dictated by structures of power, then we need to elaborate our notions of practical reasoning and practical experience.

These are not particularly new insights, which may say something about the intransigence of the task. More than twenty years ago, for example, Sherry Ortner's (1984) well known essay, "Theory in Anthropology since the Sixties," made a rather similar case. In Ortner's intellectual history of anthropology beginning in the middle of the twentieth century she foregrounds a gradual concern to attend to agents and agency and explores a growing dissatisfaction with structural-functional, Marxist, or other totalizing social models that offered wholly deterministic explanations of social action. Practice theorists have, by and large, been concerned with providing some space for the particular actor. (Though many would argue that there has been less room in practice theories for the individual agent than Ortner presumed in her discussion.) Practice theorists like Pierre Bourdieu argued against a view characteristic of earlier anthropological and sociological models "in which action is seen as the sheer en-actment or execution of rules and norms" (Ortner 1984, 150) by allowing for some level of individual improvisation.

In her review of practice theorists, Ortner suggests a serious limitation that I believe still holds true. She notes that they have not tended to develop any nuanced theory of motivation. Because structure is seen to so dominate how actors think and invent their worlds, the practical agent has agency in a very limited sense—primarily in terms of pragmatic choice and decision making, and/or active calculating and strategizing" (1984, 150). "Unfortunately," she laments, "anthropologists have generally found that actors with too much psychological plumbing are hard to handle methodologically, and practice theories are no exception" (1984, 151). "Interest theory" has largely guided the picture of the motivated actor, in which the actor is generally depicted as "self-interested, rational, pragmatic, and perhaps with a maximizing orientation as well. What actors do, it is assumed, is rationally go after what they want, and what they want is what is materially and politically useful for them within the context of their cultural and historical situations" (ibid.).

In presenting us with an agent driven by a single overriding motive, a highly strategic, endlessly calculating actor, a whole range of other emotions and values are excluded that can also be compelling motivations for action. While theorists such as Bourdieu give us some space for intentionality and reasoning (albeit a very prereflective one shaped by a pregiven habitus), he offers us a very narrow picture of a strategic agent whose conscious reasoning is highly instrumental. But if, contrary to Bourdieu, actions and the reasoning that underlies them are not merely strategic (a position I will develop in later parts of this paper), then theories of practice need much more subtle and complex theories of practical thinking and deliberation.

Ortner also looked toward other anthropological work going on at the time that concerned itself with self, body, emotion, and experience, hoping that this line of work might yield a more complex view of the psychology of actors, one that could potentially inform a more complex picture of motivation—especially the "variable construction of self, person, emotion and motive in cross-cultural perspective." She put it this way: "One may hope for some cross-fertilization between the more sociologically oriented practice accounts, with their relatively denatured views of motive, and some of these more richly textured accounts of emotion and motivation" (1984, 151). In this chapter, I try to do just this sort of cross-fertilizing by offering a concept of willing as a narrative practice, drawing heavily from certain "narrativist" moral philosophers.[1]

WILLING AS (MORAL) CHOICE

What do we mean when we speak of *willing*? If anthropologists have neglected the construct, philosophers have not. I consult several of those philosophers when thinking this through. From a western perspective, in common parlance and in philosophy, willing tends to mean "choosing to act" in some particular way. There is an emphasis on a moment of choice, and sometimes, in difficult situations, on the deliberation that surrounds that choice, as well as an emphasis on doing something—a connection between motive and some kind of public action.[2] The connection of willing to action is especially consequential when it comes to moral choice. In general, philosophers have presumed that decisions do not count as willing something if they are only privately made (I tell myself, "I will confess that I stole the money") but only if they result in public and observable action—a willing to confess that results in a public confession. It is not accidental that I have picked confession as an example. In philosophy and in everyday life, the will has also been linked to morality, the capacity, or one might say willingness to make moral choices

This picture of willing as a *moment of deliberate choice* is problematic in

making sense of the way willing seems to work among the African American families I have been following over the past seven years. These families
have children with significant illnesses and disabilities. They are concerned
with the will, especially the moral will. Parenting kin agonize over what they
ought to do and how to best care for their children. Their concerns are explicitly or obliquely connected to the problem of how to have the *strength* to
do the right thing. This strength they refer to is conceived as a kind of will
power, the power to do what is right even against inclinations to follow an
easier path—to not bother with the exercises the physical therapist has prescribed, to skip a doctor's appointment that requires a three hour bus ride
with a disabled child, to go back on drugs and leave their child for another
family member to tend to.

Such crucial moral issues may involve moments of choice, but this task
of willing the "right thing" involves much more than choosing well—and
acting well—in discrete moments. Parenting kin may, for example, criticize
themselves for not always being strong enough to care for their children as
they should. They talk about getting "tired," even "so tired," but having to
"go on anyway," underscoring how much will power is involved in living
good lives, being good parents, and simply facing the daily trials that pov-
erty, racism, and serious illness inflict. They speak about finding the will to
keep going when life is grim, to hope in the face of despair. Moral choice,
moral change, and moral achievement are fundamental and often-voiced
concerns in this African American community. As they depict their moral
choices, these are inevitably connected to selves in the process of becoming—selves created in community rather than as solo achievements.

Drawing upon several moral philosophers (especially Iris Murdoch, Alasdair MacIntyre, Charles Taylor, and Martha Nussbaum), I want to offer a
different picture of the will that, I think, speaks in a much better way to the
dilemmas and struggles these African American families describe and that
expresses their conception of the will—especially as captured by the notion
of garnering strength to do the right thing. Because the moral will is of such
concern to these families, I concentrate on willing as it is specifically tied to
moral action.

Four features are intrinsic to this alternative conception of the will.

1. Moral willing is better described as refocusing attention than making a choice at a discrete decision point.

2. The "doing" connected to moral willing is likely to be directed to internal reorientation as much as to outward action—to "emotion work."

3. Such doing requires a concept of action that is not atomistic but narrative.

4. A concept of moral willing cannot be disconnected from a notion of self. Furthermore, the "self" implied in moral willing is both a social once (created in community) and a narrative self.

Willing as Reorientation of Attention Rather than Moment of Choice

In western philosophy, the moment of choice model of willing has often been portrayed as a moment of freedom in which a private self asserts itself against the tyranny of publicly, already decided meaning. How does this division between personal freedom and public determinism play out? "I can decide what to say [thus exerting my will] but not what the words mean which I have said [for these are public, defined by the public nature of meaning and language]." Similarly, "I can decide what to do [again exerting my will, making a choice] but I am not master of the significance of my act [because the meaning of acts, like the meaning of words, is a purely public matter]" (Murdoch 1970, 20).

Iris Murdoch challenges this picture in several ways. She offers the following counter example, one that illustrates the first two features of moral willing I outlined earlier: moral willing as a matter of orientation rather than moral choice and moral willing as directed to internal work and not only publicly observable acts. Take a situation where one decides to fall out of love with someone. "Where strong emotions of sexual love . . . are concerned, 'pure will' can usually achieve little. It is small use telling oneself, 'Stop being in love'" (1970, 55). In this example, willing is connected to a kind of emotion work in which one sets out to change oneself. As Murdoch notes, the commonly pictured "neo-Kantian existentialist 'will,'" is a "principle of pure movement," that is, a kind of leap in which one adopts one course of action rather than others. Such a conception is singularly unhelpful in describing what it is like for us to change. In thinking about how one faces the task of something like falling out of love, what she proposes instead is that a notion of willing be tied to something like learning, or what she terms "orientation." Willing so conceived is a matter of learning to shift attention, to reorient, to re-envision and re-imagine.

Murdoch's position is consonant with certain anthropological investigations of personal transformation. Thomas Csordas (1994), to give a pertinent example, offers an "attentional" picture of how a change of self occurs in a religious context. He depicts religious healing among American charismatic Catholics as a reorientation of "somatic modes of attention," arguing that personal change within this tradition is fundamentally linked to an imaginative act of embodied reorientation. Recalling Clifford Geertz's description of the study of religious change as "the social history of the imagination" (1968, 19), Csordas states: "Imagination is the general capacity to transform one's orientation in the world" (1994, 74).

Willing as Internal Struggle: Emotion Work

As Murdoch's example implies, such re-envisioning or re-imagining is likely to involve internal struggles and not necessarily manifest itself only (or primarily) in changed outward acts. This, too, is something overlooked in descriptions of willing—the notion of struggle is curiously absent from philosophical discussions of the will, she notes. Willing to fall out of love involves not so much a single moral choice or even a series of moral choices resulting in some actions but a kind of practice, and one that involves significant internal work. "Deliberately falling out of love is not a jump of the will, it is the acquiring of new objects of attention and thus of new energies as a result of refocusing. The metaphor of orientation may indeed also cover moments when recognizable 'efforts of will' are made, but explicit efforts of will are only a part of the whole situation" (1970, 56). Martha Nussbaum's extensive reflections on the cultivation of moral emotions (especially *Upheavals of Thought*), drawing from ancient Greek and Roman philosophers (Aristotle in particular), emphasize much the same point.

This philosophical recognition that moral emotions are *cultivated* intersects interestingly with anthropological studies of emotion work in a variety of societies. Anthropologists have long been intrigued with the connection between culture and emotion. In a review article on the anthropology of emotions written some twenty years ago, Catherine Lutz and Geoffrey White note that rather than treating emotions as "irrational forces," a number of anthropologists were beginning to examine the culturally shaped "formulation of emotion in conscious understanding and in interactive discourse" (1986, 417), a formulation directly connected to a moral order (e.g., Rosaldo 1984; Basso 1984; Levy 1973). Significant ethnographic research has been directed to studying how children are emotionally guided as part of their socialization into society (e.g., H. Geertz 1959; Ochs 1984; Ochs, Smith and Taylor 1989; M. Goodwin 1990; Briggs 1998). C. Jason Throop points out that psychoanalytically oriented anthropologists, in particular, "have played a significant role in highlighting the importance of emotion, motivation, and early childhood experience in the cultural patterning of subjective experience and social action" (2003a, 110).

The anthropological study of how emotions are shaped through cultural practices and processes lays important groundwork for considering emotional reorientation and moral willing. More specifically relevant to my topic are examinations of how, under a variety of cultural circumstances, people take on the task of personal change and how this can involve them in a struggle to "re-orient" their emotions. For example, Lone Grøn (2005) studied a Danish "lifestyle change" health program directed at helping people with serious and chronic health problems (generally caused by being severely overweight) to modify their exercise and eating habits in accordance with more healthful routines. As part of her fieldwork, she followed a group of patients who took part in this program, to see how they experienced their task of trying to make these shifts in their daily lives. The issue of willing came up repeatedly as these patients spoke of their struggle to change basic patterns in their lives. From the health promotion standpoint, these changes were often treated as exercising will power, learning new information about the body, and making key lifestyle decisions. From the patient's perspective it was much more a matter of coming to re-orient themselves and engaging in internal struggles over how to come to a new sense of themselves and their lives. You have to, as one of these patients told her, "will with your head and your heart" to have any chance of making such big changes. It isn't simply a matter of deciding to eat less or exercise more, but one of trying to shift the

very objects of your desire, of "working on your head," as this same patient
said (Grøn 2005). Similarly, to illustrate with another example, when Carole Cain (1991) studied Alcoholics Anonymous (AA) groups in the United
States, she found that the message AA members gave themselves was not to
rely simply on "willing" not to drink—willing alone would never stop them
from drinking. Rather, the basic change had to come from head and heart,
including such things as reorienting one's beliefs and feelings about the ability to be in control of oneself or of life in general (Cain 1991; Holland et al.
1998). The famous AA serenity prayer is very much a practice of learning to
feel differently, of emotional reorientation.

Willing as a Narrative Act

Willing, treated as moment of choice out of which a specific action flows, especially fits an atomistic picture of action. Alasdair MacIntyre notes that this
is a dominant conception of action, developed within analytic philosophy
and existentialism but powerful also in sociological and psychological theories. In atomistic treatments, action is presumed to be something that can
be broken down into simple and separable parts. In an atomistic frame, one
"analyze[s] complex actions and transactions in terms of simple components"
(MacIntyre 1981, 190).

But if willing is a matter of orientation, this requires a different way of
defining action itself. A contrasting view, one I adopt here, is essentially narrative—and I draw upon MacIntyre's useful reformulation to do so. Rather
than presuming that any particular action can be broken down into basic
units, he argues, action is only intelligible as embedded within larger contexts, which MacIntyre asserts are essentially narrative: "particular actions
derive their character as parts of larger wholes" (MacIntyre 1981, 190). In
everyday practical life, an act cannot understandably be isolated into the
analytic philosopher's "basic action" but must be connected to these larger
narrative contexts from which any particular act derives its intelligibility—in
which it can be said to mean something. MacIntyre, who offers one of the
clearest arguments on this point, puts it succinctly: "in successfully identifying and understanding what someone else is doing we always move toward
placing a particular episode in the context of a set of narrative histories, histories both of the individuals concerned and of the settings in which they act
and suffer" (1981, 197). This is a fundamentally historical perspective—par-

ticular actions derive their meaning from their place in a history, or, more accurately, a number of histories.

If meaningful acts are narrative ones, that is, only intelligible as parts of unfolding narratives, then what does this say about willing? I want to build from this notion of willing as orientation rather than "acted-upon-moment-of-choice" by considering willing as a narrative act. If willing involves, in many situations, the task of reorientation, any specific moral choosing is understandable as part of a past and future, from which this particular moment derives its (moral) meaning. That is, it becomes understandable as connected to an orientation that is part of a story—one that has its own history (say, falling in love with this particular, somehow unsuitable, man) and its own wished for future (falling out of love with this man). Obviously, such a history that surrounds such re-orientation might be embedded within all kinds of larger social and personal narrative histories. There is no single correct narrative in which an action must be understood in order for it to be meaningful. Rather, the claim here is that action cannot be reduced to a meaningful unit that is disconnected from *any* larger narrative (or narratives)—whether personal ones (say, my romantic history), or social ones (for instance, a history of romance in America).[3] Since many narrative contexts can reasonably be brought to bear in answering the question, "What is she doing" or "What is she willing?", how should one sort out just which narrative history should be given primacy as an answer to these question? MacIntyre's answer is that we pay special attention to the "primary intentions" of the actor himself. How would he characterize his primary intentions in carrying out this task? This answer is likely too simple for the anthropological mind, but many would argue the need to make sense of someone's action by privileging how she would characterize her intentions, at least as a starting point for analysis. Anthropologists may choose *not* to focus upon the conscious concerns of those they study, but there has also been, within anthropology, a call to understand what is "at stake" for actors that supports MacIntyre's position (Jackson 1989, 1995; Wikan 1990, 1991; Kleinman and Kleinman 1991; Kleinman 1995; Reddy 1999). In selecting meaningful narrative frameworks for making sense of an action, there is something to be said for paying attention to what matters to those one studies, even if this is not the only narrative frame one wishes to impose as part of the answer to the question, "what is she doing?" or "what is she willing (to do)?"

Attention to the actor's personal perspective and concerns—as one critical starting point—is especially important if we are to build a picture of
willing that gives some space for the agent's own view of his moral choices,
moral dilemmas, and moral struggles. For willing, however it is defined, has
carried with it a notion of some kind of directed intentionality, especially an
intentionality that is at some level conscious to the actor, a deliberateness. I
"will" to fall out of love with someone and even if this does not materialize in
an immediate change of heart, it directs a course of change that I undertake,
a kind of personal project. Because of the deliberate and directed character of
moral willing, a narrative conception of willing needs to be especially attentive to the conscious intentions and directed concerns of the agent.

Willing as Narrative Re-Envisioning of the Self

A narrative picture of moral willing connects re-orientation to a self in
transformation. The connection of willing to a personal project of self-
transformation has special salience for the African American families I have
followed, as they struggle with how to be good parents to seriously sick and
disabled children. They very often link moral willing (or the ability to "act
from strength," as they commonly express it) to a moral project of personal
change. A primary narrative context is their own life history and the lives of
those they care about, a point made by the "narrativist" moral philosophers
I draw from here.

There is a need to connect what is at stake in any particular act to a narrative of the self, MacIntyre argues, because looking at only proximal intentions does not give us sufficient understanding of the meaning of an act. It
does not lend enough depth. We need to know something about "longer and
longest-term intentions . . . and how the shorter-term intentions are related
to the longer" (1981, 193). Longer-term intentions speak to a person's sense of
self. This self is, for MacIntyre, a narrative one—in discerning what a person
is up to by referring to their longer term intentions "we are involved in writing a narrative history" (1981, 193). Charles Taylor builds upon MacIntyre's
insight but in a reverse direction. It is not only that to understand what a
person is doing (or willing) we must refer to various narrative contexts to
decipher their intent. Taylor argues that it is primarily through having things
"at stake" that one has a self at all. So, to speak of trying to understand what
is at stake for actors is to speak of trying to understand who they are. "We

are selves only in that certain issues matter for us. What I am as a self, my identity, is essentially defined by the way things have significance for me . . . we are only selves insofar as we move in a certain space of questions, as we seek and find an orientation to the good" (Taylor 1989, 34). It is impossible to speak of understanding a person, Taylor continues, "in abstraction from his or her self-interpretations" and these concern what is of significance (ibid.). Moral willing speaks to our sense of what is significant, of what Taylor calls our "orientation to the good."

For Taylor, this orientation and the self constituted by it are essentially narrative. He further insists that this orientation only makes sense in light of a narratively understood self: "This sense of the good has to be woven into my understanding of my life as an unfolding story" (1989, 47).[4] Iris Murdoch calls us "moral pilgrims," a conceit that speaks to the quest-like narrative structure of this moral self, which is always in the process of becoming. Notably, the self that is narratively constructed is not an individual achievement but a self constructed in a community. As Taylor puts it, "one cannot be a self on one's own" (1989, 36). A self is always constructed by reference to some defining communities. This dialogical self depends upon what Taylor calls "webs of interlocution" (1989, 36).

Murdoch's discussion of moral choice that so challenges dominant conceptions of the will also depends upon an essentially narrative conception of the self, though she does not specifically speak of a "narrative self."

The place of choice is certainly a different one if we think in terms of a world which is *compulsively* present to the will [the existentialist position she opposes] and the discernment and exploration of which is a slow business. Moral change and moral achievement are slow; we are not free in the sense of being able suddenly to alter ourselves since we cannot suddenly alter what we can see and ergo what we desire and are compelled by. (Murdoch 1970, 39)

BECOMING A NEW KIND OF MOTHER AND A NEW KIND OF FAMILY: MORAL WILLING IN ETHNOGRAPHIC CONTEXT

To examine the four features of moral willing described earlier, I now turn to one of the families I've worked with. A child of one of the three mothers in the household was very badly burned.[5]

Sonya's son, Gus, was terribly burned in a household accident five years ago, when he was just a little more than a year old. Sonya and Gus live with Sonya's mother, Doreen; one of Sonya's older sisters, Mary; as well as Mary's four children. Sonya and Mary are the youngest two of Doreen's ten children. Sonya, who is now 27, has always lived at home, and theirs has been a close-knit multigenerational household, although Sonya and Mary look and act extremely differently. I met Gus and his mother just a few months after the burn accident (in September 1999). I had known this family since 1997, however, because one of Mary's children was initially enrolled in our study due to congenital hip problems.

The burn incident occurred in the kitchen. Gus was playing on the floor while his ten-year-old cousin Candace (one of Mary's girls) was cooking food. She was supposed to be keeping an eye on him, but she didn't see when Gus suddenly reached up and tipped over a pan of burning grease, which fell onto his face. His grandmother immediately called 911 and they wrapped him in wet towels while they waited for the paramedics. Sonya was not home when it happened. This terrible accident presented Sonya with a number of moral challenges and choices. These are some of the ones she has identified:

1. Should she allow Gus to have risky surgeries?

2. Should she tell him how he got burned, that it was his cousin Candace who wasn't watching him properly while she was cooking?

3. Should she talk to Candace about what happened?

4. Should she let Gus go to burn camp, where he will be with other children who are burned, and perhaps then see himself as somehow disabled? A "burn survivor"?

5. Should she make him wear the therapeutic masks and mouthpiece that he hates, even though these may help to reduce scarring? When should she insist that he wear them, and when should she allow him to take them off?

6. Should she be angry and blame her niece Candace or her sister and mother, who were all present in the house when the accident happened?

7. Should she blame herself, for leaving her year-old son in this busy, noisy house while she was at work?

Although some of these practical and moral problems required clear decisions that resulted in action, befitting the dominant notion of willing, these
decisions came only after significant reorientation of her emotions (Sonya
did decide to have the surgeries after the initial accident, and when he got
older, she decided to send him to burn camp). She had to struggle internally
in order to be able to make these decisions from a place of strength. (There is
no resonance, in any of her accounts, with any existentialist picture of a free
will acting in an otherwise determined world). Further, many of the moral
dilemmas she has named over the years (and listed above), like the ones that
have to do with whether she should be angry or not—have no obvious action consequences at all but speak, just as Murdoch insists, to an internal
struggle to envision her world in what she deems the right (most moral) way.
Notably, discussions of patient choice in the clinical literature often portray
these situations as moments of choice. But this was not how she experienced
such situations.

Re-Orientation Versus Moment of Choice

Over the years, Sonya has recounted particular dilemmas she faces in caring
for her son. Occasionally she speaks in a language of clear moral choice that
results in action. For instance, she has decided she will never tell him how the
accident happened because she does not want him to blame the cousin who
should have been watching out for him. "He don't know how he got burned
and I vowed to never tell him that . . . because I don't ever want it to be, you
did this to me." But such instances of discrete choices are rare. Mostly, even
situations that demand decisions must be faced gradually, through discussion with both friends and family about how to approach problems (how
should I feel? how should I face this situation?) and heartfelt self-reflection.
She describes in detail, for example, the agony she faced in agreeing that her
son should have his initial surgery, a horror that never quite went away in
later surgeries. "They [clinicians] told me all the bad things that could pos-
sibly happen. Like he could lose consciousness and die. You know, because
we're paralyzing his body from the neck down with medicines. . . . They tell
me that . . . his throat could swell while in surgery and cause him to lose his
breath." Sonya herself had to fight the paralysis that comes with fear at these
terrible possibilities: "I'm dealing with the idea that he got burned, and know

that I have to deal with the fact that they might come out of this room and tell me that my son died."

She presents the problem of making the right decision not as a matter of willing something, of making a choice at a particular moment, so much as taking on the larger task of how to be the kind of person capable of facing such tough choices. It is the cultivation of a way of being a mother for her son that she sees as her biggest task. She remarked once, plaintively, "everyone would say you have to be strong for him [her son]. But, I mean, how do you, you are you strong, you know? It's like, that's like, that's my kid . . . I'm vulnerable, you know what I mean? Because this is my kid and he has just suffered, you know, something I never imagined." Sonya is saying something about learning how to embody a different kind of will. In order to choose the surgeries from a place of strength, she must face her own vulnerability. Her portrayal of this experience echoes Iris Murdoch's notion of willing as "orientation," or, in this case, re-orientation.

In this community such re-orienting is almost never portrayed as an isolated individual affair. Undertaking the project of becoming strong for her son, thereby allowing her to make better decisions when things—such as new surgeries—come up, is a social project, one in which her whole family becomes involved by supporting her and counseling her when difficult choices arise. Sonya says, "My mom encouraged me [to agree to the surgery]. Mary [her sister] did too." Sonya recounts what they advised: "If it's best for him, then go ahead, and, you know, we'll deal with it . . . each step that we have to go through, we'll deal with it when we get there."

There is a "we-ness" to her account that underscores how the whole family has been faced with the moral task of reorientation. This is also evident in my interviews with Sonya's sister Mary and her mother. At first, Sonya says, this horrifying incident crippled the family: "When Gus got burned, it crippled us." But then things changed. The family "embraced" Gus and the pain of what happened; in fact, as the three mothers in this family have often said, this tragedy brought them together in a new way. They responded to it by learning to become stronger. All the children became involved with Gus's care. Everyone wanted to bathe him, to clean his wounds. Sonya described it in this way: "As a family, we've never embraced anything, so when he got burned it was just like everybody just grabbed it and hugged it and was like 'this belongs to me.' You know, even though it was like really hard and painful for all of us, but it, we had to deal with it as a family versus just me dealing with it as mom, or my mom dealing with it as grandmother. We just took it and dealt with it."

Re-Orientation as Internal Struggle

Sonya's efforts to make the right decision about, say, surgery, reveal that willing is frequently connected to a kind of emotion work in which one sets out to change oneself, to envision the world differently as a way to face tough situations and decisions as they arise. Willing, here, involves a change of heart. Overt, discrete acts of will are just a sporadic manifestation of this transformation. One of the clearest places in which the internal struggle becomes apparent in this case is in Sonya's efforts not to succumb to bitterness and anger. It was difficult for her not to be angry at the niece who was in the kitchen when Gus got burned, but she knew that her niece was not only "really really sorry" but felt horribly guilty. "She couldn't even, when I got to the hospital, she couldn't even look at me." In the hospital, Sonya acts generously—she hugs her niece. But this generous act is only a moment in an on-going effort not to become bitter or blame anyone for what happened. This internal effort is at the heart of Sonya's many stories about caring for her child. Here is one of many quotes on the matter: "It was, oh God, so, so painful for me . . . cause your first, I mean, you want to be mad. That's what I wanted to be initially. I wanted to be mad." She has had to struggle with this anger. "I tried really hard not to be angry, not to be bitter, because I know how it can make a person. . . ." She is grateful that despite her anger, the feeling of hurt is what predominated. And even her hurt has gradually subsided. She has been able to move on, even to consider herself lucky for her child who has survived his surgeries and is "so, so smart." She couches this moral re-orientation in the language of healing. As she puts it, "I healed from my hurt."

Such healing, however internal, is also not a solo task. It involves many social practices and, as Sonya makes clear, and as we have seen in carrying out this research, it is aided by family and friends, whose actions and advice are critical. Every time Gus has gone in for a surgery—and especially during the first surgery when he had a thirty-day hospital stay, he has been surrounded by his family and Sonya's friends from church. There have been problems with hospital staff because his room was so crowded with visitors. These actions, and the messages that Sonya received about how she should respond to her son's injury, have helped her in getting over her anger. No one told her to "be mad," she remembers. Instead, "I had positive people around me the whole time" and they counseled her to "just think good thoughts and . . . what you think is what will happen." Sonya notes gratefully how good this advice was, how much it has helped her to heal from her hurt and anger.

Willing as Narrative Act

The narrative nature of this moral willing, treated as moral re-envisioning, emerges in many ways in this case. There are a number of narrative contexts that are invoked in the way this incident is interpreted by Sonya and her family. There is the narrative context of Gus, the person he is becoming, someone who is strong and smart, who can comfort his mother when she feels weak, one who is not (according to Sonya) bothered by his scars, and therefore, through the way he sees himself, can teach her lessons about how to see him. There is the narrative context of Sonya's own life story, a point to which I will return in the following section. And there is, of course, the family context. The whole process of re-orientation is given a narrative treatment in interviews with Sonya and other family members. There is the shift of the family from "crippled" to "embracing" the pain of the accident, a process in which particular actions (or being willing to act), for example the cousin's insistence on being allowed to help take care of Gus, take their (moral) meaning as episodes in an unfolding family story.

There are even future stories, told by some, that help Sonya by sketching a path that she, in the midst of her pain, could not see. For instance, a particularly close cousin, and a "super Christian" spent a great deal of time with her when Gus was initially hurt. She offered her a hopeful future story that Sonya was gradually able to embrace, one that would take her from her initial anger and hurt to a place of belief and acceptance—a healing story. "She just talked to me about Jesus, and how God was gonna take care of it . . . I just have to believe that it's gonna be OK, you know? Then, and then after that, that's when the process of healing will begin."

Sonya attempts to thwart some future stories through her actions. She vows not to tell Gus that it was Candace who was careless of him and therefore, in some way, to blame for what happened. Gus loves Candace and she does not want to set such a bitter story in motion. She does her part, as do other members of the family, to knit themselves together in a closer way as a result of this accident, instead of letting it tear them apart.

Willing as Narrative Re-Envisioning of the Self

In this African American community, moral transformations of the will are often couched in a particular narrative genre, as *healing narratives*, where the self is a moral one in the process of becoming. Sonya portrays her most difficult struggle as battling her initial bitterness and anger. She describes her gradual ability to overcome these as "healing" from difficult emotions. Many personal stories are intertwined in this case. Here, I look at Sonya's, by way of brief illustration of this last point. It is repeatedly underscored in our data that one of the most significant contexts Sonya draws upon to make decisions about how to care for Gus, or to envision what kinds of moral decisions she faces, is her own unfolding life. This is a life depicted in highly narrative terms, in terms of dramatic shifts, of befores and afters, especially those centered upon the accident itself. Gus's accident, she says, "altered my total sense of being."

She recalls how unfamiliar the world was in which she was suddenly plunged. When she was pregnant, she heard about the usual childhood diseases, but no one told her "how to deal with a child when he's severely burned." This new world has confronted her again and again, for "no matter how you think you've conquered it, in one way, you know it's always something new that comes up. When you think, OK, I've got this down, you know, something new happens. Maybe there is a new surgery the physicians tell you about, and you have to face your fears all over again, or maybe he will be teased now that he's in school, and you'll have to deal with that." These situations, which must be "dealt with," could be handled theoretically as moments of moral choice. But for Sonya, they are understandable as episodes in her unfolding life story and are most deeply intelligible from that narrative perspective.

This narrative perspective of a life also provides a way for her to situate the on-going work of making good choices about how to care for Gus to a broader re-making of her own life. She believes she has become a better person because this has happened to her. While once she was rather "judgmental" of people, this has forced her to change. "It made me a better person. . . . Cause I used to be, like, really judgmental. Like, 'Oh, what's their problem?' Or, you know, 'What's wrong with them?' But it kind of made me realize that, you know, people do the same thing that I did to others." She responds to this not only by trying to protect her son, but also through a moral re-envisioning that has allowed her to embrace the pain of others.

CONCLUSION

I have challenged the atomistic picture of the will—at least in regard to the moral will. I have argued that it is too reductionistic to treat willing as a discrete phenomenological chunk of experience, an isolated lived moment of choosing and acting. Instead, I have offered a narrative picture that defines willing as re-envisioning and re-orienting, emphasizing willing at particular choice points as inextricably bound to larger moral projects. In this African American community moments of willing, of having to choose, are experienced as parts of histories—battles fought, characters changing or failing to change, moral healing engendered not only through one's own efforts but offered, as gifts, through the actions and attitudes of significant others, both human and spiritual. Above all, this moral willing is connected to the project of coming to be a different, better kind of person, one who acquires the strength to face unexpected hardships and to treat the world more compassionately. This project is a long one, and it is not guaranteed. That is why so much attention is required.

CHAPTER 4

BY THE WILL OF OTHERS
OR BY ONE'S OWN ACTION?

Linda C. Garro

W HAT IS ENTAILED BY THE CLAIM THAT volition is a generic (universal) attribute of selves (both of oneself and of other selves) while also remaining attentive to the ways in which "the world in which human beings think, feel and act is always a culturally constituted world" (Hallowell 1942, 1)? A. Irving Hallowell's articulation of this position offers a starting point within psychological anthropology for contemporary efforts, such as this volume, to move toward a more explicit "anthropology of the will." However, because Hallowell's comments on volition are embedded within his larger theoretical framework, an overview of his general approach is provided first.

In seminal publications concerning "the self in its behavioral environment" (see especially Chapter 4 and Chapter 8 in Hallowell 1955, which were originally published together as a single article), Hallowell framed the self as constituted through attributes common to all humans as well as emergent through social and cultural experience. Based on fieldwork starting in the 1930s with the Ojibwa of Manitoba, Canada, and drawing comparisons with his own cultural background and research findings from social scientists working in western settings, Hallowell noted parallels in how selves are understood, commonalities that transcended experiential variability across diverse cultural settings. He maintained that across cultures what "is held in common is a self-concept that assumes certain generic human attributes" (Hallowell 1955, 180). In addition to volition his candidates for generic attributes of self include the following: self-awareness, sentience, memory, speech [symbolization], and autonomy. At the same time, ethnographic evidence documenting variability in how self was conceptualized and experienced contributed to Hallowell's assessment of how the universal was bounded. For example, based on findings from his own field research, Hallowell considered the assumption that "human bodily structure" is a "necessary substratum for a functioning self" to be culturally contingent and therefore not universal (Hallowell 1955, 176).

Writing long before the contemporary surge of interest in the evolutionary and developmental dimensions of the cultural, Hallowell maintained that the generic attributes enable culture and development while also being transformed through culture and development. For example, self-awareness, minimally characterized as the reflexive discrimination of oneself "as an object in a world of objects" other than oneself, was put forward as "one of the prerequisite psychological conditions for the functioning of any human social order" (Hallowell 1955, 75). The capacity for "self-awareness" is necessary for human societies to "become social orders of conscious selves" (Hallowell 1955, 10). Yet, self-awareness is also "a cultural as well as a social product" (Hallowell 1955, 81), a developmental process in a specific cultural environment. Reading across Hallowell's 1955 volume *Culture and Experience*, the transformation of the generic capacity for self-awareness to the "outlook of the self in its behavioral environment" (Hallowell 1955, 89) can be seen as unfolding in time, involving a given individual, in a specific historical-cultural setting, and in the context of particular social relationships. By extension, a similar argument holds for the other generic attributes, including volition.

This jointly universal yet specific perspective is also found in Hallowell's claim that the "human individual must be provided with certain basic orientations in order to act intelligibly in the world he apprehends" (Hallowell 1955, 89). While at an abstract level the typology of basic orientations is presented as a kind of universal, at another level, these basic orientations take shape only within specific social and cultural settings as "cultural means and content may vary widely" (Hallowell 1955, 89). The "basic orientations provided by culture"—self-orientation, object orientation (including other persons), spatiotemporal orientation, motivational orientation, and normative orientation—align the experiencing self with the external world and structure the psychological field in which the self is prepared to act (Hallowell 1955, 89, 110). The socially and culturally forged basic orientations implicitly guide the perception and interpretation of experience, including what an individual takes to be reality, as well as affording a normatively informed basis for reflection, decision, and action (cf. Hallowell 1976, 391; 1958, 79). In Hallowell's framework, orientations point toward interpretive possibilities. This is essentially a processual view of the relation between culture and experience; individual experience as culturally informed rather than culturally determined.

Central to Hallowell's framework is his view that selves are in part constituted in cultural settings through interactions with "other selves." Indeed, a key insight is that experiential reality takes shape in relation to ontological reality, one that is typically shared with others within a behavioral environment. Thus, the "self in its relation with other selves may transcend the boundaries of social life as objectively defined" and involve "other-than-human selves" (Hallowell 1955, 92). As Hallowell noted: "All human cultures include classes of *other-than-human* persons that are an integral part of the psychological field of the individual" (1958, 63). That persons within a behavioral environment are seen to vary in terms of their potential powers for acting in and upon the world was not overlooked in Hallowell's work.

Hallowell's comments on volition presume the intertwining of the generic, social, and cultural. He explicitly establishes links between the volitional and the moral in the context of interpersonal relations. For Hallowell, the "universal fact" that "any human society is not only a social order but a moral order as well" means that "the members of such an order are assumed to assume moral responsibility for their conduct" (Hallowell 1955, 83). This, in turn, "implies the capacity for self objectification, self identification, and appraisal of one's own conduct, as well as that of others, with reference to socially recognized and sanctioned standards of behavior" (Hallowell 1959, 50). Given "a possible choice of alternative lines of conduct," with regard to both one's own actions as well as those of others, "implicit in moral appraisal is the concomitant assumption that the individual has volitional control over his own acts" (Hallowell 1955, 83 & 106). While much of Hallowell's discussion is couched at a general level, the intertwining of the volitional and the moral, and their embedding in interpersonal relations and local moralities, make clear that an understanding of volition cannot be divorced from particular social and cultural settings. Examining the experiential dimensions of volition, through both first-person reports as well volition-related inferences concerning the conduct of others, would therefore provide a basis for assessing similarities and divergences across cultural settings.

Before going further, it is important to note that, even though he does not differentiate them, Hallowell is advancing two positions about the relationship between the volitional and the moral. Both implicate a "conscious" or "reflective" self invested in a local moral world. The first revolves around the appraisal of conduct against local moral standards and does not require an assessment or attribution of intent, or will, to transgress. Such appraisal is consistent with a cultural proclivity, such as Robert Levy described for Tahiti, to place the "moral stress . . . on one's actions, not on one's intentions" (1973, 350; cf. Duranti 2006). Even so, if the voluntary nature of the action is not in question, the act is presumed to be a volitional act. The second position shifts the emphasis to "volitional control." In situations where "choice" is possible, Hallowell appears to postulate a link between processes internal to a self (e.g., "deciding") and subsequent action. "Volitional control" is, at least in part, a state of mind involving an "intentional" self (either oneself or another self). Conversely, it may be that in situations characterized by lack of "volitional control" moral culpability is lessened. While this does presume an understanding of oneself and others as intentional beings and reflective selves, it by no means requires that one "knows" what others are up to with regard to their intentions. Indeed, in writings on the Ojibwa (see especially Chapter 15 in Hallowell 1955 and 1960) Hallowell claims that a "generalized attitude" of caution and suspiciousness in interpersonal relations reflects the experiential reality of a cultural setting where appearances may be deceiving (such as a smiling countenance masking hostile feelings), where what is truly felt and thought by others cannot be known, and where covert means of causing harm to others ("sorcery") are culturally available. One can suspect others of harboring ill will, as well as being covert and immoral agents of harm, but it is only in the world of action that one's suspicions (hypotheses) receive support.

As elaborated in this chapter, narrative as a mode of thinking—a way of "ordering experience, of constructing reality" (Bruner 1986, 11)—offers an entrée for exploring the relevance of notions of "moral responsibility," "moral appraisal," and "volitional control" in and across specific cultural settings. In this examination of how "volition" enters social life, I rely upon Hallowell's broader conceptualization of persons, their capabilities and powers, both perceived and potential, within specific behavioral environments. My use of "behavioral environment" does not imply an "outlook of the self" that is shared by all within a cultural setting but rather reflects an appreciation that the "behavioral environment" is not the same for all individuals and may even vary for the same individual across time. I limit the ethnographic material drawn upon to two primary sources, my own fieldwork in a Canadian Anishinaabe (Ojibwa) community and some of Hallowell's writings. Among the examples examined are cases in which "volitional control" for one person's actions are attributed to another person. Because different cultural "settings" afford different narrative possibilities, in a research paper I extend this general approach to other ethnographic contexts (see Garro, n.d.).

First, though, to provide a point of comparison with the ethnographic data, I briefly review some relevant literature by American scholars with reference to primarily American cultural settings. The material covered ranges widely; some authors aspire to illuminate the nature of will as universal psychological phenomena, the work of others serves to illuminate some aspect of willing within a particular sociocultural milieu.

PERSPECTIVES ON WILLING

Writing in the late 1800s, the psychologist William James began his chapter on "will" with the following: "Desire, wish, will, are states of mind which everyone knows, and which no definition can make plainer" (James [1890]

1983, 1098). Portraying desiring and wishing as denizens of the same terrain, James asserted that *"the terminus of the psychological process in volition, the point to which the will is directly applied, is always an idea"* (James [1890] 1983, 1171, see Throop, Chapter 2). As psychological experience, willing

terminates with the prevalence of the idea; and whether the act then follows or not is a matter quite immaterial, so far as the willing itself goes. I will to write, and the act follows. I will to sneeze, and it does not. I will that the distant table slide over the floor towards me; it also does not. My willing representation can no more instigate my sneezing-centre than it can instigate the table to activity. But in both cases it is as true and good willing as it was when I willed to write. In a word, volition is a psychic or moral fact pure and simple, and is absolutely completed when the stable state of the idea is there. (James [1890] 1983, 1165)

As a "psychic and moral fact," volition represents a particular type of relation between self and "our states of mind":

I want more than anything else to emphasize the fact that volition is primarily a relation . . . between our Self and our own states of mind. . . . When an idea *stings* us in a certain way, makes as it were a certain electric connection with our Self, we believe that it *is* reality. When it stings us in another way, makes another connection with our Self, we say, *let it be* a reality. The indicative and the imperative moods are as much ultimate categories of thinking as they are of grammar. The "quality of reality" which these moods attach to things is not like other qualities. It is a relation to our life. It means *our* adoption of things, *our* caring for them, *our* standing by them. This at least is what it practically means for us; what it may mean beyond that we do not know. And the transition from merely considering an object to be possible, to deciding or willing it to be real; the change from the fluctuating to the stable personal attitude concerning it; from the "don't care" state of mind to that in which "we mean business," is one of the most familiar things in life. (James [1890] 1983, 1172–73)

In this manner, James situates willing in relation to what matters to us in life. In underscoring the way an idea makes a "connection with our Self," James opens the way for an exploration of such connections within the context of individual lives, lives as experienced in specific cultural settings. With a primary orientation toward the future, the act of willing "*let it be* a reality" is also a reflexive act grounded in the present but also related to the past. In pointing out the impossibility of certain sequelae following an act of simply willing the world to be so (e.g., instigating a table to activity), James makes even fuzzier whatever distinctions exist among desiring, wishing, and willing.

Daniel Wegner explores the sense of a causal connection between the experience of will and subsequent action (Throop, Chapter 2). For Wegner, the experience of conscious will is a feeling—an *"emotion of authorship"* (2002). He depicts conscious will as "a feeling that organizes and informs our understanding of our own agency . . . one that reverberates through mind and body to indicate when we sense having authored an action" (Wegner 2002, 318). When the willed actions are those of our own bodies, the "juxtaposition of our thought and action" provides the basis for "causal inferences about how our minds seem to be producing our behaviors" (Wegner 2005, 30). For "normal voluntary action," the "expected correspondence of action and the feeling of doing—the case when we do something and also feel that we are doing it" is "perhaps the assumed human condition" (Wegner 2002, 8–9). Importantly, we extend causal inference to the actions of others, "[w]e readily perceive agents all around us" and ascribe authorship for action to agents (Preston and Wegner 2005, 104).

Drawing on work carried out in western settings, Wegner maintains that human beings aspire to an "ideal of human agency" (Wegner 2002) grounded in a three component "thought—will—action model" (Preston and Wegner 2005, 106) with the qualities of being "conscious, effortful, and intentional" (Wegner 2005, 19). Intention "is normally understood as an idea of what one is going to do that appears in consciousness just before one does it" (Wegner 2002, 18). However, when experience does not match the ideal of human agency (one of the three components is not present), typically "we infer that the missing components of ideal agency are actually in place" (Preston and Wegner 2005, 121). With regard to intention, it "appears as though we are unable to admit or understand that we may have acted without knowing why" (Preston and Wenger 2005, 109). Given a "feeling that the action was freely willed by actor, not induced by others," there is a tendency to generate "reasons to explain our actions post hoc and believe that those reasons were our intentions all along" (Preston and Wegner 2005, 110 and 109). What is key here is that a "feeling of doing" does not depend upon prior conscious intentions. As well, there appears to be "a kind of continuum between routine practices that proceed with little reflection and planning, and agentive acts that intervene in the world with something in mind (or in heart)" (Ortner 2006, 136; cf. Haggard 2006).

At an experiential level, Wegner states that the feeling of doing "keeps our notion of ourselves as persons intact" (Wegner 2004, 658), affording the knowledge of a self with continuity through time. Further, in reminding us that we are doing something, the experience of will "serves to accentuate and anchor an action in the body. This makes the action our own far more intensely than could a thought alone. Unlike simply saying 'this act is mine,' the occurrence of conscious will brands the act deeply, associating the act with self through feeling, and so renders the act one's own in a personal and memorable way" (Wegner 2004, 658). We "do not just deduce that we did an action, we feel we did it." Such experiences "leave a residue of memories of past authorship, and give rise as well to anticipations of future authorship" (Wegner 2005, 31). Further, according to Wegner, as part of an "intuitive accounting system" (ibid.), the "feeling that we are doing things" serves "key functions in the domains of achievement and morality," helping us to "appreciate and remember what we are doing" and what we have done, while also providing a basis for "how we judge ourselves to be morally right and wrong" (Wegner 2002, 318). This "guide to ourselves" is "perhaps most important for the sake of the operation of society" in that "the sense of conscious will also allows us to maintain the sense of responsibility for our actions that serves as the basis for morality" (Wegner 2002, 328).

Nevertheless, Wegner emphasizes that while this view of the mind's role in guiding action "is a deeply important construction, allowing us to understand, organize, and remember the variety of things we find ourselves doing, it is a construction nonetheless"(Wegner 2005, 30). Further he points out that it is a construction that can be disrupted. For example, an illusory experience of will occurs when people "people feel they are willing an act that they are not doing" (Wegner 2002, x). An example consistent with this is the acceptance, as among practitioners of magic in contemporary England, that "thought affects the world directly," that "human will power is a real force, capable of being trained and concentrated, and that the disciplined will is capable of changing its environment and producing supernormal effects" (Luhrmann 1989, 120–21; see Pronin et al. 2006 for experiments promoting experiences of "everyday magical powers" in U.S. college students). For Wegner (2002, x), another illusion of will occurs when people "feel they are not willing an act that they are indeed doing." This includes situations where objects appear to move independent of human action, like the spelling of a Ouija board or the spiritualist practice of "table turning" in Europe and America in the mid-nineteenth century. These are not cases where "will" is seen to "instigate the table to activity" (or the Ouija board marker). Rather, movement occurs in the "absence of the experience of will" and may be attributed to "spirit intervention" (Wegner 2002, 7).

Similarly, for individuals, "[p]erceptions of outside agency can undermine the experience of will in a variety of circumstances" (Wegner 2005, 25). Hypnotic phenomena, trance channeling, spirit possession, and glossolalia are all examples of this, though, according to Wegner, "the most common case is obedience to the instructions given by another" (Wegner 2005, 25). Stanley Milgram (1974), whose experiments demonstrated that people would obey an experimenter's insistent instructions to deliver strong, even presumably fatal, electric shocks to another person, suggested that such obedience was produced through "agentic shift"—a feeling that agency and moral responsibility has shifted away from oneself (Wegner 2002, 94, 2005, 25). Milgram contrasted "the condition a person is in when he sees himself as an agent for carrying out another person's wishes" with autonomy, "when the person sees himself as acting on his own" (1974, 133). While in Milgram's experiments the actions performed under the experimenter's direction are seen as "alien to his nature" (1974, 147), in other contexts the feeling that someone else is the willing agent for one's own action may be a desirable outcome. Such is the case in the following excerpt from an article by Tanya Luhrmann (2004, 524) based on her fieldwork among members of an evangelical Christian church in southern California:

Answering the altar call is described by many congregants as an emotionally overpowering experience accompanied by a conscious loss of bodily control. Congregants remember that God took over their body (this can be described as submission to God's will) and carried or pushed them up to the altar. One congregant said, "It was like someone had lifted me up out of my seat and I pretty much ran down there.

I was walking real fast down there. It was like it wasn't me; it was kind of like He was pushing me up there. It was kind of cool. And I was just crying . . . I was weeping. I was crying so much. I was so happy.

With the causal impetus for action being attributed to God, such emotionally charged moments "mark God's spiritual reality in their lives" and "stand out sharply from everyday experience" (Luhrmann 2004, 525). Interestingly, contra Wegner, the embodied "feeling of not doing," the culturally and personally meaningful attribution of authorship for one's action to another with the loss of personal agency serving as experiential proof of one's special relationship with God, contributes to the emotional salience of such experiences and their status as truly memorable events.

The cultural availability and potential personal salience of an ideational reality in which believers establish personal relationships with an omnipotent being through prayer reveals another way in which the volitional and the moral are intertwined in a specific cultural setting. Prayer, for many Americans, is a means for communicating with God, a God who may be perceived as a benevolent and volitional force who intercedes in human affairs. Interpersonal involvements mediated through communications (e.g. prayer, supplication, or sacrifice) directed toward someone whom Hallowell would refer to as an "other-than-human person" are, of course, found throughout the world. What is unusual is for such connections, and for willing as a causal force, to be tested in a large-scale study using scientific methods with the results reported in the medical journal *Archives of Internal Medicine* (Harris et al. 1999). This U.S.-based study involved a large number of patients admitted to a coronary care unit and intercessory prayer groups made up of individuals who were unknown to the patients and who were randomly assigned to pray remotely for specific patients over the course of their hospital stay (all intercessors believed that God "is concerned with individual lives" and "responsive to prayers of healing made on behalf of the sick" [Harris et al. 1999, 2274]). Patients were unaware that they were being prayed for. The researchers "found that supplementary, remote, blinded, intercessory prayer produced a measurable improvement in the medical outcomes of critically ill patients" concluding that "prayer may be an effective adjunct to standard medical care" (Harris et al. 1999, 2278 and 2273).

This study is fascinating as it reveals a cultural reality where the possibil-

ity of measuring the health improvements with implied interpersonal connections between the person praying, an omnipotent being, and the person
being prayed for, are taken seriously through a large-scale study designed to
stand up to the peer review process. The reader is left to infer that there is a
causal force that makes prayer efficacious, although no direct assertions are
made about the existence or nature of God. Those praying, however, are invested in an intersubjective reality where the causal force behind the efficacy
of prayer is enabled by personal relationships with God. The person praying
is a moral actor who "wishes" or "desires" a beneficial consequence for an
unknown other and who attributes the efficacy of prayer to the response of
another (God) who wills the improvements in the sick person's health. Har-
kening back to James, volition, here, takes the form of "a psychic or moral
fact" considered to have an observable (measurable) impact on a sick person.
The close relationship between wishing, desiring, and willing is revealed in
the way that the praying person's wishes/desires are seen to be taken up by a
being with the power to will the desired end into reality.

While considerable ground has been covered in this section, two primary,
but not truly separable notions of willing have been put forward. The first,
drawing on James, highlights volition as a "willing representation," a "psychic and moral fact," a commitment of self toward "*let it be* reality." Future-
oriented and closely related to desiring and wishing, willing is bound up
with what matters to us in life. Thus the action itself may be understood as
revealing something about what matters to the actor. Such willing may take
the form of premeditated intention toward achieving some end and is associated with times when we reflexively deliberate and ultimately choose among
possible courses of action. Hallowell's discussion of "volitional control" as
tied to "moral responsibility" fits under this rubric.

The second type of willing, drawing on Wegner, is associated with voluntary embodied action and the "feeling of doing." This feeling of doing
provides the basis for remembering "I did it" but also the experiential ground
for inferences of agency to others ("S/he did it"). For much of everyday life,
the commonsense assumption is that self wills action. Though this may be
a construction common to all humans, Wegner stresses that it is a construction. Will is an "emotion of authorship" that supports the self-acceptance
of moral responsibility for actions as well as inferences that other selves are
responsible for their actions. Following Hallowell, assessing conduct, one's

own or another's, against local moral standards depends upon such attributions of authorship. In this regard, though Wegner only points to the import of having a "guide to ourselves," we also need guides for interpreting the actions of others and for understanding relations with and among others in our social worlds.

While embodied action typically supports inferences that a self is involved in action, a variety of culturally based constructions permit inferences that "volitional control" and impetus for action is situated in another person. While such attributions of interpersonal connections may decrease personal culpability, they may also serve as markers of enhanced moral standing, as when one submits to "God's will." However, in an interpersonal situation characterized by differentials in power, the perception that one is carrying out another's orders may also serve to mitigate a sense of "volitional control" and "moral responsibility" (cf. Milgram 1974). Still other cultural framings permit selves to extend influence without embodied action through internal wishes/prayers. Taken together, these constructions construe willing as a "psychic and moral fact."

Although I have noted parallels with Hallowell's position, the universalist claims made by psychologists warrant further investigation. Is it the case that, following James, willing, desiring, wishing, intending, are "states of mind" that, in some form, "everyone knows"? Is it indeed likely, as Roy D'Andrade (1987, 144–45) opines, that "certain salient areas of the experiential field will be universally recognized?" How about the "feeling of doing"? Does the model of ideal agency have relevance outside of western settings? If connections among willing, morality, and responsibility are commonly asserted, what is the range of variability with regard to the cultural construction of volition in local interpersonal worlds?

The objectives, however, for this chapter are more modest. Starting with narrative as a mode of thinking, and in light of the preceding discussion, I turn to situated contexts where "willing" enters the social arena in a specific ethnographic setting.

NARRATIVE AND WILL

As mentioned earlier, narrative, as a mode of thinking, offers an entrée for exploring the construction of "volitional control" and its link to "moral responsibility" and "moral appraisal" in specific cultural and interpersonal contexts. Through narrative, we are oriented to interpretive possibilities and moral frameworks that may be useful for navigating the world, for guiding one's own actions, and for anticipating and making sense of the actions of others (see Garro and Mattingly 2000, 1–3). Narrative "deals in human or human-like intention and action and the vicissitudes and consequences that mark their course" (Bruner 1986, 13). It offers a way for integrating temporally distributed occurrences that rely on interpretive frameworks of relevance within culturally constituted behavioral environments.

As culturally informed perspective-taking on situated experiences and events, narrative is an active and constructive mode of cognitive engagement that allies the culturally conceivable with particular circumstances. Through the narrative process, unique personal experiences become "socially forged" through "local narrative formats, recognizable types of situations and people, and prevailing moral frameworks" (Ochs and Capps 2001, 55). As resources relied on for narrative sense making, culturally available understandings both constrain and enable narrative thinking. Nevertheless, for any given situation, multiple narrative possibilities may be entertained, even by the same person and even if not given voice. Here, rather than the omniscient perspective of a mind-reading narrator, the case examples show individuals actively engaging culturally available narrative frameworks to temporally order, however tentatively, a culturally plausible unfolding of events.

Narrative thinking mediates between an inner world of thought-feeling and an outer world of observable actions and states of affairs (Bruner 1986, Mattingly and Garro 1994, cf. Mattingly, Chapter 3). Narrative plots construct two landscapes simultaneously: a "landscape of action"—focusing on what actors do in particular situations—and a "landscape of consciousness"—"what those involved in the action know, think, or feel, or do not know, think, or feel" (Bruner 1986, 14). The meaning one attributes to emplotted events reflects expectations and understandings gained through participating in situated contexts and interactions. What we understand to be culturally conceivable and/or plausible with regard to powers, limits, potential involvement and perceived intentions of agents informs our ability to relate a "landscape of action" to a "landscape of consciousness." Further, our understandings of the potential for others to author events in the world may open possibilities for our own feelings of authorship (Luhrmann 1989).

In the remainder of this chapter these narrative landscapes of consciousness and action are explored through situated instances involving misfortune, drawn primarily from my fieldwork in a Canadian Anishinaabe (Ojibwa) community; interweaving comments about the contemporary community with observations from earlier ethnographic writings.

REVISITING THE OJIBWA (ANISHINAABE)
BEHAVIORAL ENVIRONMENT

To support his theoretical claims about the self in its behavioral environment, Hallowell drew on his fieldwork in several Ojibwa communities in Manitoba, Canada, which took place over a number of field trips primarily during the decade from 1930 to 1940 (the Ojibwa are also sometimes referred to as Saulteaux by Hallowell and are known as Chippewa in the United States). Because Anishinaabe (rather than Ojibwa) is the preferred ethnonym at my field site, which is also located in Manitoba, I use Anishinaabe when discussing my own observations and Ojibwa when referring to Hallowell's work. The quotes from Hallowell in this section do convey the behavioral environment for some individuals at some times at my field site.

My field research in an Anishinaabe community was initially centered primarily around understanding how community members think about and deal with illness (fieldwork occurring at various periods from 1984 through 1989). Some earlier work (e.g., Garro 2000, 2002) conveys how some explanatory frameworks for illness pervasively known among adults in the Anishinaabe community (though not necessarily shared in terms of being deemed credible) are essentially unknown (not culturally available) among individuals in nearby communities who are descendants of European settlers. Other cultural frameworks for illness are linked to biomedical understandings and/ or are similar to others widely known throughout North America.

At the time of my fieldwork, while some children spoke only English, most adults still spoke their own language, *Anishinaabemowin* (an Algonkian language), and preferred it in most social settings. While the community is spatially and economically removed from urban areas, there are myriad interconnections and integrations with the world outside the reserve community. Important among these are linkages to the broader Canadian society through governmental relations and bilateral obligations, schools, social services, the health care system, churches, television and radio, and economic activities pursued both off and on the reserve. The highlighting of commonalities with others seen as similar—variously designated as Anishinaabe, Aboriginal, Indian, and First Nations—provide the foundation for other connections.

In portraying the behavioral environment of the Ojibwa, Hallowell claimed that "a distinction between human beings and supernatural beings" is not stressed. Rather, the "fundamental differentiation of primary concern to the self is how other selves rank in the order of *power*" (Hallowell 1955, 181, italics in the original):

The Ojibwa clearly recognize and take for granted that the knowledge and power acquired by human beings from other than human persons may vary greatly. . . . Only a few individuals acquire exceptional powers. In these cases no sharp line divides human from other than human persons. A particular man, for example, may be able to exercise a variety of specialized curing skills. . . . Such a man may have sufficient power to make his fellow men sick or to kill them as well as cure them. Exceptional men may be able to make inanimate objects behave as if they were animate. They may be able to transform ashes into gunpowder, or a handful of goose feathers into birds or insects. In such displays of power they become elevated to the same level as other than human persons. . . . Thus, despite the inherent power attributed to other than human persons and man's acknowledged dependence on them, there is an intergradation in the power hierarchy of the Ojibwa world. Some human beings seem to have been able to closely approach, if not rival, other than human persons in power. This is another factor that unifies the cosmic society of the Ojibwa rather than sharply dividing the participants in it (Hallowell 1992, 90–91).

Further, in his writings on the Ojibwa, Hallowell repeatedly emphasized the central goal as "life, in the fullest sense—life in the sense of longevity, health, and freedom from misfortune" (e.g. Hallowell 1976, 407). When they occur, illness and misfortune are events that often call for and evoke explanation. In the contemporary community, even though biomedical accounts for illness are culturally available and misfortune may be seen not to require further explanation, there are culturally available frameworks that link illness to one's own behavior or the behavior of other human beings.

In what follows, I describe two of these frameworks that are referred to locally as types of Anishinaabe sickness. Although my findings differ in some ways from Hallowell's depiction (see Garro 1990, 2000), overall I have found much of continuing relevance in Hallowell's analysis.

Ethnographic portrayals—both contemporary and earlier accounts—of the Ojibwa, as well as of other First Nations peoples living in the North American subarctic, often point to their individualism and to the high value placed on autonomy (Black 1977; Hallowell 1955, 135). Defining autonomy in terms of freedom from being controlled by other human beings, Mary Black states that "the importance of individual autonomy in Ojibwa culture can hardly be overemphasized" (1977, 150). For "the individual, a major goal is to be in control—in control of himself and of his destiny and self-determination. Stated another way, the ideal is not to be controlled . . ." (Black 1977, 145). Actions by others which are seen to compromise the autonomy of the individual are not consistent with moral standards of appropriate behavior.

Bad Medicine

At my field site, perceived threats to autonomy in everyday social interactions with other human beings, such as behaviors construed as willful attempts to boss others around or to control others (e.g., the directives of physicians and biomedical personnel), often received negative evaluation. For many, a much more significant source of perceived threat is through "bad medicine." Broadly speaking, narrative accounts involving bad medicine explain a wide range of events in the world as linked to covert and willful acts done with the intent of fulfilling the desired objectives of the user (a form of "let it be reality"). Jealousy, envy, anger, laziness, greed, desire for revenge or retaliation, desire to avoid privation, and lust are seen to motivate individuals. Within this behavioral environment, "bad medicine" is involved in covert but directed efforts to manipulate other people, objects, or events, either to benefit the user or to harm others. Consciously and intentionally wielded by covert and malevolent perpetrators, the "harming powers" of bad medicine include the ability "to cause another's death, illness, or misfortune without being present or in physical contact" (Black 1977, 149). From the culturally informed standpoint of the Ojibwa self "retaliation by this covert means was a stark reality" (Hallowell 1955, 141). Bad medicine surfaces in community life in a myriad of ways. I have heard narrative accounts commenting how an alleged user won the jackpot at a bingo game; where under the influence of bad medicine the vendor of a desired object sold it for a much lower price than its value; where the suspicious rubbing of a ballot box by a candidate for local office led to an unanticipated election result; where a courtroom judge seen to be affected by bad medicine dismissed charges against a defendant despite overwhelming evidence of the defendant's guilt. Bad medicine, like protection medicine, may, though often does not, take tangible form. Once at a community bingo game, a friend alerted me to the presence of a pungent and distinctive smell, telling me not to buy too many bingo cards as it was unlikely one of us could win.

Bad medicine may be seen as implicated when someone has unanticipated success at an endeavor such as trapping game while others nearby do not; Hallowell (1955, 286) found that this was seen as "tantamount to depriving others of part of their living." "Love medicine," a type of bad medicine, is seen to result in feelings of sexual desire and lowered resistance to the advances of the individual who uses these means. Ruth Landes (1968, 65) referred to the use of love medicine as "sneak assaults on human will" and the "ugliest sorcery and the explanation of rape." As bad medicine causes others to "perform acts or enter a state that they wouldn't have if left to their own autonomy," its use contravenes an individual's right to self determination: "If being in control is good and being out of control is bad, then 'bad medicine' is in essence the power to render another helpless or out of control, while 'good medicine' is restoring or maintaining another's state of control or autonomy" (Black 1977, 150).

"Bad medicine" is seen to involve a conscious concentration of effort, an effort localized in and controlled by a human agent who seeks to achieve certain ends. The "landscape of consciousness" is seen to involve a transformation of desire into a willed act to exercise power, a power realized only by taking control away from another. As such, it is considered a profound violation of norms governing social relationships and morally censured. Such power is actively wielded, it is intentional and it cannot be used with impunity. "Bad medicine" inevitably boomerangs back, although the timing cannot be predicted, automatically bringing illness and misfortune to the user or to close members of his or her family (without the intervention of any other "persons" including "other-than-human persons"). And the penalty may be quite serious—even fatal, in fact.

At the same time, in some cases, things may go awry and what happens on the "landscape of action" may not correspond with what was desired and intended on the "landscape of consciousness." For example, when bad medicine takes tangible form, someone other than the person intended may be harmed. Or, in some cases, more people may be harmed than intended, as was understood to be the case in a car accident that took the life of the intended victim and a person who hitched a ride at the last minute. At other times, the wearing of protection medicine may render an intended target safe. While these unintended results do not alter the act of willing harm to specific others as "a psychic or moral fact" (James [1890] 1983, 1165), the "willer" is ultimately responsible for, and suffers the consequences of, what transpires on the "landscape of action" as a result of using bad medicine. If the perpetrator of bad medicine intends only one person to die but, in fact, causes the death of two people, the "boomerang" effect is said to eventually result in two deaths in the immediate family of the perpetrator. If the bad medicine is ineffective due to the use of protection medicine, there is no boomerang. It is the actual infringement on the autonomy of others that brings the boomerang in its wake.

While the users of bad medicine are seen to actively work to bring about a certain kind of future in a fully conscious and determined way, such attributions are not based on knowing anyone who admitted to actually using bad medicine. During my fieldwork, I never met anyone who claimed ever to hear such a confession or even second-hand stories about personal revelations. Hallowell (1992, 96), however, reported:

In all the case material on witchcraft that came to my attention, there was only one instance in which an old man, mortally ill, confessed to murder by witchcraft. It is interesting to note how this man rationalized his behavior. He confessed that he had killed two people a year for half a century! He said he was commanded to do this by his guardian spirits; otherwise he would have lost his own life. Since there is no appeal from the commands of "our grandfathers," the old man had an excellent defense.

While unique, this story reveals a cultural world based on intersubjective agreement that directives of the other than human persons deflect "volitional control" and "moral responsibility" away from self, akin to the idea of "agentic shift" as discussed in an earlier section. From my own fieldwork, a similar plot, including threats to one's own life and health if commands from other than human persons are not obeyed, often underpins accounts of the process of becoming a medicine person.

The closest to a first-person account I recorded of someone deliberating the potential use of bad medicine was told to me by a young woman, Clara. Clara consulted a renowned Anishinaabe medicine man, a person who inspired both fear and respect. In this community, if a medicine person is judged a powerful one, his or her status vis-à-vis bad medicine is ambiguous. Possessing the ability to wield medicine, for good purposes or bad, means it is possible for a medicine person to use power to control others or for personal gain. During the consultation, Clara was told by the medicine man that someone had used bad medicine to get at her through harming her child. Distraught and angry, she impulsively asked the medicine person to send bad medicine after the culprit on her behalf. Although she did not report his actual wording, his reply conveyed that she was not the type of person who would ever do such thing. In telling her this, he was also assigning her the role of the "willing" agent for the potential deed; the "agentic shift" placed her as the one in command. Although she needed someone with power to carry out the deed, the moral responsibility would ultimately be hers. She would be the one, in essence, who was seeking to impose her will on the future ("let it be a reality"). The Anishinaabe medicine man's reply, without confirming or denying his willingness to wield bad medicine, also reaffirmed her as a morally upright actor in the social world, and I took this as her main message to me, for indeed she reported doing nothing, in any way whatsoever, to retaliate. But this example reveals how conscious experiences of wishing for events to take a certain course may provide an experiential ground for our capacity to become engaged with culturally situated understandings of the powers and limits of other selves to cause action in the world, even when that action is judged to be an immoral one.

Illness that comes about through bad medicine is seen to be an instance of "Anishinaabe sickness." A defining characteristic of Anishinaabe sickness is that a diagnosis can neither be confirmed nor can an appropriate course of action be determined without the guidance of other than human persons. Since most persons are not "gifted" with powers that allow for direct interactions with other than human persons on a recurring basis, the assistance of an Anishinaabe medicine person is sought as a way of entering into already established relationships with powerful beings. With their gift, Anishinaabe medicine persons are positioned to act as intermediaries on behalf of those who seek guidance and knowledge from other than human persons. Without the legitimization of a medicine person confirming a diagnosis, narrative scenarios implicating bad medicine remain at the level of suspicion. And even when bad medicine is confirmed, a degree of uncertainty remains as the medicine person does not divulge the identity of the culprit. At the same time, it is through medicine persons that victims learn whether they were the intentional or unintentional targets of the willful acts of others.

At the time of my fieldwork, there was significant diversity in the extent to which individuals deemed "bad medicine" to provide a plausible narrative frame that may be applicable in making sense of the occurrence of events in the world. At present, it cannot be claimed, as Hallowell did, that "sorcery and magic are real to the Saulteaux. Everyone acts as if they were and they thus become effective constituents of thought and feeling" (Hallowell 1955, 284). Although the reality of bad medicine was intersubjectively shared cultural knowledge in the past, at present there are many who dismiss it as superstition or anachronism. Still, for many, concerns about bad medicine and an orientation to its potentiality are part of experiential reality. And even those who are not participants in this way-of-knowing/being do understand the cultural model and its assumptive presumptions, much in the same way that E. E. Evans-Pritchard (1937) could be said to "know" about Azande witchcraft. This intersubjective understanding about the way bad medicine is seen to operate in the world can be seen as a type of resource that can be drawn upon to understand the narrative constructions of others who rely on this assumptive world.

In the following sections, I provide some additional ethnographic examples, starting with examples of divergent narratives for the same events. I then turn to an instance of another type of Anishinaabe sickness (i.e., not bad medicine) that reveals that human persons remain responsible for the consequences of their actions ("I did it"), even when they do not intend to transgress. The last ethnographic section deals with situations that may be framed in ways that absolve those afflicted of moral responsibility for their actions.

Divergent Narratives

Returning to the community after a weekend away, I learned that the son of one of my friends had won a local jigging contest in my absence. Jigging, a form of step dancing, is popular and this contest had drawn a number of contenders, many of whom had competed against each other on previous occasions. My friend, a middle-aged woman, was pleased that her son had taken such an interest in jigging and noted that it was the first time he had actually won a competition.

Later that day, during a visit to another home, the jigging contest came up again, but this time the conversation had quite a different twist. Here, the focus was on the surprise upset that resulted in my friend's son winning the competition. Another entrant had been favored to win but he had not danced particularly well. Someone made a statement alluding to the possibility that "bad medicine" had been involved in this unexpected turn of events. Perhaps, someone, someone very close to the winner, indeed as close as a parent, had wanted the favored entrant to dance poorly and lose the contest and had taken steps to ensure this possibility. In raising bad medicine as being within the realm of the plausible, a narrative scenario was advanced, one in which a legitimate wish (or desire) for a particular end was realized through an illegitimate act of will, an act where the winner's skill at jigging vis-à-vis the favored entrant was immaterial to the unfolding of events. After I left the house accompanied by yet another person who had remained silent during this conversation, he expressed his incredulity that anyone could actually believe in "bad medicine."

Subsequent events may be integrated with one's understanding of the past and taken as support for the constructed past. Some months later, just prior to another contest, an accident during a practice session left my friend's son with a broken leg. For some, like the young man who expressed incredulity, this was simply accepted as an unfortunate occurrence. For my friend, however, this was a likely instance of bad medicine perpetrated by someone

jealous of her son's abilities and she went to see an Anishinaabe medicine person for "protection medicine" to ward off future attacks. However, this same
event was construed by the person who raised the possibility of bad medicine
as the automatic consequence (or boomerang) triggered by the morally rep-
rehensible use of bad medicine—and a fitting payback at that. As seen in this
example, divergent interpretive possibilities may co-exist side by side—"bad
medicine," "payback," or "accident." It is implicitly understood that multiple
perspectives, implicating different "landscapes of consciousness" and anticipations for the future, may be held to explain what happens in the world. For
both of the unexpected events—the initial upset in the jigging contest and
the broken leg—the only external indicator on the landscape of action is the
unexpected event itself. For example, with regard to the favored entrant in
the jigging contest, beyond knowing that he did not dance as well as he normally did, there was no reported change in consciousness that could serve as
a signal of the loss of control.

BY THE WILL OF OTHERS OR BY ONE'S OWN ACTION?

As mentioned earlier, through their communications with other-than-
human persons, Anishinaabe medicine persons can diagnose whether a given
problem is due to Anishinaabe sickness or not. Sometimes, as in the previous section, someone may simply request "protection medicine" from an
Anishinaabe medicine person without asking them to make a determination
whether a given problem is indeed due to bad medicine. And, other times,
even when suspicions of bad medicine result in consultations for a determination of cause and appropriate treatment, bad medicine may not be identified. Although a variety of diagnostic outcomes are possible, cases where bad
medicine is suspected may come to be identified as another type of Anishinaabe sickness known as *ondjine.*

The term *ondjine* is used to indicate an illness or misfortune has occurred
"for a reason," with the reason attributable to something that someone did
at some point in the past (see Garro 2001 on the recollected past). This is a
very complex explanatory framework. The transgression or "bad conduct"
(Hallowell 1955, 269) may be remembered as motivated by an intention to

be helpful, as in the following reminiscence from a mother of two young children:

One time too, I was scared. I was a kid. At that time I guess I was 13 or something. I was at my mom's that time and our puppy got run over. I was scared to touch it because I was told never to touch a dog if it's suffering or something, even if you're trying to help it. But the puppy was crying and at that time what I did was I kept thinking in my mind, like nothing will happen. I just want to help this puppy. And I carried it back to the house. I always wonder if something could happen because of this.

As in this case, what is wished or desired ("let it be reality") can be irrelevant, what matters is the "feeling of doing" that supports the memory that "I did it," a feeling that perhaps is even more memorable because of the heightened cultural and emotional salience associated with the act (cf. Throop, Chapter 2). Still, while the consequences of an act or accident may be severe, one's status as a moral actor is not called into question. The act is morally wrong, but the actor is not judged immoral (unless *ondjine* arises as a consequence of the actor wielding bad medicine). In contrast, the use of bad medicine is both morally wrong and the user morally deficient.

The moral contrast between *ondjine* and bad medicine is also revealed in their concern for the potential suffering of others. In cases involving *ondjine*, there is typically a time lag, often many years, between the action and the eventual penalty, and children may suffer the consequences of their parent's earlier actions. The misdeed may date back to a time when the now parent was a young child. The mother in the puppy incident was not just concerned for herself; what she also cares about is that her children might suffer as a consequence of her action. Conversely, the use of bad medicine alone establishes a lack of concern for others; that users are not even deterred by the boomerang effect, which places close family members at risk, is a mark of their depravity. Their orientation to "let it be reality" through the use of bad medicine reveals a selfish core, and what one cares for also reveals what one does not care about, but should.

Interestingly, another form of Anishinaabe sickness is attributed to a dead person who misses the living and who desires a companion. A longed for person, who is often a child, may sicken and even die as a result. I was told that caring for and missing others was to be expected from the recently dead and that, after a close relative died, a watchful parent was attentive to signs of change in their young children. It takes no mind-reading to anticipate the possibility that the "landscape of consciousness" for a deceased self will include a longing to be with those one loves.

Returning to *ondjine*, most often the transgression involves failure to maintain appropriately respectful relations with other-than-human persons, treating animals in a proscribed manner (e.g., helping a suffering animal falls into this category but so does harming an animal), or using bad medicine (*ondjine* is the boomerang). As Hallowell first pointed out, and consistent with my findings in the contemporary community, other-than-human persons "are not characterized by any punishing role" (Hallowell 1976, 411); "their relations to man are benevolent" (Hallowell 1976, 462). An illness "thought to eventuate from the violation of moral obligations" to other-than-human persons "cannot be interpreted as stemming from their anger" (Hallowell 1976, 418). Regardless: "If a human being fails to fulfill any obligation to them, sickness 'follows him' as a matter of course" (Hallowell 1976, 462).

In an appreciable number of cases, visits to medicine persons, prompted by suspicions that illness or misfortune was caused by the ill will of others, were given a different narrative framing. In these cases, rather than receiving a confirmation of bad medicine, it is revealed that the problem results from the sufferer's (or, for children, the sufferer's parents) own misdeeds. An illustrative case involves an older woman diagnosed with diabetes. I'll call her Mrs. Stevenson. Several years earlier, one of her legs had been amputated due to diabetic complications. After developing an infection in her remaining foot, her physician warned her that another amputation might be on the horizon. Her daughter, Barbara, hoping to avert a second amputation, consulted an Anishinaabe medicine person to see if the problem was a result of diabetes or something else. For a presumed complication of diabetes, this was a quite unusual step. Typically, if Anishinaabe medicine persons are consulted about cases of diabetes, it is only to request herbal preparations seen as effective against diabetes. But Barbara saw the threat of a second amputation as unusual and wondered whether perhaps bad medicine was involved. As Mrs. Stevenson had not expressed even the slightest concern about bad medicine, Barbara, in an attempt to spare her mother any additional alarm or concern, decided to see the medicine man by herself and without informing her mother.

The Anishinaabe medicine man disclosed that the infected foot was not caused by diabetes (although the medicine man confirmed this diagnosis as well) but was due to *ondjine,* indicating that it was attributable to a past act of Mrs. Stevenson. The medicine person suggested that Mrs. Stevenson should come to see him and intimated that, upon hearing the diagnosis, she would probably remember the incident that ultimately led to the infection. And this is indeed what happened. Prompted by the diagnosis, Mrs. Stevenson eventually remembered a promise she had made when much younger, a pledge to dance in the annual Sun Dance for a three-year period. The pledge was broken when she did not participate during the third year when she stayed home to care for an ill family member. Because she intended no disrespect by her action and because she did not participate in the Sun Dance for a good reason, Mrs. Stevenson stated she never thought there would be consequences for breaking this moral commitment. Yet she never regretted the decision to stay with her ill relative, even when she learned of its link to the possible amputation. She felt the more important moral obligation was to care for her relative. Still, she willingly accepted moral responsibility for the disrespectful act and respectfully followed the steps stipulated by the medicine man for redressing the wrong.

At times, individuals may act inappropriately without knowing that they do so. For example, shortly after he got married, Mr. Clement cut down a tree to use the wood. After the tree was felled, he noticed a few bits of cloth clinging to one of the branches. A number of years later, his son was born severely mentally retarded and soon developed a serious medical condition. Although his son received extensive treatment and care from biomedical practitioners, Mr. Clement eventually sought the advice of a medicine man. He did not do this with the hope of ameliorating his son's problems but to discover if there was an explanation for what happened and, if warranted, to take steps to avert any future misfortune that might stem from the same source. It was established through the consultation that the tree he cut down was one that had been previously used by a medicine person to place cloth offerings to other than human persons. That Mr. Clement remembered the cloth on the tree suggests that he might have known it had been used for cloth offerings but this is immaterial. Regardless of what Mr. Clement knew or didn't know about the proper treatment of such trees, the manner in which he cut it down evinced a lack of respect.

Even without awareness of wrongdoing on "the landscape of consciousness," persons are responsible for what they do on the "landscape of action." In narrative terms, what one thinks, what one intends at the time of the misdeed is immaterial to the plot. However, to redress the transgression, an important component of the plot is that perpetrators own what they did; "remembering" the past incident, or accepting as one's own what is revealed of the past in consultation with the medicine person ("I did it"), is integral to the resolution of the "trouble." The plot is different for bad medicine—the use of bad medicine depends upon an illegitimate act of will ("let it be reality") on the "landscape of consciousness," even though the victim may never know whose willing was the causal force. Speaking generally, Anishinaabe sickness confirms persons as morally responsible agents—there are moral limits to what should be willed (in the sense of "let it be reality") and one must accept authorship and take responsibility for one's actions even when the consequences are not what one intends. That is unless one's self-determination is compromised.

WHO IS THE AUTHOR? IS THERE A GHOSTWRITER?

Hallowell (1942, 61) explained that some human beings, through exercising of their power, could abduct the soul of another (the self) with the explicit intention of causing the person's death. At other times, however, the powerful person's "desire" was only to "cause a temporary illness or insanity. A person who loses his senses or goes out of his mind is spoken of as *kawín òtcatcákwsī* (no soul). . . ." This condition of "no soul" or "no self," a consequence of bad medicine, takes the self out of his or her body. It is an abnormal state that can take quite dramatic forms. In one rather serious situation, a young mother started to behave in ways that were seen to be completely out of character; shouting, throwing things around, getting into fights with others, saying things that were nonsensical. Perceiving her to be "out of control" and the situation to be an emergency, family members struggled with what to do, especially as there were two plausible narrative scenarios for the young woman's condition—one involving bad medicine and requiring the help of an Anishinaabe medicine person, the other positing a biologically-based mental disorder best treated by a physician. After an incident in which one of the children might have been harmed, concern for the safety of the family as well as the young woman led to a late night decision to take her immediately to a hospital, where she remained for a number of days. While her husband rushed her to the hospital, her mother rushed to consult with a medicine person. With each diagnosis receiving independent, and divergent, corroboration from the two practitioners consulted, both of these interpretive possibilities remained open and viable even after the woman returned home. After her return, she claimed not to have any memory of the events leading up to her hospitalization, though she did remember being at the hospital and wondering why she ended up there. It was explained to me that even if bad medicine was at the root of the behavioral changes, the problem could have been interpreted by a physician as a treatable condition. The medicine person took steps to counteract the bad medicine and to ward off future attacks. There were no recurrences of the disruptive behavior during the time of my fieldwork. Under both narrative scenarios, the young woman is absolved of moral responsibility. In essence, the "biologically based medical disorder" framing places the problem within the woman's brain. In the bad medicine framing, while the woman's behavior is abnormal, the true abnormality does not lie in the brain or body but in immoral acts of another person. The woman's "self" was not present; "she" was absent from her body. The author of the behavior is a "ghostwriter" who remained hidden but who nevertheless controlled the woman's behavior.

During one of my visits to families to ask about ongoing illnesses (see Garro 1998), I noticed a toddler's face was bruised with a quite serious looking gash on her face near her eyes. The mother told me that her daughter had fallen and been injured but under circumstances that led her to believe that bad medicine was involved (the details are unimportant here). I asked the mother if she had taken her child to see someone for medical care. The mother reported that she had gone to see a medicine man but had not gone to the local health center. She was concerned that the nurse at the health center might suspect her of not taking proper care of her child and call in social services for an assessment. She surmised that having her daughter taken from her is what the perpetrator of bad medicine was trying to achieve and she thwarted this by going to consult with the medicine man and not the local health center. If one accepts the assumptive reality of Anishinaabe sickness, a parent cannot be held morally accountable or responsible in any way for the injury of a child if authorship truly lies in the willful acts of another. But if one does not accept this reality, and it was a fairly safe bet that the nurse would not, the outcome could be otherwise. Still, after leaving the home, my field assistant, who was with me at the time, wondered what had actually transpired during the consultation with the medicine man and whether it was truly the case that bad medicine was behind the child's fall. In airing this doubt, what was also being raised was a doubt about the mother's warrant of vigilance with regard to keeping her child out of harm's way. Even sharing an assumptive reality does not preclude doubts in specific instances.

The last example I'll present concerns a troubled period in married life based on what the wife, Emily, told me. Emily was someone I knew relatively well; we visited each other at home fairly often. For a period of time, Emily's husband, Frank, behaved in an uncharacteristic manner. They would seem to be getting along fine and then, suddenly, things would explode. Emily left several times, children in tow, to stay at either her parents' or her sister's home for a few days. But then Frank would promise things would be different and she would come home. Eventually, Emily suggested they go in for marriage counseling but Frank refused, so she went to see someone by herself. She wondered a few times about bad medicine but she did not take it seriously enough to either go to see a medicine person herself or to raise the possibility with Frank. Later, speaking of this time, Emily said she "didn't know what to believe." While it was possible that bad medicine was causing Frank's bad behavior, it was also possible that it was just Frank being mean. At the same time, Emily noted:

Because there were just certain times of the day when Frank was being such an idiot . . . and I always wondered why is it only at these times. Cause it started at evenings, and during the day was just OK, and evenings, like, he says, I want to go here, I want to go here, like he couldn't stay at home. It was like he was acting, like a sixteen year old, I guess. And, he was so mean at times.

What especially gave Emily pause, however, were some times immediately after he had mistreated her when:

. . . he would say, I don't know why I do that. Like, you know, he would break down and cry and he would never do that before. And he said it seems like, let's see how would I say this in English, but anyway what he said was "I don't know, I don't know why I'm doing this, I try hard not to, but, I still do it."

Even so, Emily was reluctant to even share her concerns about bad medicine with Frank as he had many times in the past expressed amazement that anyone could believe in Anishinaabe sickness and in the powers of medicine persons. Indeed, at least some of these statements were directed at Emily as Frank knew of her commitment to what she refers to as "the tradition."

One evening, when Emily's sister was visiting, Frank started treating Emily badly. Emily described what happens next:

I was going to leave right there and then, I was standing at the door and I told Frank, I'm going to leave. I'm never going to come back. Then you know, we were just arguing and all this. And then just right there in front of me and my sister he just stood there and he broke down and cried and he said, I don't know why this is happening. And, and then right there and then like I kind of knew, like I kind of believed it. Like I believed it but it's so hard to say I believed it and then again I couldn't believe it, like cause it's happened so many times that I didn't want to believe him, I guess. And then, but anyway at that time, cause he really keeps to himself. He won't tell anybody anything and that time I couldn't believe he would break down and cry right in front of my sister, cause he always tries to make himself look good in front of everybody. I was surprised that he did that in front of my sister and then I kind of, I kind of thought, you know, there really is something wrong.

Emily left but the next day she went to see a medicine man she trusted. He told her that another woman was trying to cause trouble in their marriage, using bad medicine to alter Frank's behavior. The woman's intent was to break up the marriage. The medicine man said that he would take care of it. After a few days at her sister's home, Emily decided to give Frank one more chance. What happened next was truly surprising to Emily:

Suddenly, a few days after I came back, Frank wanted to go see a medicine man and I wondered. And then he said all that time I was gone, he had seen something or he imagined this, this woman or something. He said that he had seen her in his dream and all that, and then he knew I'd take it seriously. I didn't say anything to him and he was the one that wanted to go and see a medicine man. Then we were told that someone was trying to put medicine on him again or something and then he was told to take some [protection] stuff and he was supposed to get some of that stuff you're supposed to carry with you all the time.

Since that time, according to Emily, they have had only the normal ups and downs of a married couple. Whether Frank would have wanted to see a medicine man without the "dream" experiences remains, of course, an unanswerable question. For Emily, though, his report of seeing the other woman in his dream stood as independent confirmation of what the medicine man had told her. In her eyes, it was not Frank who misbehaved. Consistent with the statements above, Frank remembered all of the altercations and how badly he treated Emily (i.e., he remembered "I did it") but, at the time that these events were happening, he also remembered feeling that he was acting against his will ("the feeling of not doing" or a form of "agentic shift"). With the medicine man's guidance, he has come to disown these actions, seeing them as authored by another. Further, the decision to seek the help of a medicine man turned out to be a turning point for Frank, who became deeply committed to "the tradition" and, to Emily's joy, to bringing up their children to share this commitment.

CONCLUSION

Hallowell's reflections on volition as generic, personal, social, and cultural represent an important early contribution to theorizing will within psychological anthropology. He suggests that volition as generic attribute may share commonalities across cultural settings as one of the prerequisites of our sociality. Volition is integral to human societies as moral orders. He outlines two forms of conceptualizing volition that are linked with self-awareness of "moral responsibility." The first is the ability to appraise one's own actions (as well as those of others) against local moral standards and the second revolves around the exertion of "volitional control" over future action within a context of local moral standards. As moralities are local and interpersonal, the volitional is culturally and interpersonally constituted.

Parallels with Hallowell's work are found in psychological writings that configure the volitional as "states of mind" linking self and, by extension, others, to embodied action ("the feeling of doing" and "I did it") as well as an "intentional" self whose acts of wishing, desiring and willing are oriented toward the future ("let it be reality"). And Hallowell's thesis that volitional assessments become intertwined with cultural frameworks for endowing personal and interpersonal experience with meaning is borne out by several examples from contemporary western settings. Nevertheless, some of the examples also highlight variability in "behavioral environments" associated with different understandings of volitional states (desiring, wishing, willing). One example is the notion that volitional states can be a force that causes observable changes in the world without embodied action on the part of the person involved. This construction is not intersubjectively shared in the west but underpins distinctive culturally available interpretive frameworks that take on moral valuation and personal salience in situated, often interpersonal, contexts (e.g., praying, using magic).

In case examples from my own fieldwork, both the construction of will-ing as a future-oriented commitment of self to "let it be reality" as well as a past-oriented acknowledgment that "I did it" were shown to be relevant to narrative framings of volitional experience. At the same time, these constructions fell short of encompassing the range of volitional states examined in this chapter. To what extent, for example, are constructions akin to those of "agentic shift" and the "feeling of not doing" found across diverse cultural settings (see also Throop, Chapter 2)? While much of what has been examined here is of relevance to Hallowell's portrayal of volition as both generic attribute and culturally constituted, as well as the linkages he postulated between the volitional, moral and interpersonal, clearly further work is needed to examine variability and similarities in varieties of volitional experience across diverse cultural contexts (see Garro, n.d., for further exploration of this issue).

A theme running through the second half of this chapter is that narrative as a mode of thinking establishes connections between a "landscape of action" involving individuals in particular situations and a "landscape of consciousness" in which the experienced, reported, or presumed volitional states of the actors involved are assessed in relation to culturally available narrative frameworks and prevailing moral constructs. As we have seen, the different narrative scenarios for bad medicine and *ondjine* afford divergent perspectives on the volitional states of the actors involved and their moral standing. When misfortune or another event in the world is attributed to bad medicine, although the identity of the perpetrator is not established beyond doubt, his or her moral character is in large measure established solely through the decision to use bad medicine in an effort to achieve desired ends. In contrast, in some cases of *ondjine*, a voluntary action may have future negative repercussions, for oneself or for one's child, independent of the intentions of the actor. Poignantly, for the person involved, there may be a sense of having been caught between competing and incompatible moral obligations. To fulfill one is to fail at the other.

Many of the accounts presented here reveal the dynamic and variable nature of assessments and attributions of volitional states in relation to events in the social world. The same event may afford different interpretations (e.g., "bad medicine," an unfortunate accident, or *ondjine*) implicating different storylines, different volitional states, and different moral status for those involved. As we have seen, unusual behavior or an unforeseen misfortune may raise suspicions that the trouble is but a symptom of an underlying problem that cannot be addressed without the assistance of a medicine person, but alternative narrative framings are also possible and are often aired, at times by the same person. Further, for bad medicine and *ondjine*, the degree to which their causal framings are intersubjectively understood far exceeds the degree to which they are intersubjectively shared with regard to interpretive salience and motivational force in everyday life contexts. While it is a premise of everyday interaction that one cannot know what another thinks or feels or desires, many also hold that it is vital to remain attentive to the possibility that another's willful acts are impacting on one's own or another's autonomy. Even those who reject this assumptive reality participate in a social world where the potential for interpreting troubling events along such lines can easily arise, as can negotiations and contestations about how to account for such events. Divergent views of the volitional, with accompanying moral loadings, coexist. If, in other settings, it is also the case that the moral and the volitional are intertwined, then to sideline the volitional by only viewing it as a private mental state limits our ability to examine the ways in which the conjoining of the volitional and the moral is revealed, understood, negotiated, and contested in everyday social contexts.

CHAPTER 5

WILLFUL SOULS

Dreaming and the Dialectics of Self-Experience Among the Tzotzil Maya of Highland Chiapas, Mexico

Kevin P. Groark

Obviously one must hold oneself responsible for the . . . impulses of one's dreams. What else is one to do with them? Unless the content of the dream . . . is inspired by alien spirits, it is a part of my own being.

Sigmund Freud (1925)

AS THE EPIGRAPH SUGGESTS, IN WEST-ern ethnopsychology the ultimate responsibility for the dream is understood to lie within the mind of the dreamer. Despite the apparent alterity of dream experience, it is seen as an expression of the individual's unconscious desires and drives. For Freud, this assumption opened the door to the study of the dreamwork and a focus on mechanisms of dream formation: condensation, displacement, symbolism, secondary elaboration, and so on (Freud 1900). But what happens when local theories posit more than one self (or rather, an extension of one's self) as the subject of the dream? And what is the relation of these models of self to the exercise and experience of will?

In this chapter I discuss the link between dreaming and "disavowed volition" among the Tzotzil Maya of highland Chiapas, Mexico.[1] Through a close examination of the psychological and social dynamics of "dream investiture" (in which individuals are divinely appointed to specialized vocational and religious responsibilities), I illustrate the ways in which basic epistemological and ontological assumptions toward dream experience yield a culturally distinct approach to willfulness and self-assertion; one in which the most experientially "willful" component of the person—the waking self of daily life—is also viewed as only partially agentic, subject to the intentions, desires, and wills of other agents, located both internally and externally. Among the highland Maya, dreaming facilitates a form of action and experience that shifts agentic responsibility away from the waking self, recentering it in the essential soul—the experiential self of the dream. In the case of investiture dreams, the resulting social and psychological transformations are not seen as mediated by individual desire or will; rather, they represent submission to a divine mandate communicated in dreams. Such dreams are understood to reveal both the will of the deities as well as the previously unknown potencies of the dreamer's essential self. They are, in short, disclosures of the dreamer's fate.

Owing to its unique phenomenal properties, dreaming offers a special vantage point for addressing shifting modes of self-experience and their relation to willful social action (see Kracke 1991). I propose that this particular form of self-transformational dreaming opens up an experiential space allowing the individual to pursue highly valued personal and social goals (such as becoming a curer) while simultaneously disavowing any agentic responsibility for choosing to pursue those goals and vocational aspirations.[2]

In developing my argument, I juxtapose highland Maya ethnotheories with contemporary psychoanalytic understandings of self, experience, and personal agency. The chapter opens with an introduction to highland Maya investiture dreams and local models of self and dreamspace. I then move on to an exploration of the psychoanalytic notion of "intermediate areas of experiencing" (as exemplified in the work of D. W. Winnicott, Christopher Bollas, and Thomas Ogden) in order to explore the unique experiential qualities of dreaming and the complex dialectical relationship of the dreaming self to the waking self. These analytic models provide a framework for thinking about the psychic displacements engendered by the movement from one experiential mode to another, and the ways in which local Mayan ethnotheories condition both the experience and social uses of dreaming (in this case, in the service of negotiating complex questions of personal agency or willfulness). In support of this argument, I briefly discuss Tzotzil dream talk, in which this experiential split between the waking self and the dream self is explicitly indexed, giving rise to a decentered narrative frame in which it is understood that the dreamer is not responsible for the narrated content. I close with a discussion of the complex relationship between the exercise of "mitigated agency" in investiture dreams and local notions of fate or destiny, particularly as these bear on the pursuit and assumption of high-status vocations in a strongly egalitarian—yet deeply stratified—social setting.

HIGHLAND MAYA INVESTITURE DREAMS

The highland Maya recognize a special class of investiture dreams in which a Catholic saint appears, asking for assistance (which is usually interpreted as a request for the dreamer to assume some religious office) or informing the dreamer that he or she has been "named" or "chosen" for a specialized or high-status vocation (such as a curer, midwife, bonesetter, or ritual musician). To a significant extent, these visitational dreams are culturally stereotyped—in the case of shamanic investiture, the person is "visited" three times and presented with the insignia and tools of his office. During these visits, the curer is often given specialized knowledge of prayers, remedies, and curing ceremonies (see also Fabrega and Silver 1973; Page Pliego 2005). These dreams may emerge spontaneously, taking the person by surprise, or they may come as the result of a more-or-less conscious (but secretly held) desire to attain the new role. This process of investiture is explicitly theorized as taking place in the realm of souls; it represents divine recognition of the essential nature of the dreamer. In "seeing" and "respecting" these dreams, the individual subordinates himself to the will of the deities, accepting the divine burden of office in the service of community.

The saints who choose the dreamer are felt to possess penetrating insight and an ability to see the true nature, abilities, and motivations of each person. They perceive individuals as others cannot, discerning hidden qualities and aptitudes that have heretofore gone unnoticed. When a saint appears in a dream to "show someone his work," this nomination reflects a divine assessment of integrity and calling—official recognition that one is, indeed, not like other people. For many, the very fact that the person sees these dreams is evidence that his soul is indeed "clever" (*bij*), and was chosen for that very trait. When one of my informants told his wife about a dream in which he had been presented with curing paraphernalia, she exclaimed, "Ah, your soul is really clever! As for me, I've never seen [dreamt] like that. But you, you see everything that's given to you. . . . This is because your soul is very clever!" However, not everyone sees clearly in dreams; in fact, curers are virtually the only people to whom clever souls are attributed. Perhaps this is why the local name for curer (*j'ilol*) translates literally as "the one who sees." Despite small variations in the process of dream investiture, the key element is the personally and socially transformative quality of divine election and the importance of the quality of the person's soul in this process. Such visitation dreams form part of the "phenomenological armoury" of the individual (Ray 1992, 68), simultaneously authorizing and legitimizing their new social role to both self and society through the idiom of soul-based encounters with powerful others. If the person recognizes the dream as one of investiture (and does not resist the call), he or she may begin a regimen of fasting, prayer, and petition in order to be "given more power." During this extended process, which can span several years, the dreamer quietly puzzles through the possible meanings of the dreams, often with the help of his or her spouse. The initial sessions of dream sharing allow the aspirant to test social opinion, gauging reactions among family members to these reports of divine election. Often, the aspiring curer begins to test his diagnostic and curative powers by surreptitiously curing family members.[3]

This early period in the curer's career is a time "characterized by concern, anxiety, preoccupation, and social withdrawal . . . a critical and stormy period in the life of the individual" (Fabrega and Silver 1973, 33). The principal questions with which the nascent curer wrestles relate to the social and political implications of shamanic election, professional competence, and public opinion. Many worry about being forced to publicly acknowledge their status before feeling prepared to assume the responsibilities of curing community members for payment—should they fail in their cures, they run the risk of public humiliation, being labeled a fraud, or worse yet, being accused of witchcraft. Once a curer has debuted (and is accepted as legitimate), he cannot decline his services without a very good reason—he is obligated to use his gifts of curing power and divine access in the service of his community. Moreover, he cannot resist the appointment of the deities—illness, injury, and death are sent as punishments for failing to subordinate one's self to divine will.

VISIONS OF THE SOUL: HIGHLAND MAYA
THEORIES ON SELVES, SOULS, AND DREAMS

In order to provide a cultural grounding for the following discussion, I present a thumbnail sketch of Tzotzil views on the self, the dream, and the social world. Three broad ontological and epistemological premises underlie the Maya approach to dreams: 1) a tripartite model of the self; 2) an objectivist construction of dream experience; and 3) a cultural emphasis on destiny or fatedness.

In a classic statement on highland Maya models of personhood, Peter Manning and Horacio Fabrega (1973) claim that the Tzeltal and Tzotzil Maya "seem to lack a conception of the self which is internally located, autonomous, and separate from that of other 'objects'" with a corresponding lack of a theory of mind or person as possessing volitional efficacy for "ordering, monitoring, and controlling human actions" (1973, 266). Based on these questionable assertions, they conclude that, for the highland Maya, "body and self do not possess logically independent status" (ibid., 267). While it is true that the Maya configure the self and theorize experience in a culturally distinct manner, they are clearly aware of an authorizing subjective core that overlaps comfortably with a more-or-less monadic sense of "self," but which is not co-extensive with the physical body.

Tripartite Model of Self

Highland Maya metaphysics posits a conjunctive self consisting of three components: the waking self, the essential soul (or dream self), and a co-natal animal companion.[4] In my analysis, this tripartite conception of the individual articulates three distinct forms of self-organization and experience. These local aspects of self (and their relationship to varying forms of self experience and volition) constitute a distinctly Maya construction of subjectivity, in which some components of self are internal, while others are characterized by varying degrees of externality and independence (see Pitarch Ramón 2003 for similar observations among the Tzeltal Maya). Moreover, these constituent elements of self are theorized as possessing very different volitional or agentic potentials.

First, there is the self of waking life, psychically complex and self-reflective. This is the unmarked seat of "me-ness," indexed by the first person pronoun "I" (vo'on). The waking self is closely identified with the physical body (bek'talil), an otherwise inert form animated by the essential soul (ch'ulel) and its attendant warmth (k'ixnal), as well as the emotive and intellectual contributions of the head (jolal) and heart (o'ntonal), which work together in the production of both feeling and thought. This body-based social self is characterized by a sort of "mundane" or everyday volition. Through deliberative or emotionally motivated choice and action, the person charts a course through daily life and is generally held accountable for the outcomes of their actions.

This corporeal self is clearly distinguished from a radically simplified "essential soul" (ch'ulel), the experiential self of the dream. During the day, the soul resides in the heart, animating the body of its bearer with consciousness, character, personality, and vitality. While inside the body, the impulses and desires of the soul are modulated and tempered by the dictates of sociality, propriety, and reason (all of which are seated in the head). At night, the soul quits the body in search of adventures, yielding dreams. Wandering disincarnate, its actions and encounters take place outside of the volitional control of the waking self. Indeed, the soul is characterized by an unpredictable willfulness of its own, an oneiric volitional potential that often takes the dreamer by surprise. Freed from its social fetters, the soul's "essential nature" is made manifest in interaction with others.

Finally, we have the co-natal "animal companion" (chon, vayijel). This extracorporeal alter, linked to the individual from birth, resides on the sacred mountain of Tzontevitz, and its identity is thought to determine social dominance and power, serving to naturalize the unequal distribution of skills among supposed equals. Powerful people are said to have large carnivores (jaguars, coyotes, etc.) as animal companions, while humble or "poor" people have smaller animals such as rabbits, squirrels, opossums, or skunks as companions (see Gossen 1975, 1976, 1999). In addition to its role in naturalizing social inequality, this animal co-essence is thought to be the primary target of supernatural attack for witches and demons. In this context, it functions as an extrasomatic locus of vulnerability, playing a key explanatory role in many forms of illness. Like the essential soul, the co-natal animal companion lies outside of the volitional control of the person, and like any wild animal, its actions are unpredictable. Should the animal soul be injured or killed during its adventures, its human companion would soon sicken and die; their fates are inextricably linked. However, unlike the essential soul—which is, above all, an experientially based alter—the experiences and vicissitudes of the animal co-essence remain generally unknown to, and uncontrollable by, its human counterpart; it does not provide a vehicle for any form of direct experience, although it is sometimes encountered by the dreamer's essential soul in dreams.

The Nature of Dream Experience

In the Chamula dialect of Tzotzil, the word for "dream" is *vayichil*, a noun derived from the verb "to sleep" (*-vay*). As Robert Laughlin (1976) points out, dreams are—quite literally—derivatives of sleep. The verb "to dream" occurs in intransitive (*vaychinaj*) and transitive (*vaychinta*) forms, suggesting both active and passive accents on the nature of dream experience. Laughlin (1975, 139) provides several Zinacantec Tzotzil terms meaning "to dream" which derive from the noun *ch'ulel* ("essential soul"). Among these are *ch'ulel* ("soul/dream"), *ch'ulelaj* ("to dream"), and *ch'ulelta* ("to dream about").

Although the latter are not common in Chamula, they precisely parallel the aforementioned cognate terms derived from (*-vay*) "to sleep" and serve to underscore the intimate connection between the soul and dreaming. Sleep (or loss of consciousness in general) occurs when the soul leaves the body. Although people are uncertain as to where the soul goes, most agree that it leaves "the earth's surface" (*sba banamil*) and travels to "the other earth" (*yan banamil*), or "the other heaven" (*yan vinajel*)—the realm of souls or essences (Arias 1975, 53). The consciousness of the dreamer is carried in the vehicle of the soul to this numinous realm, yielding dreams.

The transition from sleep to waking represents a literal "return of consciousness," a movement of the soul from outside the body, back to its home in the dreamer's head or heart. This newly returned component or extension of self carries with it the memory of its experience, which (at least in the telling) has a quality of revelation, of just-arrived news. These dream memories are then actively reflected upon by the waking self in an attempt to understand where he has been, what he has seen, what he has done, and what it all means.[5]

For the highland Maya, dream experience is generally conceptualized as continuous with mundane daily experience—however, this does not imply that they fail to distinguish the two, that they confuse dreams with waking experience, or that they consider the two to be phenomenologically equivalent. In emphasizing this continuity, I want to highlight the fact that the social relations and motives for action that characterize waking life "on the earth's surface" are thought to seamlessly transition from the realm of physical bodies to the realm of souls (and vice versa).

Seen through the eyes of the soul, the dreamspace offers a crucial "glimpse behind the curtain," allowing direct access to the normally hidden webs of individual motive and feeling underlying everyday waking life. Through correct interpretation of the dream (which, as Laughlin [1976] points out, is not such a simple matter) the dreamer gains valuable information about the true qualities of others—and often of themselves. Given that events on the earth's surface are inextricably rooted in the realm of the essential—a nocturnal domain accessed every night, by every person—dream experience provides an experiential (and evidential) basis for both interpreting events and framing action in the waking world.

Fate, Destiny, and Personal Agency

Gary Gossen (1975, 1999) ties Tzotzil soul beliefs into a broad argument about the role of fate and destiny in the Tzotzil worldview. According to his analysis, highland Maya soul beliefs constitute a "native metaphysics of personhood," which acts as an "extrasomatic, coessential, nonlocal nexus of causality and destiny" (1999, 244). The waking self of everyday life is, therefore, little more than "the passive bearer of forces over which it really has no control" a self which is, moreover, "subject to the agency and will of others, both human and supernatural" (ibid., 240). Since individual destiny is always linked to extrasomatic forces that are outside of one's direct control, Gossen concludes that "the exercise of free will and acting only in one's own self-interest [is] probably doomed to failure" (ibid., 260).

While Gossen's characterization captures something fundamental about the highland Maya outlook on fate, it fails to recognize the complex ways in which individuals do indeed exercise volition and take action in their everyday lives—and the importance of dreaming in this process. For our purposes, the question is not whether the highland Maya possess or lack "agency." Rather, we are interested in the ways in which a sense of personal agency or volition is either brought to the fore and emphasized or shifted to the background where it fades from view. Far from reflecting a simple fatalism, Maya soul beliefs serve to maintain a dynamic tension between fatalism and volition, often mediated through dreams.

I suggest that the distanced and decentered action of the dream is experienced by the dreamer as mediated by a quasi-autonomous agent within the self, a sort of sub-ego. In an ironic twist, the most experientially "willful" component of the person—the body-based self of waking life—is also viewed as the most constrained, subject to the intentions, desires, and wills of other agents, located both internally and externally. Indeed, in many contexts the culturally preferred location of transformative agentic potential is situated beyond the confines of the physical body in the quasi-autonomous essential soul; a component of self that is only ever partially and provisionally known to the dreamer, but whose actions reflect back onto the self in sometimes profound ways.

Paradoxically, the "fatalism" that Gossen identifies as stemming from these soul beliefs can actually *facilitate* individual choice, volition, and willful action by framing it in terms of the culturally acceptable idiom of "success-dreaming" (Ray 1992, 68). In the highland Maya model of a tripartite self, we find an explanatory construct that allows the experience of willfulness to be decentered away from the waking self of everyday social life and located in one of several extensions of self, all understood—somewhat paradoxically— as lying outside of the volitional control of the waking self to which they are connected. Further distancing is achieved through the radical objectification of dream objects, which in the case of visiting saints, can also bear aspects of the individual's willful desires. When taken together, these ontological models of self and dream experience lay the foundation for a phenomenologically grounded approach to the experience of willfulness within its cultural matrix. By removing the question of individual desire and will from the pursuit of certain high-status social roles, both the individual and the larger social group can enjoy the security—the fatedness—of knowing that dream nomination represents the discovery of the true nature of the dreamer in the realm of the essential. Turning Freud on his head, the highland Maya dress waking life in the fabric of their dreams.

In the following sections, I provide a psychoanalytic approach to the phenomenology of highland Maya dream experience, emphasizing the ways in which local ontological assumptions serve to open up the dreamspace for use as a unique experience structure in which the locus of responsibility shifts from the consciously organized self of waking life to the quasi-autonomous essential soul. I will argue that this experiential shift plays a key role in allowing for a sort of mitigated or displaced agency in which a secondary or ancillary will—that of the soul—becomes foregrounded in its interactions with agentically powerful deities in the dreamspace.

ESSENTIAL SOUL, TRANSITIONAL SELF: A PSYCHOANALYTIC READING OF THE HIGHLAND MAYA DREAMSPACE

In recent years, much of contemporary psychoanalysis has shifted from a focus on conflict-based psychopathology to an emphasis on the constitution of personal meaning and the problem of "disordered subjectivities"—difficulties in rendering a subjective life that feels rich, vital, and authentic (Mitchell 1993, 21–25). The most interesting development has been a sustained attention to the nature, texture, and elaboration of subjective experience, and the processes through which this is accomplished. Perhaps the earliest and most influential analytic thinker concerned with these questions was D. W. Winnicott, who focused attention precisely on the complexities of subjectivity and the problematic epistemological status of subject and object in psychoanalytic theories of experience (see Winnicott 1951 [1958], 1959 [1989], 1971). In recent years, Winnicott's foundational insights have been extended and more fully developed in the work of Christopher Bollas and Thomas Ogden, both of whom focus on the complex relationship between subjectivity and objectivity as constitutive poles of experience. In particular, these theorists are concerned with the potentially transformative dialectic underlying dream experience and the mediating role of the dream as a *particular kind of experience structure* that exists in dialectical relation to waking life, both facilitating and foreclosing certain forms of self experience, understanding, and knowledge.

Winnicott's Transitional Phenomena

D. W. Winnicott is perhaps best known for his work on "transitional phenomena," particularly his characterization of the familiar transitional object (Winnicott 1951 [1958], 1959 [1989], 1971). For Winnicott, transitional objects are "the first not-me possessions," physical objects that are not clearly experienced as either subject or object, straddling the permeable boundary between "me" and "not-me." While "objectively" external to (and ontologically independent of) the subject, at the experiential level the transitional object begins life as an extension of the subject. Over time, the integrity of the object asserts itself, and it is gradually understood to exist independently of the self. Despite the name, it is not the object that is transitional, it is the subject—the infant—who is transitioning from a state of *merger with*, to a state of *relation to* (Winnicott 1971, 14).

While Winnicott is most closely associated with the concept of the transitional object, his conceptualization of the "transitional area" or the "intermediate area of experiencing" (Winnicott [1951] 1958)—the space between subject and object, the space of subjective objects—provides a particularly useful heuristic model for understanding Maya soul beliefs and the dreamspace. Winnicott postulates the existence of three metaphorical "areas" of experience—the first and second areas correspond to the inner psychic world of the subject and the external "reality" of the object, respectively. But in between these extremes lies the "third area," a porous zone in which subject and object merge in the immediacy of experience. The mental space occupied by the transitional object is precisely this intermediate area, a space that is neither subjective nor objective, inner nor outer, illusory nor real. For Winnicott, this third area lies "intermediate between the dream and reality" (1965, 150), on "the knife-edge between the subjective and that which is objectively perceived" ([1968] 1989, 206).

Although initially introduced as an account of infant development, in his later papers Winnicott emphasizes the role of transitional processes in inaugurating the development of two different modes of organizing experience (1971, 95–103). At one pole, the space between subject and object disappears—the object is an extension of the self. At the other pole, the separation between the subject and object is complete—the object is seen as independent, though in relation to the self. In health, the transitional area of experiencing remains alive and freely accessible throughout the lifespan, producing a "potential space" Winnicott closely associates with the "cultural" life of symbolism, creativity, illusion, imagination, play, and dreaming (1971, 100). One mode does not replace the other—rather, they exist in a dialectic, as poles of experience between which we oscillate throughout our lives. Drawing on these later developments, M. Masud Khan explicitly links the dream to the third area and to transitional experiencing, arguing that "the dream-space is the internal psychic equivalent of what Winnicott has conceptualized as the [physical] transitional space which a child establishes to discover self and external reality" (1974, 314).

Dreaming and the Dialectics of Self-Experiencing

In a series of provocative monographs, Christopher Bollas (1992, 1995) puts forward a model of the subjective elaboration of experience based on the claim that *all* experience represents this mutual interpenetration of subject and object—the creation of subjectified objects. A basic component of Bollas's vision of human subjectivity and meaning-making is his bifurcation of the subject into two complementary selves: the "complex reflective self" (CRS) of waking life and the "simple experiential self" (SES) of immersive experience (1992, 17):

The simple experiencing self and the complex reflecting self enable the person to process life according to *different yet interdependent modes of engagement: one immersive, the other reflective.* When I am "in" the dream, although as a simple self I perceive dream objects, even more importantly I endure deep experiences there. Recollection and interpretation of the dream's meaning do not necessarily address the essence of self experience gained by the simple self's movement through the events of the dream, but the complex self possesses a different psychic agenda: the aim of this position is to *objectify* as best as possible where one has been or what is meant by one's actions. (Bollas 1992, 15; emphasis added)

In essence, Bollas replaces Winnicott's spatial model of movement between "areas"—the subjective, objective, and the transitional—with a model of temporal cycling between these two distinct experiential selves. Everyday life represents a continual shifting between these two self states, one characterized by "psychic density and thoughtfulness," the other by "a suspension of such complexity in the service of simple immersive participation in experience" (Bollas 1992, 15).

Experiences in the "third" or "intermediate area" occupy a key position in Bollas's "dialectics of self experiencing"—an oscillation between subjectification and subsequent objectification (1992, 31). When the simple experiential self is lost in self experiencing—whether in waking life or in the dream— "the distinction between *the subject who uses the object* to fulfill his desire and the *subject who is played upon* by the action of the object is no longer possible. The subject is inside the third area of self-experiencing. His prior state and the object's simple integrity are both 'destroyed' in the experiential synthesis of mutual effect" (ibid.). Emerging from such immersive experiences, the complex reflective self takes himself as an object of reflection, considering where he has been, and objectifying these experiences in terms of more-or-less consciously articulated theories of self and other.

Also working within a Winnicottian framework, Thomas Ogden (1986) proposes a similar model of dream experience. For Ogden, the ability to dream is crucially mediated by the ability to maintain a "psychological dialectic process" in which the dream experienced as *thing presentation* in one experiential mode is processed and symbolized as *word-presentation* in another mode. For our purposes, thing-presentation can be understood as referring primarily to unconscious eidetic internal sensory material (e.g., a mnemic representation of an external object), while word-presentation refers to the language-based meanings that become attached to these internal object representations in the process of becoming conscious ("The conscious presentation comprises the presentation of the thing plus the presentation of the word belonging to it, while the unconscious presentation is the presentation of the thing alone" [Freud 1915, 201]). Through this linking process, otherwise unconscious thing-presentations are linked into a conscious or preconscious language-based network of associative meaning, thereby entering more fully into a system of cultural meanings and becoming both individually and culturally inflected representations. In other words, the *dream as thing* is only transformed into the *dream as experience* when it is drawn into a dialectical process of language-based differentiation and distancing. By means of this process, the wild night-dream of the immersed self is *objectified and interpreted* according to local ethnotheories of experience, yielding the domesticated daydream of the waking self.

In both Ogden's and Bollas's model, the dreamer who generates and experiences the dream might, for analytic purposes, be understood as distinct from the dreamer who understands and interprets the dream. The former represents the self given over to primary process mentation based in fantasy and imagination, while the latter represent a secondary-process thinker whose mental operations are governed by a culturally informed, reality-oriented, logical mode of understanding that is oriented toward objectifying the dream as a *certain kind of experience with a certain kind of relation to actuality.* Bollas stresses the potentially transformative effects of this oscillation between the complex and simple selves—when we shift from one mode to the other, "we change the nature of perception . . . subjectivity is scattered and disseminated into the object world, transformed by that encounter, then returned to itself after the dialectic, changed in its inner contents by the history of that moment" (1992, 18). These selves—the complex reflective self and the simple experiential self—should therefore be understood as reifications of two very different modes of processing experience that exist in a dialectical and mutually transformative relation.

In this dialectical model, health is conceptualized as a free movement or oscillation between these poles of subjectification and objectification, a process that allows some regulated overflow and interpenetration between these artificially segregated domains. Indeed, Winnicott (1971, 2) conceptualized the segregation between these experiential "areas" in terms of a semi-permeable membrane, a sort of skin that connects as it divides, allowing measured diffusion from one area into another. If one pole of experience comes to predominate, however, this porous membrane becomes a solid barrier, and experience ossifies into either the hallucinatory realism of the psychotic or the reality-based disenchantment of the normotic.[6] In such cases, the connection between the dreaming and waking self is severed: The dream becomes either a concrete reality that is interchangeable with waking experience, or conversely, it degenerates into a sterile and denatured fantasy bearing no relationship to waking life.

In many ways, the highland Maya essential soul is the structural opposite of Winnicott's transitional object: Instead of being an external object that is not perceived as wholly external, dream objects (including the dream self) are internal objects that are not perceived as internal. Moreover, in Winnicott's model we see a self moving from a state of undifferentiation toward one of "reality-based" differentiation through the use of the transitional object. For the highland Maya, the transitional quality of the semi-autonomous essential soul functions in the opposite direction, moving the subject back toward unity by incorporating more "primary process" dimensions of experience (imagination, fantasy, etc.) within the boundaries of everyday consensual reality.

The Dream as Processive Experience Structure

When viewed in light of this oscillatory model of dream experience, the dreamspace can more readily be understood as a "potential space" or "intermediate area of experiencing," a liminal experience structure through which we move on a nightly basis; one that processes us according to a dialectical logic based on the experiential shift from the simple experiential self of the dream to the complex reflective self of waking life. In the dream, we become a simple experiential self, return to a state of unintegration, ". . . loosening [the] self into an archipelago of many beings, acting various roles scripted by the ego in the theatre of the night. Waking, we rise from these regressed states . . . from the plenitude of selves to the discerning 'I' who reflects on his odd subjects" (Bollas 1992, 15).

Seen from this perspective, dreams reclaim a protosymbolic integrity as "real" experiences through which the dreamer is "gathered and processed" as he "wanders amidst the seemingly objective dream objects through which he thinks himself" (Bollas 1992, 14):

In the dream we are immersed in our own selves. Freud rightly saw the dream as a condensed event with suggestive force disseminating in a thousand directions, leading to an infinite reading of its meaning. His admonition that we must not regard the manifest text as the meaning of the dream unfortunately led to a crucial failure to see in just what ways the dream also had an integrity of its own: after all, the subject is living his own ego organization! As such, each person is graced by the visitation of the dream, which brings him into his self, right into the structure of his being, taking him through its processional logic and character. . . . [The dream] has an integrity unto itself, and when this integrity is allowed to stand, the dream can also be seen as the only uncontested moment in which one experiences the self that one is as one lives *through* one's psychic structure. (1995, 178; emphasis in original)

As this quote suggests, the dream functions as an experience-structure with its own particular "processive effects" on the subjectivity of the dreamer; the dream proprioceptively engages the dreamer with the dream object on all levels (Bollas 1995, 43). In fact, dream objects derive a special processional potential precisely because they have been *experienced* in the "real" of the dream. They are thereby endowed with a singular uniqueness and importance deriving both from their integrity of form and their seeming independence from the dreamer.

Within this generative "potential space," subjectified dream objects arrive as though by chance. Coming unbidden as they do, these dream objects have the potential to sponsor and elicit units of self experience that may be novel but feel deeply responsive to the wishes, worries, fears, and fantasies of the dreaming self. Such objects represent the metamorphosing of a "latent deep structure into a surface expression" that is often puzzling precisely because of its seeming "itness" and externality (Bollas 1992, 54). Such "transitional" dream objects cannot be neatly assigned to either "the real" or the illusory—they partake of both. Yet for the highland Maya, they represent the hyper-real, the essential. This, then, is the paradox of dream object arrival, "the double experiencing of [dream] objects as [simultaneously] vehicles of wish and spontaneous elicitors of inner experiences," a process in which we are both "the initiators of our own existence as well as the initiated" (Bollas 1992, 27–28).

As Bollas points out, this variable "placing" of the self in relation to dream experience is the work of the complex reflective self of waking life, and as such, it is a process that depends crucially on local ontological and epistemological propositions. Among the highland Maya, the essential soul (*ch'ulel*) is, in many ways, an objectification of this simple experiential self— a nonreflective, radically stripped down "particle participant" in dream experience. It mediates encounters with dream objects locally understood to be essentially real and unquestionably objective to the dreamer, bringing their influences and effects back into the physical body of the dreamer here "on the earth's surface." Moreover, the essential soul has marked "transitional" qualities—it is an intermediate construct that is simultaneously "me" and "not-me," subject and object, manifesting qualities of both internality and externality—allowing for varying degrees of estrangement from, and rapprochement with, the consciously organized self of waking life.

In the following section, I explore a set of domain-specific lexical, discursive, and pragmatic features of Tzotzil dream narrative. I suggest that these linguistic devices serve to decenter the speaking self as the primary author of oneiric actions, reflecting instead a focus on the soul-based agentic self of the dream. This variable "placing" of self through the establishment of a distanced and decentered narrative frame serves to mitigate questions of dream authorship, sidestepping questions of responsibility for the narrated dream experiences. As philosopher Edward Casey has argued, personal agency is not a dichotomous "thing" that one either has or lacks; rather, it reflects "a broad spectrum of ways in which the [individual] becomes implicated via self-projection or by proxy in his own imaginative presentation" (1976, 45). Thus, the narrative and conceptual positioning of the self in relation to its own experience becomes a critical datum for any discussion of agency or will (see Schafer 1973, 1976).[7]

PLACING THE SELF: THE NARRATIVE NEGOTIATION OF AGENCY IN TZOTZIL DREAM TALK

At the moment of waking, a fascinating experiential shift occurs. For the first time, the person reflects on his dream experiences from the perspective of the waking self. He has gone from deeply immersive, embodied, disseminative first-person experiences in the dreamspace, to a wakened state in which he "realizes" that these were the experiences of his soul, not himself. As discussed, this simple self exists in dialectic relation to the complex reflective self of waking life, who both bears the soul and interprets the meaning and significance of its wanderings. It is at this point, in the transformation from the *dream as dreamt* to the *dream as understood*, that the articulation of the simple experiential self and the complex reflective self can be most clearly seen. Through this dialectical process, the wild nightdream translated into a language of action and experience that is both personally and culturally intelligible. Highland Maya dream narratives explicitly reference this split subjectivity, drawing it into discourse where it can be used as a domain-specific language for framing action and making claims (and in many cases, for disavowing any meaningful volitional role in having chosen to do so).

The perspectival tension between the first-person immediacy of the dream and its reframing as a quasi–third-person experience of the soul finds expression in dream narrative, where it is indexed in a number of ways—all of which serve to shift the speaker from a central experiential position to one of distance and marginality. This indexical shift is accomplished through a variety of lexical and discursive devices, including opening and closing codas that employ deictic adverbs to mark the departure and subsequent return of the experiencing self (the quasi-autonomous essential soul); the liberal use of evidential particles that mark dream experience as epistemologically distinct from waking experience; as well as a marked preference for heteroglossic quoted speech that maximizes the distance between the narrator and his or her "quoted voices" (see Groark 2009 for a detailed discussion of the lexical, discursive, and pragmatic features of Tzotzil dream narrative and their psychological implications).

I suggest that these devices shift the focus from the corporeal presence of the waking, speaking self to the essential body of the dream self or soul—a "self" which is marked as clearly "mine," but also "not quite mine"—or better yet, a "me" experienced under the distinct phenomenal conditions of the dream, with all the epistemological and ontological entailments that such an identification suggests. This narrative framing serves not only to mark dream experience as pertaining to a distinct phenomenal order, but also to position the self in relation to these experiences.

By locating experience at a distance from the speaker (or perhaps as originating in a separate narrated subjectivity) this "cross-world identification" (Langacker 1985) or "decentered framing" (Hanks 1990) provides a narrative resource for managing—mitigating, diffusing, or even disclaiming—a sense of agentic responsibility for described events or experiences on the part of the speaker. By drawing attention to the dream's twilight valence (as both fundamentally "mine" and "not quite mine") the focus tacks between the here-

and-now narrator and the implicitly or explicitly referenced soul. Through these shifting frames, the speaker is subtly relocated from the center of the dream to the margin, *from experiencer to observer.*

This framing of the dream as relatively distant and differentiated from the waking self as organizing agent, gives rise to a potentially generative "duality of consciousness" (Ray 1992, 64), allowing both dreamer interlocutor to locate responsibility and ownership of the dream (especially those with implications for self-definition) in the quasi-autonomous "essential soul." By dampening the illocutionary force of the narrative, these discursive devices promote the appearance of independence and distance from the speaker. The narrated dream thus becomes a discursive frame in which it is understood that the speaker does not bear authorial responsibility for the actions and experiences described. Somewhat paradoxically, by shifting the indexical ground to the realm of the dream and the dream self, the speaker can actually claim greater significance for the narrated content. By grounding the experience in the realm of soul or "essence," dream events and interpersonal transactions take on a heightened actuality. This augmented significance derives precisely from the fact that the experience took place in a dream—a space of a different phenomenal order.

I suggest that the imaginal distance created between the waking self and the dream self opens up a sort of Winnicottian "intermediate area of experiencing." Indeed, the Maya soul has strikingly transitional qualities. It is both essentially "me," yet in some ways strikingly "not me"—a flexible continuum along which self experience can be placed. Just as the infant moves through varying stages of merger and differentiation with the transitional object of childhood, so too the dreamer can occupy variable subjective positioning in relation to his transitional self, the essential soul.

At one extreme, the dream experiences and actions of the soul can be appropriated and incorporated as isomorphic with the waking self (emphasizing connection and identificatory merger). Ego syntonic experiences—those in line with the values, wishes, and phantasies of the waking self—can be drawn closer, gradually folding into the very fabric of self through identification with the soul as the manifestation of one's true nature. At the other end of the continuum, dream experience can be clearly differentiated from the waking self (emphasizing detachment, disavowal, and projection). Ego dystonic experiences—those at odds with the person's consciously organized theory of themselves—can be externalized and objectified as uncontrolled and unbidden actions of the soul framed as relatively distant from, and un-controlled by, the waking self. And of course, much dream experience falls somewhere in between; in uncertain relation to the dreamer. It is precisely this variable positioning of the transitional self along a "me"–"not-me" con-tinuum that potentiates the use of dreams as vehicles for identifying (and, perhaps, for identifying *with*) alternative or future self-states—states con-ceived of not as potential, but as essential, reflecting the most basic nature of the dreamer.

SOULS, DREAMS, AND MITIGATED AGENCY: SOCIAL USES OF INVESTITURE DREAMS

In this final section I explore the social uses of this distanced and decentered construction of dream experience, emphasizing its utility for context-specific negotiations of volitional responsibility and willfulness. Returning to the phenomenon of investiture dreams, with which I opened the chapter, I argue that this particular dream genre provides a cultural affordance allowing for the exercise of a sort of "disavowed volition." Drawing on the cultural mod-els and expressive resources described earlier, the investiture dream becomes a vehicle through which highly motivated individuals can pursue prestigious vocations while, simultaneously, sidestepping any sense of direct volitional responsibility for having chosen to pursue them (see also Ray 1992).

The Chamula Tzotzil have been accurately characterized as possessing a "deep skepticism about individual autonomy and the very idea of the 'self-made' individual who is guided only by pragmatic self-interest" (Gossen 1999, 242). This conviction leads to anxiety about being seen as overly self-assertive, resulting in an "unwillingness to undertake new endeavors," a "re-luctance to act publicly in ways that might be perceived by others as overtly self-serving," as well as a "reluctance to engage in instrumental acts that sug-gest individual volition and exercise of power over others"—unless somehow legitimized in the eyes of the community (Gossen 1992, 240). As we have seen, soul beliefs (and related ideas of soul-based ascription) provide one such resource for legitimizing certain high-status pursuits and undertakings. The otherwise divisive effects of social inequality resulting from such actions are neutralized—paradoxically—by highlighting and essentializing the individual's difference; by locating it in the very fabric of the self, the soul.

As discussed, this ambivalence toward striving and self-promotion is especially clear in the domains of curing and religious service. Within these realms, evidence of divine dream election is part of the authorizing discourse that both signals selection and legitimizes the person's emerging status. For the call to be viewed as authentic, the complex reflective self of waking life— the seat of everyday volition and striving—cannot be seen to have chosen the path (see Ray 1992). The individual must be chosen by the saints; an election experienced in dreams, by the "soul." Since this dream self is understood to be outside of the volitional control of the individual, questions of choice, ambition, and strategy are (at least theoretically) precluded.[8] Tzotzil dream talk subtly draws attention to these disjunctive self states, emphasizing the soul-based locus of dream experience and vocational election.

Dreams are valuable resources for the highland Maya. Through them, one can account for and legitimize willful acts—to both self and society. Drawing on these experiences, the individual can articulate and pursue deeply desired goals, while paradoxically experiencing this as compliance, obedience, and subordination to divine authority in the service of community. Volitional responsibility is placed in the deity or saint, the exceptional qualities of the self are placed in the soul, and the self is recast as a passive object of these essential forces. This constitutes what M. C. Jedrej and Rosalind Shaw (1992b, 11) refer to as the "duality of agency in dreaming" in which the actions of the self are experienced as subsumed within the agency of another, an experience of being acted upon even as one acts.

CONCLUSION

In a short addendum to his general theory of dream interpretation, Freud writes, "Obviously one must hold oneself responsible for the . . . impulses of one's dreams. What else is one to do with them? Unless the content of the dream . . . is inspired by alien spirits, it is a part of my own being." (1925, 133) We have seen how Mayan ontological premises yield a very different theory of the dream—one characterized by objectivity, externality, and the involvement of a semi-autonomous essential self. The Maya do not, as Freud sug-gests, hold "one self" responsible for the content of the dream—rather, they postulate a radically simplified essential self as the subject of the dream. And the content of the dream is not to be found inside of the dreamer, but in "the other earth, the other sky," a numinous realm of souls, all of whom act as agents in the theatre of the dream.

From the perspective of Western scientific psychology, Highland Maya dream metaphysics transform the dream from an intrapsychic experience (in which one encounters eidetically rendered internal objects) to an extra-somatic, non-psychological experience (in which one is in direct interper-sonal exchange with real others).[9] From the Tzotzil perspective, the dream-space could more accurately be described as an intersubjective relational field in which one comes into contact with the true nature of self and others. Yet the dream remains the creation of the dreamer. Despite elaborate cultural theories of the self and the dream, the complex reflective self of waking life and the simple experiential self of the dream are, in truth, two facets of one self—a single self experienced under the very different phenomenal condi-tions of waking life and the dream. We have seen how this experiential split is theorized at the local level, how it is mobilized in discourse, and how it functions as a resource for both self-elaboration and social legitimization, allowing individuals to sidestep troublesome questions bearing on the asser-tion of ambition, desire, and willfulness in a social setting that discourages these qualities in favor of an ethos of homogeneity and equality.

As this chapter illustrates, a fine-grained ethnographic focus on the so-cially and individually preferred location of the subject in relation to his own experience—in this case, in relation to the experience of volitional efficacy and willful action—is a basic element in the development of a truly "cul-tural psychodynamic" approach.[10] Such a focus bridges the often disparate worldviews of anthropology and psychoanalysis, yielding a deeper and more nuanced understanding of the complex ways in which human subjectivity is shaped—and is, in turn, shaped by—the cultural world in which it is always embedded.

CHAPTER 6

TRANSFORMING WILL/ TRANSFORMING CULTURE

Jeannette Mageo

The social categorizations that establish the vulnerability of
the subject to language are themselves vulnerable to both
psychic and historical change.

Judith Butler (1997)

S AMOANS HAVE A WORD FOR "WILL"—
loto—but anthropologists have not always translated it
thusly, which puzzled me when I first began doing ethnography in American
Sāmoa in the 1980s. I was taking a language class kindly offered to stateside
teachers by a high-ranking member of the government. He decided to teach
us a love song, chanting the language into our heads. He gave us the Samoan
version and an English translation with every word glossed but one—loto.
After class, I asked him to translate it. He hesitated. Pondering, he told me
that loto meant, "to think." Vaguely remembering my predecessor and men-
tor Bradd Shore had translated loto as "to feel," I stuffed the song into my
pack. Several days later, I asked another Samoan to translate this line of the
well-known song for me. He translated loto as "to will." Now really confused, I became doggedly persistent. Carrying the song and its confounding
line to a host of Samoan friends, I asked each to make the translation. They

produced the same variety I had already encountered. I showed them the discrepant translations. All insisted those too were correct.

HYPOCOGNITION AND HYPERLEXICALIZATION

Loto is the word for depths, such as the depths of a pool, and the word for "inner." The interior of a house, for example, is *lotoifale*, literally the house's loto. The person's loto is the inner depths of the subject. Confirming Robert Levy's model of hypocognition, Samoans say "One cannot know what is in another's depths" (Gerber 1985, 133). Intellectual inaccessibility is one of Levy's gauges of hypocognition; lack of fine distinctions is the other (1973, 1974; see Throop, Chapter 2). As a verb, the term loto conflates what we consider subjectivity's distinct activities: willing, thinking, feeling, and desiring—for "to desire" is *tauloto, tau* being a prefix that denotes intensity or endeavor (Pratt 1977, 295). As a noun, loto refers to an organ in the chest, which is not the heart but which is the place of memory (Pratt 1977, 205). Memory, *lotomanatu*, literally translated, is personal thinking/feeling in the loto. *Ta'uloto*, "to tell the loto," is "to repeat from memory" (Pratt 1977, 301). *Manamanaloto* is "to cherish in remembrance."

Willing is the most salient activity of the loto. So, in Samoan *fai* makes a noun into a verb. When one adds fai to loto—literally "to do loto"—one does not get "to think," "to feel," "to desire," or "to remember," but "willful," a word that implies judgment and hence a moral problem. While people deny they can know a hypocognized territory of self, this very lack of knowledge makes such territory morally treacherous. Thus, Samoans frequently invoke *lotoleaga* as an explanatory principle for people's bad behavior; *lotoleaga* refers to envy but translates literally as "ill will." When a person has unexpected trouble in social circumstances, Samoans often attribute this to the "ill will" of others, meaning that people's envy of that actor's possible future or actual past success inspired a desire to harm. Indeed, to the extent that people hypocognize subjectivity or sociality in their models of *being* a person, the neglected aspect is hyperlexicalized in their moral models: They produce a profusion of moral terms to corral this dubious dimension of self. These prolix moral terms reflect anxiety about irremediably deficient information, in contrast to the cliché about Eskimo's making a multitude of useful and accurate distinctions between kinds of snow.

Loto terms with moral denotations, like failoto and lotoleaga, combine loto with another word that either aims at distinguishing a manifestation of loto that Samoans view as morally deficient or a form of control over the loto that they regard as virtuous. Arrogance and hysterical bouts of feeling, for example, are ways to express loto and moral deficiencies; humility and stoicism indicate a subdued loto and are virtues. Yet, Samoan's discourse on the will seems to heighten its illicit expression. Thus, in Samoan social theory, everyone has their established post: They play their role, performing their duty by serving those above them in the hierarchy. In fact, people tend to challenge the hierarchy at every credible opportunity: This is *lotofa'amaualuga*—a desire for self-aggrandizement attributed to the loto. Samoans believe it dignified to suppress personal feeling in favor of conventional sentiment, yet visitors to Sāmoa have long documented displays of strong personal emotion (Turner 1861, 133; Pritchard 1866, 147–48). At nineteenth-century funerals, Samoans would pound their heads with rocks until the blood flowed, wailing that their dead relative had deserted them. Still today, they may collapse in tears, kiss the corpse, and throw themselves upon it. They are then *lotovaivai*—too weak to contain the overflowing pool of their inner life.

People are incorrigibly subjective *and* social: Although they may have a culturally shared and elaborated tendency to assume they are more significantly one than the other, their actual behavior will belie this assumption. When it does, they exhort one another to better conform. U.S. Americans, as documented by their court system, tend to assume that individuals are responsible for their actions. When others do not assume individual responsibility, Americans exhort them to exercise will power and "stand on their own two feet." Samoans tend to assume that people are part of larger collectives and responsibility for their acts is collective. Traditionally, should a person commit a serious offence, villagers burned his or her family's house and ring-barked its trees, driving out the entire group. When others do not assume their proper place in the collective, Samoans exhort them to desist from willfulness and "stand at their post."

WILL AND REFUSAL

Will is inevitably a political concept because of its hand-and-glove relation with subjection—being forced to defer to another's will. Samoan childrearing is a battle in which youngsters learn to relinquish their individual wills and follow orders. After children become verbally competent, elders are likely to communicate with them in the imperative form (Sutter 1980, 37–38). Those who fail to obey orders are usually beaten. Beating continues until the child sits down and suppresses all emotion, which elders read as conveying a demurring will.

When people in a culture aim at suppressing individual will, will goes underground and is accommodated in a negative sense. In Sāmoa, this photographic negative of the will is *musu*. Most simply, musu means that the subject does not want to do something, as in this line from a song: *"Auē musu'e fa'alogo o le tala pa mai ia* Afono" (Alas, I don't want to hear the story from Afono). Literally musu means "to refuse"; in practice, it often means "to refuse to answer" or to act like one did not hear an order. More generally, musu refers to mute noncompliance (thus a doubling of the base musu, *musumusu*, means "to whisper"). Or, musu may refer to a passive-resistant attitude conveyed by mute social performances—from grimacing to stamping the feet—through which a person expresses his or her will. Thus, Eleanor Gerber tells us that young people who linger in the back of the house to be available to serve elders during a meal:

. . . will talk together, play guitars and sing quietly, the girls may comb each other's hair. When a call comes from the front room, all this pleasant interaction ceases; the look of annoyance can be plainly read on all faces. Typically, the girls will arise clumsily with an exaggerated show of exhaustion, and sometimes they will whisper "Alas." Genuine anger may flash briefly as the servitors grimace and quietly mimic the words of the command. (1975, 67)

In the nineteenth century, Krämer ([1902] 1995, 61) reports similarly that youths:

. . . mostly carry out their parent's orders punctually and without murmuring even when they are inconvenienced by them. I have often observed that girls were removed from a dance or shaken out of their sleep to prepare a kava for some thirsty gentleman, and they always went to it without a murmur, although their displeased features expressed more than words.

Musu performances are acceptable because it is rude to talk back to authorities; to speechlessly fail to comply is to resist with discretion. Authorities, therefore, often tolerate wordless refusals. Gerber, for example, tells of a girl who calls to her younger sister to bring water from inside a house. In the Samoan age-grade hierarchy, the elder sister is a superior.

There was no response. The older girl called several more times, with increasing irritation, and finally threatened "to get the broom" [with which to beat her junior]. At that point, the head of the little girl's friend appeared in the window: "She's musu." Without any further comment, the older girl got up and fetched her own water; and did not either scold or hit the small delinquent. When I asked the older girl why her sister had refused, she said she didn't know because she hadn't asked. I also asked why she had not gotten angry at her sister's disobedience—which would have been the normal course of events. She said: "The little ones, when they're musu, sometimes we let them go" (1975, 231).

Musu is a politic and sometimes accepted way of circumventing authority. Deference itself, then, charts out a protected arena for the exercise of musu: one's right—not to carry out one's own will per se—but to silent noncompliance. In settings where authority is absent, musu is also an inviolate preserve of the will—a kind of game reserve, if you will, where an animal normally hunted and subdued survives. Margaret Mead, for example, describes a girl who travels several miles to go on a picnic and then returns home immediately merely because she is "musu to the party" ([1928] 1961, 124). As musu is mute, no explanation for refusal is expected.

Musu, individual will in a negative sense, places the structure of authority in Sāmoa in high relief—a structure that Samoans are apt to contest. Before Christianization, families, villages, and districts frequently warred to contest the proper ownership and ranking of titles and the proper exercise of authority that went with them. This chronic fractiousness has shaped Samoan politesse. To ask in Sāmoa is implicitly to order and to assert authority; to decline, to say "No," is to contest authority. In ceremonial speech or any polite exchange, therefore, one treats others as if they were of higher status (whatever their actual status) by never saying "No." One simply agrees; then if one judges the asker lacks authority, one does whatever one likes.

Being polite, however, muting one's will, can in effect be consent. When asked to dance, young Samoan women cannot politely decline. A Samoan woman once told me she married a man because he begged so often she became ashamed to refuse. Indeed, women often use this as a facetious ex-

planation for why they married their husband (Cluny Macpherson, personal
communication). This situation can be a joke. It may also be a nightmare.
The dream of one young woman, whom I call Pese, reported in English, is
an example.

I had a pretty bad dream. . . . I was walking a long the highway and suddenly a guy
came up and accosted me under the tree. I tried to get away but he's holding me
against my *free will*. He told me that he wanted to talk to me for a long time but
I always give him the . . . look. Later he told me that he's going to marry me but I
completely refused. Then I freed to run away. I prepared all my things and the day I
was leaving. I was so glad and relieved that I am going away.

While I was walking to the plane, I was sitting at my seat and the plane took
off on the air. And the other passenger was sitting next to me. And suddenly he said
"Thanks for coming with me." I was so shock when I turned it was the same guy I
met and wanted to marry me. Then I fainted and suddenly I was awake by my alarm
clock. (emphasis mine)

Pese starts out politely: She does not say "no" but only gives her pur-
suer a "look"—presumably one of those grimaces mentioned by Gerber and
Krämer as musu performances. When that does not work, Pese becomes ad-
amant, linking her right of refusal explicitly to "free will," an English phrase
that in Anglo-American locales denotes legitimate exercise of individual will.
The better to refuse, Pese appears to be leaving Sāmoa, land where mute
compliance can get you married, and leaving furthermore on an airplane—a
symbol of modernity. Yet, for all that, polite compliance Samoan style seems
inescapable!

Musu is also a word for a common, transitory psychological state that
people believe is involuntary: The person sits in almost catatonic silence and
is generally left alone until he or she spontaneously recovers. As hinted by
the preceding dreamer's faint, a young person pushed too far may slip into
a more severe form of dissociation—spirit possession. One of my former Samoan sisters-in-law whom I call Easter described such a course of events.

My mom was scolding me while I was outside . . . picking rubbish . . . and then she
said I was just blanked out . . . the next thing, I was in the middle of the house. . . .
She [her grandmother] was really telling my mother not to treat us like that . . . .
She [her mom] gets angry . . . usually pulls our hair and gives us spanks. To me, I

didn't think it was *ma'i aitu* [spirit possession] . . . but to them . . . my grandma was really in me and talking about those things my mom . . . has to do . . . . They only splashed water on me when I fainted . . . . The only thing I remember was . . . I was all wet. . . . She must of smacked me . . . with something that really hurt me. My mom . . . really tells us what to do.

Those who do not become possessed by a protective grandparent, who simply descend deep into a musu state and are further harassed and reproached by an elder, may commit suicide (Freeman 1983, 219). Samoans call suicide "power over one's own life" (*pule i lona ola*)—it is the last refuge of the will.

HISTORICAL VICISSITUDES OF THE WILL

At any rate, people recognized this version of volition/subjectivity as the Samoan way when I resided in Sāmoa during the 1980s. When missionaries and colonists came to Sāmoa, however, they brought their own model of the will. To trace its effects, let us begin at a point of conflict, the family.

Missionaries aimed at recasting Samoan family relations into a nuclear mold. Sāmoa has a generational kinship system: There are no aunts and uncles only mothers and fathers. In pre-Christian times, these multiple mothers and fathers might have lived in different houses or villages. Because another "mother" or "father" wanted a particular child or because of children's preferences, little ones often grew up in households other than those of their biological parents. Writing about "those who become converts from heathenism," the missionary George Turner ([1861] 1986, 86) describes his efforts at reform.

No sooner are their eyes opened to see their parental responsibility, and that they must give account at the judgment-seat for the manner in which they have trained up their children, than they wish to collect their offspring from the families into which they have been adopted. But then the parties who have adopted them will not give them up; and often, too, the children are unwilling to leave their adopted parents and go among strangers—for, alas! Such to them are their real parents. Christian parents, however, are to some extent succeeding in their efforts to recall their children to their proper home; and the consequences are delightful. A sense of parental responsibility is making way among the whole population.

Even when Mead was in Sāmoa in the 1920s (1961, 42–43), children moved readily between households as a way of refusal when parent figures became overbearing; in many cases this is no longer an option for young people. The family, transformed by mission influence and politically adaptive redefinitions of authority, became an increasingly constrictive locale. In the westerly islands, villages grew top-heavy. Titles proliferated because until 1991 only titled people could vote: It was in candidates' interest that as many of their supporters as possible bore titles (Macpherson and Macpherson 1985, 1987). Even elders who did not have the right to the deference and service that titles conveyed became demanding: Young men were the village's labor force, producing agricultural surpluses that allowed elders to buy the foreign goods on which they had come to depend (O'Meara 1990).

Adolescent girls were likely to escape the labor demands that weighed upon their brothers because of a Christian elevation in status. Before Christian times, only the highest status girls (tāupōu) were virginal, awaiting ceremonial defloration when they wed a highly titled man. Missionaries preached that all girls should be virginal, like the tāupōu, implicitly elevating the girl's status. Samoans embody dignity as erect immobility; therefore, the higher in status one is, the more immobile one is; nimble inferiors become one's hands and feet. As elders came to see adolescent girls as tāupōu-like, their authority in the household increased and the labor expected of them decreased (Mageo 1992, 1994, 1998, 141–217). While these virginal expectations enhanced a young woman's domestic power, they thwarted her will by lessening her discretion in choosing a mate.

Traditionally most girls had married at their own discretion by simply following the boy of their choice back to his family's estate (āvaga)—although they were supposed to choose with family status considerations in mind (Mageo 1998, 2008). Christian girls, in contrast, were to marry at their parents' behest. For parents, a male's status was likely to be his most attractive feature. Although marriage by elopement remained extremely common during the mid-to-late twentieth century, elders and brothers guarded girls more vigilantly. During this time as well, there was a spirit possession epidemic. Frequently girls were possessed by "spirit girls" who were known for following boys back to their households and seducing them—having their will with them one might say. In the mid-twentieth century, suicide and possession became epidemic—arguably because of a less bearable economy of the will (Bowles 1985; Macpherson and Macpherson 1985, 1987; Mageo 1991, 1994, 1996, 1998, 164–90).

DREAMING AND THE WILL

If colonialism in Sāmoa violated the traditional preserve of subjectivity and its signature aspect, willing, the dreams I collected during the 1980s also suggest a new enfranchisement of the will. In these dreams, dark passageways or crowded closets represent subjectivity, apt images for a hypocognized area of self, but so does glittering wealth secretly shared with a "true" friend or relative. In these dreams, subjectivity also appears as the site of the "real" me. One girl I call Tutu dreamed she was walking in a dark passageway with faces flying past her. She commented:

[The] real me . . . likes to keep hidden . . . away from crowds. Yet, I force myself to go to public places and to be [with] everyone. If I had it my way, I would rather stay by myself. . . . The point is why am I in the dark again? Yet, I'm happy. Maybe . . . I should be more private.

Another girl I call Penina dreamed that she was in the United States with her aunt. In the dream she brought home stolen "coins, money, jewelry, diamonds, pearls, and gold necklaces." Her aunt accepted half this loot. It signified their close personal relationship but also that Penina was, in her words, "a real selfish person" because she wanted to oppose her father's demands to stay in Sāmoa and "give us a good name for our family . . . putting other people's feelings before mine," which would mean "ignoring my true feelings."

Hypercognized feelings, Levy argues, seek expression in art and dreams. In these two dreams Samoans' hypercognized subjectivity makes a debut, but these dreams also mark historical wrinkles in cultural categories tracing back to missionaries and their invasion of Samoan language and thought. These dreamers deploy what I call a "discourse of sincerity" against an ethos of sociality—a discourse missionaries imported, characterized by a privileging of subjectivity and individual will. In this discourse, people describe inner thoughts and feelings as "real" and "true," attributing them a context-transcendent quality. Michel Foucault (1990) associates nineteenth-century evangelical discourse with confessing sexuality, but the aim in missionaries' discourse of sincerity was to confess subjectivity. One of Reverend Murray's converts (1839), for example, confesses that "Formerly . . . we uttered love . . . with our mouth while our hearts were full of hatred and murder": In other words, formerly she was insincere—expressing prescribed social sentiments, acting her part in the group rather than privileging inner experience. This association of sincerity and Christianity is still in place. One of my informants had the following dream:

I was sitting in church all alone. My eyes were closed quietly saying a prayer. A strong wind blew inside the church. The windows were pulled by some invisible power. The whole building rattled and I heard a voice saying: "You are a hypocrite; you are a hypocrite again and again. You will die like all hypocrites in this church."

"Soul," referring to the individual's personal feelings, thoughts, and volitions, was a cultivated aspect of self in eighteenth- and nineteenth-century England. The Industrial Revolution precipitated the migratory employment pattern that characterizes capitalism, breaking down many stable agricultural communities. Values that had once resided within the community needed internalization (Levy 1973, 347–54; 1974). Evangelical religious practices helped to achieve this effect. Evangelicals preached that original sin sullied people's souls. One could be good, therefore, only through constant introspective vigilance (Davidoff and Hall 1987, 88). The attention thus directed illumined and expanded that internal space we call subjectivity—a kind of psychic valise in which people came to port their values. Subjectivity was not only ported from British town-to-town but also to the fringes of empire by missionary teachers.

When Samoan village chiefs converted to Christianity, they often ordered their villages to convert. Missionaries made them rescind these orders because they believed conversion was genuine only if it was the individual's own will (see, for example, Turner 1861, 23). Moral choice, they believed, was the function of the will and the essence of subjectivity. I argued above that subjectivity and will are favorite topics in Samoan moral discourse: Terms suggesting quiescent subjectivity are morally positive; terms suggesting active/intrusive subjectivity are morally negative. One acts as a Samoan moral agent by controlling subjectivity, particularly personal willfulness, in deference to authority and to the necessities of social life, *not* by making personal moral choices. Yet missionaries implanted meanings in Samoan language that fostered just this exercise of personal will. London Missionary Society (LMS) ministers took Samoan terms that had a social character and gave them newly subjective nuances (Mageo 1998, 141–63). The word *soul* itself is an obvious example.

In Samoan, *aga* means "face" in the sense of facing someone and in the sense of persona (Mageo 1989). In pre-Christian Sāmoa, a doubling of aga, *agāga*, meant what one became after death—a spirit (Pratt 1977, 22). Thus what Samoans took to be the essential part of the person, their persona, remained after less essential parts decayed. Missionaries translated agāga as soul. Such translations gave subjectivity new significance within Samoan language because missionaries entangled them in literacy itself. Reading the Bible was the very signature of Protestant practice in Britain; this was particularly true for the independent churches that made up LMS (Gunson 1987). Missionaries, therefore, opened schools as soon as they did churches, teaching "Reading" and "Writing" along with "Moral and Religious Education" (Mills 1844, Turner 1861, 48–60). Mission services became a daily social event where high-ranking Samoans gave speeches employing terms to which missionaries had given Christian meanings (Holmes 1974, 60–62). Religious texts translated by LMS ministers iterated these meanings and were the only published material in Samoan until early in the twentieth century (Huebner 1986).

Samoans still associate the kind of will promulgated by missionaries with modernity and the west. A girl dreamt, for example, of a white-robed prince from outer space who came to her village, speaking a foreign language no one understood, presumably as colonists once did. Colonial westerners were termed *pālagi*—literally sky busters—for so their ships appeared on the horizon. Full of loving kindness, as the missionaries proclaimed Christians to be, the dream prince transformed the village by his very presence such that: "The people of my village were no longer sad but just happy. They were no longer poor, but rich. Everyone has their *free will* to do anything they wish" (emphasis mine). In other words, this combination of Prince Charming and ET condenses western colonization, fairytales, and science fiction, and deliv ers all that evangelical missionaries and other western interlopers promised; one of those promises was a new disposition of the will. This disposition was symbolized in the dream of an American Samoan boy I call Galu as a magic carpet.

I was on a flying carpet. I started to fly over . . . DC because I saw the White House, monument, and many other land marks. I kept on going higher and higher until I was in space. There were meteoroids all over the place. I could see stars. There was a very bright one. I don't know if it was the sun or just a very unusually big star. Then I woke up because it was so bright it hurt my eyes.

Role-playing the carpet, Galu described himself:

I never get tired. I'm magical and have my own will power. . . . The flying carpet is my top gun. It is the headstrong part of me that always wants to be the self-righteous part of me. The part that wants to be more and doesn't let anything get in the way.

Galu uses words that in English and Samoan have negative connotations to characterize an apparently positive part of him, betraying ambivalence beneath the enthusiasm of his confession. "Headstrong" is a negative English word for willfulness; its Samoan translation, *lotomālosi*, is a term with which parents condemn a youngster's willfulness. Yet, for Galu, as in the western model, will is also synonymous with masculinity ("my top gun") and an inexhaustible magic power that transports Galu to what must seem to him the center of the western world. Will power allows him to rise higher and higher, a U.S. metaphor for success, without letting "anything get in the way," like not being able to say "No" to his family requests for help, service, and money, as they do for so many Samoans. Like the girl escaping her suitor on the airplane, Galu leaves Sāmoa. His exit seems more effective than hers, at least until he reflects on space and the meteoroids:

On the other hand, outer space and the meteoroids did not want to be willful. On the contrary, space just wants to kick back and relax. Sure, I think about the future and what I need to do to be successful. The meteoroid likes to stop and smell the flowers along the way. It plays the take life easy role.

Instead of insisting on the "I" who needs to be successful, the meteoroids play a role. The more individualistic a culture, the more people identify with their "I"; the more social a culture, the more people identify with their role—like Galu's meteoroids (Mauss [1938] 1985, Dumont 1966, Shweder and Bourne 1984, Markus and Kitayama 1991, Mageo 2002). Here, registers of the will correspond to two models of personhood circulating in Galu's post-colonial world. At first will power is a real trip, transporting, freeing him from parental complaints about headstrong, disobedient children and social demands that might get in the way of achievement. Yet, will on the western model is so effortful. Galu associates not being willful with taking life easy, relaxing, not too much responsibility resting on his individual shoulders, although the phrase Galu enlists to justify this presumably Samoan orientation comes from U.S. discourse as well—"taking time to smell the roses." Here what one might call a hybrid American-Samoan way charts a path of resistance to a western model of will power as a tireless ascent to "success."

WILL, AGENCY, AND THE DREAM

Samoans, then, see individual will as the signature aspect of subjectivity. Will and subjectivity with it are hypocognized in Samoan models of being a person and for this reason are hyperlexicalized in moral discourse (see Throop, Chapter 2). Moral agency, however, is not exercised through individual will but through its abnegation. Will is also granted a place in a negative sense: as a subordinate's way of evading a superior's imperatives, as a right of refusal when authority is not at issue, as a mute performance, and as a quasi-dissociated state tolerated as a temporary aberration. In colonial and postcolonial times, a Christian expansion of parental authority and elders' consumer needs have so constricted this traditional refuge of the will as to fuel psychologically extreme expressions of it—spirit possession and suicide.

Samoan dreams also suggest that subjectivity and the will are newly valued. Dreamers' associations to them manifest a discourse of sincerity that privileges personal sentiments and volitions and a linked discourse in which "free will" and "will power" are validated. These discourses, a legacy of LMS missionary zeal and U.S. colonial presence, have given Samoans a dual model of the will. On the one hand, will is still a suspect aspect of the person that must be corralled in deference to authority; on the other, will is now a heavenly cargo that can descend like riches—a free gift from outer-space or a way to escape Sāmoa and ascend into space, to become, so to speak, a star.

The Samoan case suggests that "free will" is a phenomenon recognized not only in more egocentric but also in more sociocentric societies; in both it is associated with individuality. As people regard individuality (positively, negatively, or variously), so also they regard the will. Yet, here I would like to distinguish between will and agency, and to suggest that, unlike "will," agency has no necessary relationship to the ego.

Foucault challenges ideas of agency as "individual will": Power and resistance are only discourse effects (1980, 1990). Galu's dream and dream play display post-colonial interplays of power and resistance. He enlists a U.S. discourse in which "will power" is identified with success, but within which one finds traces of a Samoan discourse in which will is stubborn noncompliance. One might say he resists the power of Samoan discourse, through which others overrule his will, through an imported discourse—one that he hopes has transporting power, a hope that Pese, fleeing her dream suitor, initially shares. Yet, Galu also resists the U.S. discourse on will, symbolized by a rise to hurtfully bright stardom and characterized by tireless assertion. He does so through a hybrid discourse, symbolized by space—a limitless (oceanic?) expanse—and by what we perceive from earth as falling stars, meteoroids. This discourse favors relaxation and enjoyment of life's beauty. Praxis theorists argue that cultural structures in discourse and elsewhere amount to a game that one can play to advantage. Galu's dream and role-playing seem explorations of various advantages and disadvantages associated with U.S. and Samoan discourses of the will.

Is Galu's dream justly encompassed by the terms "discourses" and "practices"? Dreams traffic in images: Dream reports are translations (Crapanzano 1980). Recounting a dream is a reflective, even contemplative activity, although doing so may also have immediate practical and social aims (see, for example, Garro Chapter 4 and Groark Chapter 5). Western understandings of agency tend to place it within what Jacques Lacan would call the world of the Sign—that is, the realm of language and goal-oriented strategizing (1968, 1977). Dreaming, however, is the primer site of the imagination: Dreams think in images.

In western societies, our sense of self rests on our ability to control our circumstances, the ego's famous penchant for acting upon reality. Our experience of dreams is one in which we lack agency. Thus, Lacan says that the dream consists in "the absence of horizon . . . and, also, the character of emergence, of contrast, of stain, of its images, the intensification of their colours. . . . [I]n the final resort, our position in the dream is profoundly that of someone who does not see. The subject does not see where it is leading, he follows" (1977b, 75). In short, the dream is where the egocentric version of agency—willing—fails.

The eye is a symbol for consciousness and in the dream, according to Lacan, one "does not see." Indeed, we close our eyes in sleep. Lacan's stance on the dream iterates the classic psychoanalytic idea that dreams manifest primary process (meaning "unconscious") thinking. In recent decades, many psychologists and anthropologists have questioned this idea (Noy 1969, Tedlock 1987, Mageo 2003, Lohmann 2003). Yet, I suggest our model of agency remains based upon an equally derogatory notion of dreams as a form of inaction. Further, revising this notion entails dissolving the western equation between agency and willing and, further, altering our model of the dream. Like Groark's Mayans (Chapter 5) and Garro's Anishinaabe (Chapter 4), we need to reconceive the dream as a mode of action and agency, albeit a mode that is latent in most westerners. In the western "free will" model, people understand will, predominately, as exercised in efforts to gain an end. In the traditional Samoan model, people understand will, predominately, in terms of resistance. Dreams are mental acts: as dreamers, we act to re-conceptualize cultural orientations and understandings, re-conceptualizations that may move us to effort or resistance but are not, strictly speaking, coincident with them.

If the ego, à la Freud, thinks about reality, what does the dream think about? Contemporary psychological and anthropological studies of the dream (Palombo 1978, Hunt 1989, Foulkes 1985, Stephen 2003) argue that dreams are a kind of remembering whereby dreamers sort experience into memory schemas. Yet, the dream according to Levy (1984, 225) is a repository of all that is hypocognized in culture—that for which we have no schemas!

Dreams, it seems to me, "remember" by abstracting schemas from the mélange of daily, lived experience. Pese's and Galu's dreams abstract schemas of and for "willing." Their dreams consider will's power (or a lack thereof) to free people, helping them rise above the constraints of their time and place—to be context transcendent, as many westerners aspire to be. Dreams then represent cultural schemas in the personal symbolic world of the dreamer.

Personal symbolic worlds are best understood as unique ensembles drawn from a vast common of cultural images—like meteoroids and magic carpets, villages and spaceships. Dreams select images from this internalized cultural common that signify schemas to the dreamer: as Pese's "look" signifies musu and getting away on a plane signifies her free will; as Galu's carpet signifies "will power" and his "space" signifies taking life easy. Pese and Galu deploy these dream images, along with the stories that flow from them, to illustrate and discover their emotive and embodied responses to these schemas and to the cultural models of the will that these schemas constitute. Galu dreams of a magic carpet carrying him over the earth, rising heavenwards, because it depicts his exhilaration with a Western "will power" schema. Pese dreams of getting away on an airplane because it captures her terror that even modernist escapism will not free her from Samoan schemas for compliance.

The very act of abstracting cultural schemas from experience and casting them in one's own symbolic world is a way of considering them as orientations for real-world strategies that iterate, vary, or combine these schemas and the models to which they refer. Thus, the "free will" schema and the "will power" schema refer to a western model of willing as agency; a musu schema and today, a "taking time to smell the roses" schema, refer to an American/Samoan model of will as resistance both to Samoan authorities and western pressures. Dreams react to these schemas and attendant models in ways that clarify what is wish fulfillment and what is nightmare. These realizations, however nonverbal, cannot but subtlety affect our directions in waking life. Indeed, imaginal deliberations in the dream may be a wellspring of waking agency.

Samoans and many peoples who anthropologists study believe the person's spirit self acts in dreams in ways that have weighty consequences for waking reality (see, for example, Lohmann 2003, Mageo 2003, Tedlock 1987). What is a spirit but a person as pure meaning? In dreams, we are like spirits: for all practical purposes, the body is gone; only our memories of the day remain. What we remember is what the day meant to us. Spirits and dreamers, then, inhabit what one might call a "higher" realm of pure meaning. By reacting to cultural schemas, symbolizing them in ways that capture personal experience, people act as agents of meaning in dreams. The Samoan dreams and interpretations cited here betray dreamers' wills and their reactions to a Samoan ethos of sociality *and* a western ethos of individuality, but more than this: They contribute to an imaginative cultural recalibration of subjectivity and the will. In dreams, we change cultural forms by rendering them in terms of our experience, remembered through the morphing images of our imaginations. These renderings suggest interpretations—as the hidden passageways and stolen treasure give meanings to subjectivity, or as outer-space princes and meteoroids give meanings to the will.

People make dreams; to make a dream is to remake cultural meanings. Such acts precede and follow the world of the Sign, as the night precedes and follows the day. If the Imaginary, as Lacan argues (1968, 1977a), recedes into the background of the mind in the course of human development, in dreams it continues to oversee the world of the Sign, just as a magic carpet overseas the land.

CHAPTER 7

HOW CAN WILL BE EXPRESSED AND WHAT ROLE DOES THE IMAGINATION PLAY?

Pamela J. Stewart and Andrew Strathern

T HE IDEA OF THE WILL IMPLIES AGENCY and choice between possible actions. It also implies a kind of determination to carry out an action once it has been chosen; a positive drive or desire to accomplish an action. The saying "Where there's a will there's a way" expresses this notion as a piece of folk wisdom. These are pragmatically and experientially informed dimensions of the idea. But in addition, the concept of the will as it appears in a number of cross-cultural and historical contexts implies a further framework, the framework of cosmology. In the Judeo-Christian traditions, great emphasis is placed on the notion of "free will." Although the emphasis appears to be placed on a notion of freedom here, actually a major component involved is that of responsibility, and beyond that the fate of the soul. Free will implies responsibility for actions and, hence, constraints upon choices of action in terms of their likely outcomes. In this chapter we look at a cross-cultural range of examples, all of which deal with the question of the will in relation to cosmology and morality, and the possible results that flow from the exercise of the will. We deliberately choose examples from both ethnographic and literary sources, because for our purposes here—which are thematic, not methodological— these examples all point in the same direction: awareness of the constraints on, and results of, the exercise of the will. Our choice of examples from different cultures and periods of time is also deliberate. We want to show that there are important continuities across otherwise quite diverse cultural terrains. We also wish to show how imagination comes into play as a creative force in shaping how people exercise their wills. Dreams are one pathway in which the imagination enters and intersects with the will. The comparisons we make in this chapter thus aim to illustrate similarities across terrains of cultural difference without neglecting the cultural differences themselves. We are aware that our discussions touch on several of the classic themes in psychology and religious studies. Our intent, however, is not to review the literature, but simply to make a contribution to the study of such themes by deploying a range of comparative cases seen from the perspectives of cultural anthropology. We expect that our approach will intersect with particular ethnographic cases discussed by other contributors to this book (see Chapter 1 of this volume).

We begin by employing a literary example that turns on the significant consequences of exercising free will. Throughout the chapter we also want to show how the cosmological dimension implicates the will of the spirits in relation to the willed actions of people.

THE CASE OF COUNT DRACULA AND FREE WILL

Looking at the concept of will reveals several possible pathways to approach the topic. For instance, in Chapter 2 of Bram Stoker's novel *Dracula*, the novel's main protagonist, Mr. Harker, and we, the audience, first meet Count Dracula. His now famous opening line is, "Welcome to my house! Enter freely and of your own free will!" As the scene continues, Count Dracula does not motion to Mr. Harker in any way until the threshold of the castle has been crossed—that is, Mr. Harker has entered of his own free will. After this action, described as being taken by free will and uncoerced, the novel depicts a train of events that involve a cosmological world in which human beings and spirits of the dead are seen to exist in a particular landscape, and humoral substances, especially blood, are involved in the transformative relationship between the living and the dead (Stoker [1897] 1997). (Count Dracula is a blood-sucking vampire who needs regular meals of human blood to remain in an un-dead state. The blood is obtained from living victims.) In this novel, the action of expressing free will had profound implications both for Mr. Harker and for Count Dracula, who allowed Mr. Harker to enter his castle in the first instance.

In this example, we are explicitly confronted with the notion of free will. But an important theoretical question must be: Is there such an entity as "free will"? Or is "will" a response to learned modes of interacting within social, religious, and political systems that constrain or drive action? If this is the case, then all action must be considered in terms of the "cost" to the actor in relation to positive and negative social feedback and the cost to those impacted by the particular action other than the actor. The examples that we present are used to look at the forces that eventuate in a decisive action. These forces are intimately bound within the cosmological framing of the actor's awareness of the world. This framing presents the actor with potential outcomes that must be imagined by the actor in anticipation of the event. But imagination is limited by not knowing enough about the agency of other actors, which can radically alter the outcome of particular actions. Hence the well-known theme of "unanticipated consequences." Our further examples explore this line of thinking about contexts of action from various materials, highlighting the role of cosmology throughout.

ARJUNA AND KRISHNA: LEGITIMIZING WAR

A particularly intriguing case study for examining will is that of the battle-field conversation between Arjuna and Krishna in the Bhagavad Gita (translated as *The Song of God*), which is a part of the Mahabharata, an epic tale composed between 300 BCE and 300 CE. The story is of a great war between two sides of an extended royal family whose members all trace their heritage back to an earlier ancestor, Bharata. The narrative is filled with episodes of revenge seeking, deception, bribery, and killings between the two sides. The warrior Arjuna, who is a master of arms, especially the bow, doubts the moral correctness of his impending actions (i.e., killing warriors on the other side of the battle who are his extended kin) and thus he becomes overwhelmed with grief and indecision. At this point in the narrative, the deity Krishna appears to Arjuna and has an extended dialogue with him. The eighteen chapters of the Gita have been interpreted in numerous ways, but one commonly put forward is that the dialogue is between two inner selves or voices. At the end of the dialogue Arjuna's self as expressed by Krishna (or transcendental self) is told by Arjuna's other self that Krishna's will is to be done. Krishna instructs Arjuna to enter the battle to re-establish *dharma* (translated variously as social duty, righteousness, or universal order) and keep it strong.

Arjuna thus confers legitimacy on the war, including the killing of his own relatives, in the name of a greater cause, whose tenets remove individual responsibility or blame in the name of a transcendental cosmological order of things. The cosmological thought world presented in the Gita defines actions as right or wrong through doctrinal codes expressed in the Vedas and the Upanishads, but the dialogue between the inner selves is not unlike the following case studies. In the conversation between Arjuna and Krishna, internal struggle is resolved by external cosmology, just as it is in Christian ideology with the expression 'Thy will be done' in the Lord's prayer.

Thus, a part of the complexity of exploring will is identifying how constructs of ideological thought worlds constrain will and how will (individual and notionally group) sometimes reshapes ideological thought worlds through changing practices. We will see this process exemplified in the next example, drawn from ancient Greek tragic drama and mythology.

AGAMEMNON AND IPHIGENEIA: THE WILL TO SACRIFICE

A parallel to Arjuna's dilemma is found in the story of the ancient Greek king of Mycenae in Argolis, Agamemnon, who was leading an expedition of allies to recover Helen, wife of his brother Menelaus, who had been abducted and taken to Troy by Paris, son of King Priam (the subject of Homer's epic *The Iliad*). The Greek fleet was gathered at Aulis, a beach in the Euboean straits, where it was becalmed. Calchas, a prophet, declared that the wind would not rise unless Agamemnon sacrificed his beloved daughter, Iphigeneia, to the goddess of the hunt, Artemis. Agamemnon's supporters were growing restless, and although he was in anguish at the thought of sacrificing his own daughter, he finally agreed to do so (Graves 1960, 290–95). The poet Aeschylus in his drama *Agamemnon* recounted the scene and the King's thoughts:

> My fate is angry if I disobey these [commands],
> but angry if I slaughter
> this child, the beauty of my house,
> with maiden blood shed staining
> these father's hands beside the altar
> What of these things goes now without disaster?
> How shall I fail my ships
> And lose my faith of battle? (Aeschylus 1960, 11, lines 206–13)

"When necessity's yoke was put upon him", the poet continues, Agamemnon "endured then to sacrifice his daughter," in spite of her piteous supplications (ibid.). Even if this was in a sense "against his will," in another sense it took "will power" to carry out the act that he believed to be necessary and in accordance with the will of Artemis. Curiously enough, one version of this narrative suggests that at the last minute Artemis herself took pity on Iphigeneia and removed her from the sacrificial altar, substituting in her place a white hind. This, however, is not how Aeschylus portrays the event, since he sees the sacrifice of Iphigeneia as contributing to the rage of Clytaemnestra, her mother, against Agamemnon, and to Clytaemnestra plotting with Aegisthus, her lover, to murder Agamemnon on his return from Troy, thus working out the curse on the house of Atreus. (Aegisthus had earlier murdered Agamemnon's father, Atreus, enabling his own father, Thyestes, to gain the throne in Mycenae for a time.) Artemis is depicted as having her own grudges against the house of Atreus and for this reason to have demanded the sacrifice of Iphigeneia.

Agamemnon is thus faced with the same sort of dilemma as Arjuna. If he follows his inclinations toward his own kin, he must spare his daughter; but if he does so, his enterprise against Troy will fail, and his prestige as a king and warrior leader will be lost. He chooses political status over kin ties, and this is depicted as a product of necessity, because the will of the gods and goddesses cannot be brooked with impunity. Yet the ultimate choice is his own. It is the paradox of free will once again. He is coerced, but he must make his own choice and take the cosmic consequences, which in this case include his own subsequent death at the hands of his wife and her lover. And in an even later consequence, his son Orestes kills Clytaemnestra in revenge. The curse on the house of Atreus entails a series of killings and revenge killings within three generations of the family. Little wonder that the Chorus observes that "by suffering we learn" (*pathei mathos*, in Aeschylus's condensed phrase—*Agamemnon*, lines 176–77). The curse was imposed by deities displeased at human actions, and continued over a number of generations, as we have discussed. Human choices, and the exercise of will, were made within this framework; and, if in some senses free, they were also always coerced.

ANCESTORS AND THE WILL: THE TALLENSI AND THE MELPA

These ancient Greek ideas of fate, necessity, prophecy, and inter-generational conflict can further be compared with ideas regarding ancestors and destiny among the Tallensi people of Ghana, studied by Meyer Fortes (1987). Fortes supplemented his detailed ethnographic accounts with interpretations based broadly on psychology. He saw the concept of the ancestors as founded on the jural control of parents, especially fathers, over their children. He also recognized the "controlled ambivalence" of inter-generational relations (1987, 199) and saw the "latent antagonism between father and first-born son," who would succeed to the father's position in his lineage after the father's physical death, as underpinning the concept of their respective Destinies. Father's and son's Destiny are in conflict, Fortes notes, and the conflict "invites interpretation as a symbolical acknowledgment of a conflict of potencies" (ibid.). At the father's death, although the son succeeds to his father's position, the father is reincorporated into the family shrines as an ancestor, "in his morally coercive aspect" (Fortes 1987, 202). These references to jural capacities and moral aspects of the parent indicate that Fortes considers that only certain dimensions of the living person are preserved in the concept of the ancestor. In the Tallensi case jural and moral aspects were apparently to the fore, but in other cases we can discern the aspect of the ancestor's will, similar to the will of Artemis in the Greek example. This will may, of course, be put further in the service of morality, as Fortes himself notes (Fortes 1987, 205). In any case we see in this Tallensi example how will may be imputed to ancestral figures as well as to living humans.

We consider next how concepts of will and morality are expressed among the Melpa-speaking people of Mount Hagen in Papua New Guinea. Melpa symbolic concepts foreground issues of decision-making. They also show the cosmological intersection of human choices and the actions imputed to ancestors and spirits.

The closest Melpa term for what we call the will is *noman* (Stewart and Strathern 2001, 113–37; Stewart and Strathern 2000, 46–47; 53–54; 83; Strathern 1981). The noman is emblematic of conscious mind, encompassing stimuli that shape the noman through experience or "being." In addition, aspects of what we might call the unconscious form and shape the noman throughout a person's life. The noman is defined as both the transpersonal and the contemplative aspects of self. It also signifies intentionality and decision-making.

Spatial imagery predominates descriptions of the noman, even though it is said not to be visible in the body as a separate organ. It is said to have an "upper" and "lower" aspect, either of which can prevail over the other. The imagery of upper and lower parts to some extent correlates with a conscious/ unconscious distinction, but is better represented as a notion of that which is immediately accessible versus that which is submerged.

These differing aspects of will are arenas in which a person can establish a dialogue between inner selves in determining what particular action to take or not take. A person's noman is said to lie "straight" if the person's particular actions are seen as being in accordance with what is accepted as proper, effective, or correct. Socialization is supposed to inculcate notions of what constitutes a "straight" noman or its reverse, a "crooked" noman. Not only right and wrong are involved. Conflict is also implied, between upper and lower and between singular and multiple intentions. A strong noman is one that is firm and unitary in the face of conflict. This, in effect, corresponds to will. A dilemma is expressed by saying *nanga noman e rongenem*, "it cuts my noman in two." Something that hurts the noman is expressed as *na noman ronom* "it strikes me in my noman." Dramatic turns of phrase like these indicate the force with which issues of decision-making are imbued and experienced.

Ideas about the interaction of will with other aspects of the person, including bodily aspects, are of great and enduring significance in Hagen. This does not mean that such ideas are unchanging. Actually they are rather fluid and accommodate shifting ideological stances as Hageners try to work out their own models of fundamental realities, basing these models both on experience and on interpretations of experiences.

Issues regarding the noman can also be described in humoral terms since it is said that if the "grease" of persons mixes through fertilization the outcome can be a good or a bad noman in the child that is born, depending on the type of noman that the parents have. But it is ultimately the experience of persons and their own decision making throughout their lifetime that shapes their *noman* and guides them in future selections of pathways to follow.

The cosmological dimension is also involved here. Although exercise of decision-making via the noman is ultimately an individual matter, each person's noman is also thought of as linked to the ancestors and spirits, and to the person's group as a whole. Wrong choices emerging from a crooked noman lead to punitive action by ancestral ghosts, allowing wild spirits of the bush to inflict sickness on the person. In a different way, anger and frustration in the noman of someone who feels wronged or victimized may also lead to their becoming sick. Here the spirits mark the person out in order to induce compassion on the part of those around him or her and to instigate ways of redressing the wrongs that have been caused. The cosmological framework thus "takes care" of the individual.

As times change, so do individual ideas about will and freedom of decision-making. Among Hageners, Christian theology and teaching has altered ideas of will in terms of moral considerations for individuals that overlap in some ways and differ in other ways from past considerations of this sort. The dialogue between the inner selves incorporates the belief that God's will can be learnt through prayer and that this can guide one's actions in opposition to being driven to take action through desires outside of the Christian normative ones. "God" here substitutes for the role played by ghosts of the dead, with whom communication took place through dreams, among other ways.

The imagination (mind's eye) plays a key role in determining how individuals evaluate the potential outcome of their actions (Strathern and Stewart 2006a). The example that we use next is that of suicide—the willful taking of one's own life to obtain a strongly desired end result that seems not to be obtainable by continuing to live. Suicide is often a protest statement and can effectively point a finger at an individual or individuals who are seen to have committed an injustice. It can actually function as an extreme case of "sickness."

THE DUNA: SUICIDE AS AN EXPRESSION OF WILL

An example from the Duna area of the Southern Highlands of Papua New Guinea demonstrates this point (further information on the Duna can be found in Stewart and Strathern 2002a; Strathern and Stewart 2004). A young Duna man had been accused of interfering with a Duna girl of the local parish. The girl was considered by the community to be too young for a relationship of this sort. Parish councilors and leaders decided that the young man should pay a largish sum in compensation, of which he was able to raise half of the requested amount. The leaders reportedly suggested to the girl's family that they should accept this amount and close the issue, but an uncle (father's brother) of the girl later and suddenly accosted the youth, while he was with a group of his age-mates, and publicly shamed him by demanding that he pay the remaining amount of the compensation payment. That night the youth went missing and was found dead early the next morning. He had hanged himself from a tree. The uncle was blamed for the young man's death, and a heavy demand for compensation was placed on his family. The harsh words of the uncle were found to be responsible for the suicide of the boy. We describe this sort of network of actions as "chains of agency" because of the various expressions of agency that go into an event. Also, there is interest in what causes a person to willfully take their own life. Through an examination of chains of agency the question of "who or what drove them to it?" can lead to re-evaluating wider social issues.

Typically the context of suicide is one in which shame is said to have been involved, and shame is a powerful, culturally shaped emotion in many societies, including those of Papua New Guinea (see Stewart and Strathern

2002b, 132 with references given there). But along with shame, there often goes the element of willful protest. And where a suicide is seen as a protest, further issues of responsibility come into play (see Stewart and Strathern 2002b, 132–36).

A second example from the Duna area involves a young woman who had decorated herself elaborately and hanged herself from a tree near the settlement of a young Duna man with whom she had a relationship and had wished to marry. This man, as it turned out, already had one wife, and his parents had rebuffed the girl, who subsequently killed herself. The father of the young man had in particular spoken harsh words to the girl, and she had been shamed as well as disappointed about the demise of her relationship. Her act of killing herself was clearly seen as an act of protest against the family of her lover, who were brought to a local moot and ordered to pay compensation to the dead girl's kin. This would be seen as her way of exacting revenge.

In a rather different example, we cite the case of the orator and politician Cicero in ancient Rome, who, after being betrayed by Octavius, thought of going into Octavius's house and killing himself on the altar of his household gods in order to bring supernatural vengeance on Octavius himself (Stewart and Strathern 2002b, 133). Here the idea was that the domestic gods, the Lares and Penates, would be offended at the desecration of their altar by the act of suicide and its spilling of blood, but would direct their ire not against Cicero but against Octavius. The act would thus have been an act of revenge involving the Lares and Penates as offended witnesses and agents of vengeance against the man whose household they were otherwise expected to protect. Suicide as a protest to the spirits, with an appeal to their pity, concern, or retributive powers, is an idea that would resonate well with Papua New Guinean ideologies.

COUNTY DONEGAL, IRELAND: GHOSTLY WILL

In our examples of suicide in this chapter we have seen the dead expressing their will and agency, much as ghosts are reputed to do in popular contexts in western Europe. Following are two examples of the putative will of ghosts from our recent research in Donegal, Republic of Ireland.

The first is a story told to us in August of 2004 by an elder man. The narrator told us that as a boy his father had often taken him to see an old vacant house nearby. He was then conducted to a room on the second floor and shown a yellow stain on the floor that had caused the floorboards to decay. The stain was said to be the place where a drunkard had slept off his excesses and had relieved himself on the floor while asleep. People said he had died eventually from delirium tremens (a fatal form of alcohol withdrawal marked by severe shaking of the body). The story was a cautionary tale for the benefit of the boy about the shaming and lethal consequences of immoderate drinking. Over the years various people rented the house. One had heard a ghost in the house and had financed a local Catholic priest to perform an exorcism that was said to have driven the ghost away from the house. But later, after the narrator had grown up, the old house was purchased by a family: a man, his wife, and their child. This family reported that the house was haunted by a ghost that frequented the room with the stain at regular intervals. They called the ghost by the name Joe after a former owner of the house, and they reported hearing him enter the house and walk up the stairs to the room with the stain. The wife and her son also both said that they saw the ghost on several occasions, regularly in fact, expecting him to come in at a certain time of night. They gave descriptions of his appearance and clothing.

The narrator of this story said that he knew the ghost was actually of the man who was said to be the drunkard who stained the floor. He explained that the man had died in his early thirties and that the dead man's family had a very high proportion of individuals with juvenile onset diabetes. He said that the ghost kept returning to the house because his spirit had remained unsettled owing to the story of his supposed drunkenness. The narrator believed that this man actually died of untreated diabetes, and that he would continue to return to the house until the truth of his death was acknowledged by his surviving kinsfolk. The imputed will of the ghost is thus adduced to explain its continuing manifestation of itself.

The second story is also from Donegal, Republic of Ireland. It is the Ulster-Scots (see Strathern and Stewart 2005) story/ballad of "Stumpie's Brae," which is a tale of how the consequences of wrong actions cannot be escaped as long as the will and agency of ghosts are concerned (see Strathern and Stewart 2006b). The storyline is of a man and a woman who are visited by a peddler or traveling salesman who wants to rest in their home overnight. The couple allow the man to stay but become envious of the wares that he has in his bag and they kill him while he sleeps to steal his goods. Thus, they were very bad hosts. They stuffed his body into the bag that the man had carried his goods in, but since he was too long for the bag they had to defile his body by cutting the legs off at the knees. After this act they buried the body on a nearby *brae* (this is Scottish and also the Ulster-Scots term for hillside) and returned to their home. But the unquiet spirit of the murdered man returned every night to haunt the couple. The ghost could be heard clomping across the wooden floors of the house as it moved on the bloody stumps of its legs. The ghost was referred to as Stumpie because of this. The story ends with the couple attempting to escape the ghost by emigrating to America, but the ghost follows them across the sea and drives them insane and into an early grave.

Here is the moral warning:

Young man, it's hard to strive wi' sin
An' the hardest strife o' a'
Is where the greed o' gain creeps in
An' drives God's grace awa'.

And here is the denouément:
In the woods of wild America
Their weary feet they set
But the Stumpie was there the first, they say,
And he haunted them on to their dying day,
And he follows their children yet.

Stumpie's ghost here is an instrument of revenge and justice rolled into one. The part of his dead body that has been subjected to the outrage of mutilation becomes the agent that creates terror against his murderers. There is poetic or ironic justice in this point alone. Moreover, the peddler's death, far from obliterating his agency, increases it. As a ghost he is enabled to move around more surely and freely than living human beings. He can enter the couple's house literally "at will," unbidden and unbarred. He can circumvent flooding and reach the house in spite of water levels in streams around it being raised. And, most importantly, he can make his way across the ocean to reach America on the same boat that the couple had taken to escape him.

Thus, he pursues them at each turning where they had hoped to be free from him. This image of the pursuing ghost is a veritable representation of human will—that aspect of the person that can transcend disabilities and difficulties in order to impress its agency on others. Ghosts are the shadowy embodiment of will power.

BRITAIN: THE CASE OF DR. DAVID KELLY

Parallels to the Duna suicide cases, and less directly perhaps to these Donegal narratives, are found in the case of the senior weapons scientist in the Ministry of Defence in Britain, Dr. David Kelly. He was found dead in July 2003, apparently by suicide, following the revelation that he was the secret source used by a British Broadcasting Corporation (BBC) reporter. The reporter had suggested that the British government's picture of the threat posed by Saddam Hussein's weapons in Iraq had been overstated ("sexed up"), perhaps as a means of persuading the British parliament and public that the war against Iraq was legitimate. Dr. Kelly was a quiet person who shunned publicity, and he had suffered during the government's Parliamentary Committee investigation of this matter. The death of Dr. Kelly immediately forced the government to authorize a fully independent inquiry (led by Lord Hutton, a senior judge) to examine the circumstances surrounding the event. As a result, aspects of the government's war policy and the levels of validity of its intelligence information inevitably came to light. The independent inquiry, like a Duna moot, provided an opportunity for many more facts and opinions to emerge that would write themselves into British political history in the way that major compensation payments inscribe themselves on Duna political consciousness. His death caused the public at large to look for the chains of agency involved. And by his death, Dr. Kelly magnified greatly his own agency.[1] This magnification continued regardless of the fact that the Hutton Inquiry exonerated the British government of any deliberate deception over the weapons of mass destruction issue. Indeed, this issue, as a nemesis of political decision-making, itself came back as a kind of ghost to haunt the British Labour government headed by Tony Blair as prime minister.

The relevant issues were reopened when a later inquiry under the leadership of Lord Butler found that the government's intelligence had actually been deficient and that it had been overstated, just as Dr. Kelly was reported to have indicated. Particularly at issue here was the point that the government's claim that Saddam Hussein could deploy weapons of mass destruction within 45 minutes related only to battlefield weapons, not to long-range missiles that might threaten the British population. Even if Saddam had such weapons then, this claim could not stand as a reason for declaring that the war was necessary to protect the public.

Prime Minister Tony Blair nevertheless appointed John Scarlett, the official who "took responsibility" for the pre-war intelligence advice, to succeed to the position of the head of foreign security intelligence in the United Kingdom (*The Independent*, May 7, 2004). When the new report from Lord Butler came out, so did the "ghost" of Dr. Kelly, in the shape of remarks made by the former BBC executives who had resigned in the wake of criticisms of the BBC's reporting by Lord Hutton, author of the earlier report. Kelly's "ghost" in this sense came back to haunt John Scarlett, threatening either his new appointment to a high-level post or the government's credibility in making that appointment.

This discursive regeneration of issues through the invocation of names of the dead by the living remains a powerful way of augmenting the agency of both the dead and the living. The same holds for all those contexts in which killings are remembered and used as a means of furthering conflict, for example in the sectarian politics of Northern Ireland and its relationship to Britain and to the Republic of Ireland. Relatives demand justice for the dead in unsolved cases of suspected sectarian killings, focusing their distrust often on the police investigators and imputing their bad faith. Those who were killed while fighting in a particular cause may be held up as martyrs (i.e., continuing witnesses after their death) to that cause, and therefore as a reason for continuing the fight—again, implicitly or explicitly, as a part of the struggle for a vision of justice which at the level of practical action becomes entwined with motivations for revenge.

WILL, COSMOLOGY, AND THE IMAGINATION

The theme of the willful taking of one's own life to dramatically alter the outcome of events is also found in the September 11, 2001, attacks on the

World Trade Center and the Pentagon in the United States and by suicide bombers generally. During the events of 9/11, the suicide missions were undertaken by individuals who had a clear intent to alter events through the taking of their lives and, in this example, the lives of many others. Likewise, suicide bombers in general are prepared to kill themselves and others to express their will to alter events. These suicides are invariably associated with cosmological purposes and ideologies of seemingly correct action within the wider context of relationships between peoples and often religious entities.

The role of imagination in individual action is pivotal, as we have noted, because an action that is the product of the will is also the product of imagining its desired outcome, as an aim to be secured against other alternatives or against opposition. Imagination is brought into play in the process of overcoming opposition. As a concept, the idea of the will mediates between intentions and desired outcomes, overcoming resistance and ambiguity. Therein lies its power and its danger, as well as the responsibilities that go with power and danger. Referring such responsibilities to the cosmological level is one way of dealing with them. Locating them entirely in the individual is another. The doctrine of free will runs in counterpoint to the idea of God's will, attempting to recognize both the individual and the cosmological poles of action by proposing that individual actions may have cosmological causes and results. The image of crossing the threshold of Dracula's house encapsulates all of these points.

Further, human responses and actions are often generated out of various emotions that are conditioned by influences from experience in which the imagination has played a part as the site where fears, desires, and fantasies have grown, been nurtured, and often silently, to the outside listener, influenced the way that an individual interacted within their world. This role of the imagination can be noted in the conversations that people have with deities and spirits who are a part of their thought worlds, as noted for the Hagen example above in relation to Christian prayer (see also Strathern and Stewart 2009).

This world of the imagination also includes "iconic codes"—codes that are embodied or expressed "outside language" (Aijmer 2000, 3). Göran Aijmer discusses this point in relation to violent acts, pointing to the "symbolism of iconic codes and their use in the visionary building of possible worlds, forming the *imaginary order* of a society" (ibid.). Violent acts, Aijmer argues, may embody complex aspects of symbolism that relate to both order and disorder in a given social context, and it is these symbolic aspects that give violence its many potential meanings. This is an important point when we consider the acts, including both violent and nonviolent ones, taken by peoples around the world in the name of a particular religion or in a belief that these acts conform to a set of "moral" teachings directly linked to specific cosmological ideologies (see also Strathern and Stewart 2008).

The imagination is important in religious teachings and in general in individual emplacement within a cosmological thought-world that is bounded by a set of "moral" normative prescriptions. Vincent Crapanzano's concept of "imaginative horizons" and "frontier" is applicable here, especially when considering frontiers "that postulate a beyond that is, by its very nature, unreachable in fact and in representation" (2004, 14). This frontier can be the arena of the afterworld seen as unreachable during life but filled with particularly tangible features that await the recipient after death.

Imaginative capacities direct and drive the will and the actions that result from this process of interaction with the world around us. Arjun Appadurai asserts that "the imagination has now acquired a singular new power in social life" (1996, 53), which he links to the accelerated transnational flow of images. These flows are a part of what produces historical and cultural changes in how the will is conceived and transformed.

The will is attached to self-awareness, which is in a constant interplay with information coming from the "social semiotics" that the individual is surrounded with. In the previous examples from the Bhagavad Gita and the concept of the *noman* in Hagen, we can see that an "individual semiotics" is at play in which "the will" must act upon what on balance appears to be the "correct" path to follow. This "individual or internal semiotics" is also expressed in dreams. For example, among the Melpa speakers in Hagen dreams are thought to represent the actual observations and experiences of the person's *min* or spirit while they were asleep (Strauss and Tischner 1962; Stewart and Strathern 2003). In Melpa the phrase *ur kumb etepa köni* (make a sleep-likeness and see something) describes the way that the individual self interacts with and learns from the dream world. The dream period is one in which a dream-time "social semiotics" includes the dreamer's dead kin's transformed life-spirits (*min*), the living, and nonhuman spirits. This interaction with the dead through dreaming is very important for the Melpa because it is believed that the dead are able to "see" (perceive, understand) more than the living and they are also able to make events occur through their own agency. This heightened ability to "see" extends, in some degree, to future events that the dreamer would not be aware of by other sensory means. Dreams can thus be valuable signs of things to come, directing the individual to take one course of action rather than another. The will of the person can be extensively informed by the dream world, just as the dream world reveals the wishes, or will, of the dead, often informed by resentments against the living.

CONCLUSION

In our discussion we have stressed the point that ideas about the will belong to the general domain of choice and intentionality in human action; but within this broad domain they pick out questions of freedom, constraint, internal argument, and connections with cosmological notions that provide an ultimate framework of right and wrong. In many ways the idea of will is linked to questions of responsibility for action. This is the case in the examples presented from diverse ethnographic materials from Highlands Papua New Guinea, ancient Greece and Rome, Africa, the United Kingdom, Ireland, Christian ideology, and Hindu cosmology.

Interestingly, for Hageners, aspects of the noman, including the thoughts that specifically induce a particular action, are said to be hidden from others (although not from the dead/ancestors and nowadays from God). Given this, people read intentions, and the responsibility that goes with them, from actions themselves and their results. For them, will is thus seen as projected into the world, while at the same time it is deeply introjected in the individual. Cosmology steps in to close the gap between an observable world and an inscrutable source of willed action. As we have noted, dreams and their interpretation are often cited as giving important clues to this process of attributing meaning and direction to actions.

In conclusion, the concept of the will offers up a number of phenomenologically interesting cross-cultural questions. Can we find correspondences across cultural and historical contexts that reveal patterns going beyond the specifics of this term in the English language? Questions of this kind tend not to be susceptible to simple answers. However, we can recognize clusters of concepts regarding action and choice that clearly belong to the same broad domain of experience in life. People act according to their inclinations or the pressures placed upon them. The idea of the will expresses the notion of active agency, often in circumstances of resistance or difficulty. And while the will might seem to be a quintessentially individualistic notion, issues to do with it are always framed within some wider morality or cosmology.

Will thus mediates between the private aspects of individuals and their externalized social lives. Since this mediation is a process common to many, if not all, societal complexes, we may conclude that the term has a useful cross-cultural reference. It forms a core around which elements of morality, responsibility, legitimacy, desire, and theodicy can all be fashioned into a complex vision of human action and its concomitants.

CHAPTER 8

EMIL KRAEPELIN ON PATHOLOGIES OF THE WILL

Byron J. Good

T HIS CHAPTER EXAMINES THE ROLE OF the will in the writings of the great nineteenth and early twentieth century German neuropsychiatrist, Emil Kraepelin. When I was invited to participate in the AAA panel on the "anthropology of the will" that led to this collection, I immediately thought of something that had long puzzled me. Kraepelin is often cited as the "father" of contemporary psychiatric classification, the originator of an "objective-descriptive" approach to diagnostic classification that claims to be theoretically neutral and shapes the current American Psychiatric Association's Diagnostic and Statistical Manual (DSM-IV). However, Kraepelin's writings on mental disorders refer explicitly to pathologies of the "will," a term that seems anachronistic today and suggests that Kraepelin's writings are not theoretically neutral but rather reflect an older psychology. An examination of the place of the "will" in Kraepelin's writings opens onto a vast scientific literature on the will in nineteenth century neurology, as well as a popular literature on the will of the German people and the link between psychopathology, pathologies of the will, and the social and genetic bases of degeneracy. The concept thus opens onto the darker history of racial ideology in German medical science, suggesting that psychological anthropologists should take care in advocating a new anthropology of the will. This paper uses Kraepelin's neuropsychiatric writing as well as his reflections on German society as a basis for examining these issues.

Kraepelin's *Lectures on Clinical Psychiatry*, first translated into English in 1904 (references here are to the 1913 edition), provides easy access to his views of psychopathology and makes clear why his work is thought of as largely descriptive. Each of the lectures was devoted to a particular form of mental disease—"melancholia," "depressed stages of maniacal-depressive insanity," "dementia praecox," "katatonic stupor," and so forth. Within each lecture, Kraepelin provided several brief case vignettes, describing in great detail the patient's symptoms, something about their onset, and often some details of the patient's life history, as well as providing a short discussion about how these patients differ from those suffering from other related conditions.

I have always been struck by Kraepelin's description of the pathology of the will in the chapter on "depressed stages of maniacal-depressive insanity." Let me quote briefly from the case, then say why I find this reference to the will intriguing. Kraepelin opens Lecture II with the following case:

Gentlemen, The patient you see before you today is a merchant, forty three years old, who has been in our hospital almost uninterruptedly for about five years. He is strongly built, but badly nourished, and has a pale complexion, and an invalid expression of face. He comes in with short, wearied steps, sits staring in front of him almost without moving. When questioned, he turns his head a little, and, after a certain pause, answers softly, and in monosyllables, but to the point. We get the impression that speaking gives him a great deal of trouble, his lips moving for a little while before the sound comes out. (1913, 11–12)

Kraepelin points out that the patient has intact cognitive functions, and that he has no apparent delusions, unlike the patients he described in the previous chapter, who suffer "melancholia" or a severe, psychotic depression. He goes on:

. . . it must strike us that this patient is not apprehensive, but only "low-spirited," and still more that, unlike the patients already considered, he is apparently unable to move and express himself freely. In those cases [i.e. the melancholia cases], there were lively gesticulations, lamentations, and complaints, and a certain necessity of giving vent to the oppression within, while here it is hard to draw any remark from the patient. . . . This very circumstance, that the answers come so slowly, even on matters of indifference, shows that in this patient we have not to deal with a fear of expressing himself, but with some general obstacle to utterance in speech. Indeed, not only speech, but *all action of the will is extremely difficult to him.* For three years he has been incapable of getting up from bed, dressing, and occupying himself. . . . But as he has the most perfect comprehension of his surrounding, and is able to fol-low difficult trains of thought, the disturbance must be essentially confined to the accomplishment of voluntary movement. . . . Under these circumstances, it will be permissible here to speak of an *impediment* of *volition*, in the sense that the transfor-mation of the impulses of the will into action meets with obstacles which cannot be overcome without difficulty, and often not at all by the patient's own strength. This constraint is by far the most obvious clinical feature of the disease, and compared with this, the sad, oppressed mood has but little prominence. No other psychical disturbances can be made out at present. [italics in the original]

In the late 1960s and early 1970s, a group of American psychiatrists, led by Robert Spitzer at Washington University in St. Louis, set out to reform the psychiatric diagnostic system. Calling themselves "Neo-Kraepelinians," this group sought to emulate Kraepelin in providing clear, symptomatic de-scriptions of psychiatric diseases, defined in clinical terms but with the goal of ultimately finding specific disease etiologies, assumed to be neurophysio-logical, for each diagnostic category (see, e.g., Blashfield 1984; Klerman 1978; Weissman and Klerman 1978; Wilson 1993; cf. Good 1992 for a discussion of this movement). In contrast to psychoanalytic or existentialist or interper-sonal assessments, the so-called "objective-descriptive" approach to diagnosis aimed at being theoretically neutral, disavowing efforts to base categories on psychological or functional origins of symptoms, providing instead objec-tive clinical descriptions that could serve as a basis for research into genetic markers, neurophysiological dysfunctions, or responses to drugs that might indicate biological markers distinguishing diagnostic groups from one another. Given this disavowal of psychology and the claim to emulate Kraepelin in being a-theoretical, it is thus intriguing to find Kraepelin's description of depression as a "pathology of the will," reflecting an older psychology. The language of the will has almost entirely disappeared in that great neo-Kraepelinian compendium, the Diagnostic and Statistical Manual 4th edition of the American Psychiatric Association (1994)—the DSM IV. However, the presence of the will in Kraepelin's writings should not go without notice.

The will was an important category in nineteenth and twentieth century German philosophy—one only has to think of Schopenhauer (*The World as Will and Representation*) or Nietzsche. It was also crucial in the language of German National Socialism and Nazi ideologies, as in Leni Riefenstahl's infamous film *Triumph of the Will* (see, e.g., Barsam 1975, Sontag 1980). But what is its place in the history of psychiatry? Knowing that Kraepelin's categories dementia praecox and manic-depressive psychosis were used, well after his death in 1925, by the Nazis to identify categories of hereditarily "degenerate" persons who should be eliminated from the German gene pool, or that Kraepelin's student and close colleague Ernst Rudin was a staunch advocate of racial hygiene theories and later a dominant figure in Nazi psychiatry (Roelcke 1997), lends urgency to understanding the social history of the ideas underlying Kraepelin's apparently non-theoretical classification of psychiatric diseases. It also adds irony to the proud claim of contemporary descriptive psychiatrists to be neo-Kraepelinians.

What then was the place of a psychology of the will in the psychiatric theorizing and classification of Kraepelin and his contemporaries? Is there a relation between nineteenth century notions of *degeneracy* and the *will*, both present in Kraepelin's *Lectures*? Are pathologies of the will relevant for current thinking about culture and mental illness? What does a critical historical reading of the place of the will in German writings about psychopathology tell us about the history of the concept more generally and about the potential benefits and hazards of its use as a category within psychological anthropology? The following is not intended to be a full explication of these issues. It is rather a brief report of an initial survey of the place of the will and pathologies of the will in Kraepelin's psychology, as well as in his reflections on social and political issues in Germany following World War I.

EMIL KRAEPELIN

Emil Kraepelin lived through a complex, interesting period of political transformation in German history. Born in 1856, he lived for forty years under
the rule of Bismarck, witnessed the freeing of Prussia from Austrian influence and the unification of the German kingdoms, watched the dissolution
of the monarchy and Germany's defeat in World War I, and followed the
political crises in the postwar era with great dismay, before dying in 1926.
He was a political conservative and maintained his support for Bismarck's
vision of authoritarian leadership to the end of his life (sources include Berrios and Hauser 1988; Engstrom 1991, 1992; Roelcke 1997; cf. Brink & Jelliffe 1933; Kahn 1956; Braceland 1957). While a medical student (1874–78),
Kraepelin attended a summer course on experimental psychology taught by
Wilhelm Wundt in Leipzig, was an assistant to the professor at the University of Wuerzburg in charge of the psychiatric and dermatologic clinics, and
wrote a dissertation in 1877, "Concerning the Influence of Acute Diseases on
the Causation of Mental Illness," reflecting his work with Wundt, to whom
he remained faithful throughout his life (Kahn 1956, 289). In his dissertation
he sounded a theme that was to be central to his life's work: "The most important achievement which the advance of scientific research has brought to
psychiatry in our century is the firm foundation of the notion of the somatic
basis of mental disorders" (quoted in Kahn 1956, 289).

Kraepelin delivered his inaugural lecture for his initial professorship at
the University of Dorpat in 1886, further elaborating his vision. "He an-
nounced his intention of combining psychiatric research and patient care
and set the objectives for the former: in the short term he was to search for
valid disease groups, and in the long term seek the 'laws' linking anatomi-
cal and psychological data" (Berrios and Hauser 1988, 815). This broad commitment—to research-based classification, primarily through careful clinical
description, with a longer term goal of seeking somatic bases for disease—
ran throughout his life. His greatest contribution was the careful, longitudinal description of the symptoms of his clinical cases, following patients over
years, writing notes on specially designed index cards, and analyzing the
symptomatic differences between those who had differing courses of illness.
He is best known for his description of *dementia praecox* and its subtypes,

which he distinguished from both melancholia and manic-depressive insanity, and the general structure of his classification system, with categories not that different from those in today's diagnostic systems.

When he was twenty-seven years old, Kraepelin wrote a "Compendium of Psychiatry," which became the first of many updated editions, first of the Compendium, then of *Psychiatry: A Textbook for Students and Physicians* (see Braceland 1957). With each volume, he refined his thinking and his description of categories and causes of mental illnesses. A brief review of the 6th Edition, published in German in 1899 and translated and published in English in 1990, indicates the broader place of the category "the will" in his thinking. Volume 1 of the 6th Edition provides an overview of mental illnesses—"The Causes of Insanity" (both "external" and "internal"), the "Manifestations of Insanity," "Course, Outcome and Duration of Insanity," "The Diagnosis of Insanity," and "Treatment of Insanity." His discussion of the will falls in a subsection of Manifestations of Insanity entitled "Disorders of Volition and Action," which follows his descriptions of disorders of perception, mental functions, and emotional life. Here he has sections on the reduction and the increase in volitional impulses, disorders of the release of volitional impulses (which he distinguishes from the impulses themselves), increased and reduced suggestibility of the will, compulsive actions, instinctive actions, morbid instincts, disorders of expressive movements, and behavior due to morbid motives, which ends with a discussion of the forensic implications of the loss of "capacity to control oneself" and for "responsibility." In Volume 2, which provides detailed descriptions of particular disorders, discussions of the will or of volition are fairly rare and appear only in the context of clinical descriptions of syndromes.

How then does Kraepelin's discussion of the will relate to what was being written within medicine and psychology of the time? And perhaps of greater interest to anthropologists, what was the relation between this rather technical and descriptive discussion of disorders of the will or volition as part of clinical syndromes and the more general discussions of the "will" as a social or spiritual phenomenon of a people, particularly of the German people, discussions to which Kraepelin actively contributed?

PATHOLOGIES OF THE WILL IN NINETEENTH
CENTURY PSYCHOLOGY AND PSYCHIATRY

Even a quick search in the history of psychology and psychiatry makes it
clear that the will and disorders of the will were major categories in nineteenth and early twentieth century neurology, psychology, and neuropsychiatry—in France, Germany, and the United States. Although anachronistic
for today's reader, Kraepelin's use of the language of the will and its pathologies was unexceptional in his time. The best review of this literature and
discussion of the disorders of the will in psychiatry is in an essay entitled
"Will and Its Disorders: A Conceptual History," published in the journal
History of Psychiatry in 1995 by the historian German Berrios (Berrios and
Gili 1995). Berrios and Gili trace the concept "will" through philosophy and
psychology into nineteenth century neurology and psychiatry. They argue
that in the nineteenth century, the will "was an important descriptive and
explanatory concept, naming the human 'power, potency or faculty' to initiate action" (1995, 87), but that it came under attack at the turn of the century.
By the first World War, with the rise of experimentalism, psychoanalysis,
and behaviorism, the will was no longer a fashionable concept. Berrios and
Gili express the opinion that this decline "created a conceptual vacuum in
the 'domain of the voluntary' which has since been unsatisfactorily filled by
notions such as 'instinct', 'drive', 'motivation', 'decision-making', and 'fron-
tal lobe executive.'" They go on to suggest that "the decline of the will also
led to neglecting the study of aboulia, impulse, agoraphobia, and obsession
as 'pathological disorders of the will'" (1995, 88). But more important than
this conclusion—aimed at urging the reader to take this work seriously, suggesting more than a passing historical interest—is the broad review of the
philosophical, psychological, and psychiatric lineage of this domain, and the
insight into the debates that developed, particularly during the nineteenth
century.

Rather than attempting to summarize this literature and the debates or
provide a historical review of the writings on disorders of the will in psychiatry and neurology in Kraepelin's era, here I can only make four summary observations concerning that literature. In the end, I return to a discussion of
the close link between Kraepelin's understandings of psychopathology and

its causes, his views on the disorders of the body politic, and the place of the will in this discussion.

First, the literature—particularly in French and German—is vast. There were well-worked-out debates about the nature of the will, the neurological defects producing these disorders, the potential for localizing the will and deficits of volition in the brain, and classification of clinical signs and symptoms associated with disorders of the will. Much of the psychological and neuropsychiatric literature is more interesting than the philosophical writing (for purposes of an anthropology of the will), because it is laced with clinical examples and description of life stories. In one important thread of this literature, analysis of the will was linked to the rise of neurology and neuroanatomical understanding of how nerve impulses are carried to the muscles. The French psychologist Theodule Ribot (1894) has an entire treatise titled "Diseases of the Will" (published first in 1883 as *Les Maladies de la Volonte*), which attempts to link clinical phenomena to the growing understanding of the nervous system, raising questions of whether disorders of the will are linked to the executive function of the brain or to the ability of the nerves to adequately translate volition into muscular action. As Berrios and Gili (1995, 98) point out, "Ribot's work is the point of convergence of positivism, antimetaphysical psychology, Spencerian evolutionism and clinical analysis."

As this comment suggests, even though quite technically linked to emerging understandings of the functioning of the nervous system, medical discussions of the will were never far from concerns about the role of modern civilization or degeneracy or political activities in producing disorders of the will. Disorders of the body and of the body politic are closely linked, even in writings on neurophysiology. These themes are most explicitly expressed in writing on the depletion of neural energy (this was, of course, the period in which George Beard's writings on neurasthenia became popular), the loss of inhibition as part of crowd behavior (again, this was a time of popular writing about mass psychology), and the debates in Germany about whether World War I resulted from a "war psychosis" or to the contrary was linked to what Kraepelin called "the vitality of our collective psyche" (Kraepelin [1919] 1992). The "will" was thus a critical concept bridging neurophysiology and neuropsychiatry, philosophy, and social and political writing.

Second, one of the primary debates revolved around what Berrios and Gili

(1995, 91–94) call "reductionist" versus "non-reductionist" accounts of disorders of the will (see Murphy and Throop, Chapter 1; Throop, Chapter 2). At stake was the general question of whether the will is an independent faculty or mental power, or whether what we call will or volition, the force that leads to action, can be fully accounted for by the emotions and "understanding," that is affect and cognition. (Note that William James weighed in on the side of non-reductionist accounts, arguing that willing produces movement, which often in turn produces feelings or affects.) It is in this context that Kraepelin's case, quoted at the opening of this paper, should be understood. Kraepelin argues that in the case of this patient in the depressed phase of a "maniacal-depressive insanity," which we would now call manic-depressive or bipolar disorder, the depressive affect is not primary, as it is in cases of melancholia, and that the man's thinking was intact, again unlike the delusions suffered by those with melancholia or dementia praecox. Thus, in his *Lectures on Clinical Psychiatry* Kraepelin argues that patients with "maniacal-depressive insanity (circular stupor)" are suffering a primary disorder of the will. Although he does not use the term, "aboulia" was widely used for a diminution of the will that produced the symptoms of apparent passivity and inability to carry out action that Kraepelin describes. Thus, for Kraepelin, description of the depressed stage of a patient with manic-depressive illness in terms of the will and impediments of volition, both highlighted in italics, is a critical theoretical claim about the etiology and nature of this disorder and its relation to other forms of psychopathology.

Third, the scientific and clinical literature at the turn of the century was filled with detailed classifications and descriptions of disorders of the will, by neurologists, psychiatrists, and psychologists of the day. One of the major axes for classification distinguished disorders reflecting an overly weak versus an overly strong will. Wilhelm Griesenger, a German psychiatrist who preceded Kraepelin, wrote that disturbances of the will ranged from "total absence of volition" to increase in power (quoted in Berrios and Gili 1995, 97):

Weakness of the will may result from incapacity to reach conclusions which may be due to troubles in perception or to the lack of a strong ego . . . these states manifest themselves in passivity and apathy, or in great hesitation and irresolution . . . and are frequent in the stage of melancholia.

Increases in the power of the will, on the other hand,

Take the form of inordinate desire, a thirst for action, a passion for making plans . . . and a pathologically increased sense of self.

Here then we see the origin of Kraepelin's desire to show that manic-depressive disorder is a primary disorder of the will—with the depressive phase resulting from a weakening of the will, the manic phase indicating a pathologically active will.

But disorders of the will were also seen as associated with other disorders as well. Eugen Bleuler, leading scholar of schizophrenia, analyzed "disturbances of centrifugal functions," including detailed analyses of the distinction between what was popularly called "weakness of will" and "hyper-function of the will" (Bleuler 1924, 142–56). "Weakness of the will" provided a basis for distinguishing what are now called "negative symptoms" of schizophrenia, whereas "hyper-function of the will" was associated with impulsive acts separated from rational control—as when "schizophrenic patients sometimes develop a special energy or will, as, for instance, when they pull out their own teeth, squeeze out one of their eyes, or do something similar without analgesic." Other psychiatrists spelled out specific pathologies of impulse control, of obsessions and compulsions, or of phobias as pathologies of the will. Thus, although explicit reference to "the will" has disappeared from psychiatric classification and theorizing today, many of the symptom clusters associated with particular diagnostic entities continue to reflect this older psychology. In these terms, Berrios and Gili are right: The absence of a robust conception of the will or volition in psychiatric nosology and theorizing has indeed created a "conceptual vacuum in the 'domain of the voluntary'," but even in its absence an older concept of the will continues to influence contemporary psychiatric classification.

DISORDERS OF THE BODY POLITIC:
SOCIAL AND POLITICAL DIMENSIONS OF THE WILL

Finally, I want to turn to Kraepelin's interest in the social and political dimensions of the will and to a more obscure link of discussion of the will to the larger ideology of degeneracy. Here the story becomes both more interesting and much darker. As we noted in the opening, Kraepelin grew up an admirer of Bismarck and was a political conservative and nationalist. Very early on, he saw alcoholism and syphilis as both social and moral pathologies, which does "damage to the germ" and "can result in the degeneration of entire lineages," thus weakening the German nation, and actively campaigned against them (Kraepelin [1908] 2007). And he argued that one of the few means of preventing mental illnesses in future generations was "to make the coming generations strong and resistant and to prepare them for the struggle for existence [*Kampf und Dasein*]" (Kraepelin 1896, quoted in Roelcke 1997, 389). By 1919, with the defeat of the German army, the collapse of the monarchy, the rise of leftist and democratic forces which threatened the previously elite classes, and national politics in disarray, Kraepelin took it upon himself to publish an essay, "Psychiatric Observations on Contemporary Issues" (Kraepelin [1919] 1992), in which he voiced his strong opinions about the causes of the loss of the war and the future of Germany.

Kraepelin opened the essay with a clear attack on those who were criticizing Germany's commitment to the war as a "mass psychosis" or "war psychosis." As to the war effort, Kraepelin began,

there can be absolutely no talk whatsoever of a morbid disorder. The drive of self-assertion is the primal and most powerful force behind all individual and group action. When this self-assertion appears threatened all the forces of the will are naturally roused in order that . . . the danger be dispatched and the opponent wrestled to the ground. Only an ageing and decrepit people would, in feeble deference, evade the fight for survival . . . ([1919] 1992, 257)

Kraepelin contrasts this with "combat neurosis," which he argued "afflicted less stable, emotionally excitable, nervous and infirm personalities," immediately comparing it to "accident neurosis," which he defined as "the reluctance of weak-willed persons to return to work after suffering an injury" ([1919] 1992, 258). The increase in levels of combat neurosis over time, he reasoned, grew out of the fact that the desperation for recruits required that "more and more incompetent, mentally deficient, infirm and morally inferior persons had to be drawn into service, thereby eventually adversely affecting the fighting spirit of the troops" (ibid.). What was more, he argued, "it came to pass that an undesirable collection of individuals remained on the home front who possessed neither the ability nor the desire to commit themselves to the defence of the fatherland" ([1919] 1992, 259). Economic hardships were exploited by "ruthless smugglers, . . . generally recruited from the ranks of the failures, decrepits, loiterers and swindlers, for whom this form of parasitism came naturally, in accordance with their entire predisposition" (ibid.).

Even though alcoholism almost disappeared during the war, Kraepelin noted, hunger, disease, and the "gradual grinding down of the collective psyche" led to the "unexpected collapse and resulting upheaval" ([1919] 1992, 260). Popular sentiment demanded an escape from the war and peace at any price, leaving Germany at the mercy of its enemies. But more than this, what followed was "a wave of senseless destruction and self-laceration which compounded in the extreme the misery created by the war" ([1919] 1992, 261). Here, Kraepelin is referring to the November Revolution of 1919 that demanded an end to the war, repeal of the wartime statutes, and the abdication of Emperor William II, as well as the political rise of the Social Democratic Party calling for the establishment of the Republic. Some of Kraepelin's harshest language is reserved for the leaders of this movement, which stimulated mass actions that he characterized as *hysterical disorders*, in which individuals' "own will" is taken over by the impulses of the masses and "the activation of the will is dominated . . . by ancient herd instincts," as in epidemics of hysteria ([1919] 1992, 262). In this setting, those with the most hysterical traits often stand at the head of mass movements. "Dreamers and poets," "busybodies," and "professional swindlers" all emerge as leaders, followed by a swarm of "inferior personalities." And here he further asserted his clinical experience: "I have found in the recent demonstrations a number of the leading personalities and their followers whom I have either been able to examine or of whom I acquired more precise information, belonging to one of the above groups. The active involvement of the Jewish race in such upheavals has something to do with this. The frequency of psychopathic predisposition in Jews could have played a role, although it is their harping criticism, their rhetorical and theatrical abilities, and their doggedness and determination which are most important" ([1919] 1992, 264).[1]

Kraepelin continued with a final outburst against the *Raterepublik,* which, he argued:

brought us the 'dictatorship of the proletariat'. . . . In this ludicrous governmental nonsense one cannot but recognize the final perversion of the idea that the abilities of all social classes are essentially equal and that only external causes, oppression, exploitation and artificial deprivation inhibit the awakening of the intellectual powers slumbering in the masses. . . . The development of every child teaches us that this conviction is false. ([1919] 1992, 265–66)

He concludes with his alternative to the republican or socialist vision of the future of Germany and the "true people" or *Volk*.

If our people is to prosper, then its leaders must be its most noble and diligent sons. Popular rule must become the rule of the best. Therefore it is necessary that . . . we rear the most superb personalities to guide our destiny in the difficult days to come. Unfortunately the prerequisites for the realization of this urgent demand are extremely unpropitious. ([1919] 1992, 268)

The war has "carried out a terrible selection," killing many of Germany's finest men. "It was above all the unfit and selfish individuals who remained unscathed." Humanitarian efforts to help the "suffering, sickly, and the decrepit" add further to the burdening of those most able, a burden "we cannot afford to increase . . . indefinitely" (ibid.).

His final prescription is "to work systematically and employ all of our resources in the physical, mental and moral regeneration of our people" ([1919] 1992, 269). Attention must be focused on fighting influences that will threaten future generations, particularly "hereditary degeneration and genetic defects resulting from alcohol and syphilis" (ibid.). In addition, the next generation needs to be cultivated by encouraging early marriage, protecting the young from "physical, mental and moral neglect," "the strengthening of the body, of the mind, and in particular of the will, by means of their regular and appropriate engagement," and on "a selection of the most valuable and capable portions of our progeny" (ibid.).

It is quite clear that Kraepelin speaks as a member of a generation committed to Bismarkian ideals, and that his ideology is in defense of class privilege. But where does his language of *degeneration* and *regeneration* come from, how is it linked to his ideas about the will, and how is it related to his categorization and understanding of psychopathology? In a book called *Faces of Degeneration: A European Disorder, c. 1848–c. 1918*, Daniel Pick (1989) outlines the importance of the theme degeneration and degeneracy in France, Italy and England. Linked to evolutionary theory, particularly Lamarckian views (Engstrom 2007), degeneration accounted for both the status of some societies encountered by colonialists—degenerate societies—as well as pathological families and individuals, families whose degenerative hereditary processes produced increasing numbers of mentally and morally defective individuals, idiots, the mentally ill, and criminals. The perspective was central to evolutionist theorizing about race, class, and society and was a popular frame for psychiatrists as for others. Henry Maudsley (1835–1918), British neuropsychiatrist, held positions similar to Kraepelin's, expressed most directly in his 1883 book *Body and Will* (see Pick 1989, 203–16). It explained potential causes of mental illness—one class of mental illnesses in Kraepelin's *Textbook* were the "Degenerative Psychoses." And it also helped to explain why some disorders were chronic.

For German neuropsychiatry, and Kraepelin in particular, the question of why some forms of mental illness seemed to produce chronic deterioration, while others were cyclical or allowed recovery, was thus inevitably caught in the ideology of degeneracy. Kraepelin wrote about "degenerating psychological processes" and "dementia praecox," commenting:

The common feature of those illnesses which we group under the name of degenerating psychological processes is the rapid development of a lasting state of psychological weakness. . . . What we call dementia praecox is the sub-acute development of a peculiar, simple condition of mental weakness occurring at a youthful age . . . (quoted in Berrios and Hauser 1988, 817)

In Kraepelin's *Textbook*, dementia praecox stands as its own category, not under the heading Degenerative Psychoses, and Kraepelin says explicitly that hereditary factors seem to be present in about 70 percent of the cases and that the "real nature" of dementia praecox remains "totally obscure" ([1899] 1990, 153). Nonetheless, one source of the long-standing idea that dementia praecox or schizophrenia is a disease for which there is little or no chance for recovery, an idea that still holds sway today, may be its link to degeneracy articulated by Kraepelin and others of his generation (cf. Zubin, et al 1985; Barrett 1996).

Roelcke (1997, 389) argues that Kraepelin made a significant shift from a

position of being "concerned with the ambivalence of life in a rapidly changing world," in the 1880s and 1890s, to "interpreting behavior and institutions
which did not correspond to his traditional outlook on societal life as 'consequences' of degeneration, i.e., of quasi-biological laws." And he argues that
this position is first made explicit in Kraepelin's reports on his trip to South-
east Asia, including to Indonesia, where he visited patients in what is now
the Bogor State Mental Hospital, just north of current Jakarta, to investigate
whether these cases fit the classification system he was developing (Kraepelin 1904a, 1904b). Roelcke suggests that this report, often described as an
early model for cross-cultural or comparative psychiatric research, actually
expresses clearly for the first time his interpretation of the role of "nutrition,
climate, and racial attributes" in determining clinical presentation. He explained his observation that delusions are relatively rare among those patients
with dementia praecox he saw in Java as being due to a "racially determined
deficiency of psychological differentiation of both the affected individuals
and their culture" (Roelcke 1997, 389). Indeed, it may be that this trip, far
from leading Kraepelin to a serious recognition of cultural differences in the
presentation of psychopathology, actually crystallized or strengthened his
views of the power of racial difference. Whatever the case, the trip apparently affected his views on the importance of the will.

Shortly after his return from his trip to Java, Kraepelin wrote:

the fundamental importance of the will in nature, which to that point I had only
dimly perceived, assumed more definite shape and tangible boundaries. On the basis
of thousands of individual observations it became forcefully clear to me that, above
all else, the instinctive urges of the will (*triebhafte Willensregungen*) slumbering in
every living creature determine not only its living expression but also its future development and ultimately its very constitution. [quoted from his *Memoirs* in Engstrom 1991, 111–12]

Kraepelin does not specify how his travel brought him to these conclusions,
but it was following this trip that he redoubled his efforts for social reform—
for penal reform, for the control of alcohol, and for the control of sexual behaviors associated with syphilis. All of these were linked, for him, to weak-
nesses of the will, and all were both an indication of social degeneracy and a
cause of further degeneration of society.

In 1908, four years after his trip to Dutch East Indies, Kraepelin wrote an essay *Zum Entartungsfrage* ('On the Question of Degeneration,' Kraepelin [1908] 2007), which Roelcke argues represented a "turning point" in the debate about the legitimacy of degenerationist theorizing: "It implied a major shift in the focus of concern, namely from the social origins of a disease that affected individuals, to the biological processes that threatened the collective 'culture' or 'folk body'" (1997, 390). And this shift turned in part on Kraepelin's ideas about the will and pathologies of the will both in individuals and in the body politic.

It is not easy to neatly tie all of this together—much of Kraepelin's medical texts read as though they might have been written recently, while his social and political writing reads as if from a distant era, clearly reflecting a powerful climate of eugenics theorizing and pointing forward to some aspects of National Socialism. But though his psychiatric observations and his political reflections remained distinct and the latter do not invalidate the importance of his clinical observations, Kraepelin's psychiatric interests in the pathologies of the will must be understood in a larger social and political context. His psychiatric observations provided a language that mediated his interpretations of the social and the political, even as his broader understanding of degeneracy influenced his increasingly pessimistic views of dementia praecox or schizophrenia.

Kraepelin was disappointed by his failures in the public arena in his interests in both alcohol abuse and syphilis. He was a follower of Bismarck, believing in the "rule of the best" and leaders of a people to be drawn from "its most noble and diligent sons" (quoted above, Kraepelin [1919] 1992, 268). He saw political revolution and democracy as unleashing irrational forces of the masses, a form of hysterical disorders that "ultimately explode with enormous power and which in their blind rage can no longer be controlled by the forces of reason" (Kraepelin [1919] 1992, 261), thus calling for leadership with a strength of will. Pathologies of the will, linked ultimately to degeneracy, were thus found in political life as well as in his psychiatric wards, in both the bodies of the patients he followed over the years and the body politic of his beloved Germany.

Germany's defeat in World War I heightened the concerns of intellectuals about the potential loss of spirit or will of the people and the threats of degeneracy to the nation's future. Roelcke shows that even persons such as Alfred Hoche, who had strongly criticized the writing by Kraepelin and his followers on degeneration on empirical grounds, changed their positions and developed ideas that would be taken up under National Socialism. Hoche joined with Karl Binding, former professor of law in Leipzig, and published a booklet, *Die Freigabe der Vernichtung Lebensungwerten Lebens* ('Legislation of the extermination of undeserving life'), suggesting that the "unproductive" who had no "self-awareness" were "human ballast," and that in particular historical moments it is a national duty to eliminate this burden from the society (Roelcke 1997, 397). This picked up themes expressed ten years earlier, in more tenuous fashion by Ernst Rudin, Kraepelin's follower and colleague, and in 1919 by Kraepelin himself in his essay cited above.

CONCLUSION

Kraepelin died in 1926, before the Nazis came to power. He was a great scientist and clinician, whose classificatory work has had a permanent influence within psychiatry. I make no claims for Kraepelin's responsibility for the use by the Nazis of his categories and theories of mental diseases: Kraepelin was scientifically accurate in claiming that both schizophrenia and bipolar disorder have a genetic component, and to the best of my knowledge he never argued for the "elimination" of persons suffering these conditions. I do agree, however, with Roelcke, who concludes his paper "Biologizing Social Facts," (1997, 398) arguing that "historical development suggests that the Kraepelinian nosology and the ensuing conceptualizations, more than competing approaches, carried with them a particular intrinsic potential for political abuse (though not as a *necessary* consequence)." The "disturbing political overtones of proto-fascism" (Shepherd 1995, 180) of Kraepelin's writings, the eventual use of Kraepelin's categories by the National Socialists, the conviction that dementia praecox is linked to degeneracy and genetic decline, and the more general use of these theories and categories by eugenics movements throughout Europe and the United States of Kraepelin's long-standing claims of the link of genetics to the major mental disorders, understood within a degenerationist framework, lends powerful irony to the claims of those who fashioned the DSM system to be neo-Kraepelinians.[2]

Examination of the place of the will and pathologies of the will in late nineteenth and early twentieth century writings on neuropsychiatry are a reminder of the prominent role once played by psychological theorizing of volition and human action. One might well agree with Berrios and Gili that the disappearance of this concept leaves a "conceptual vacuum," poorly filled by other concepts. For medical and psychological anthropology, this work suggests possible directions for research, exploring local accounts of volition or the will and their relation to both psychopathology and more general concerns about disorders of modernity. It is imperative, however, that anthropologists look critically at the social history of the concept of the will and its pathologies. It may be that the concept disappeared from explicit psychological theorizing in part because of its role in National Socialism. Any effort to rehabilitate the term as a critical concept for cross-cultural research thus needs to include a critical review of the social history of the concept. The place of the will and its pathologies in the neuropsychiatry of Kraepelin and his followers, as well as in Nazi ideologies, should give psychological anthropologists concerns as they explore the possibilities of a 'psychology of the will' as a legitimate category for comparative study.

AFTERWORD
Willing in Context
Douglas W. Hollan

I HAVE WANTED TO WRITE THIS AFTER-word for a long time now. Not only because the topic is a stimulating and challenging one, but also because I made a promise to the editors to do so. Many things have intervened and have made it difficult for me to accomplish my task, however. At least I tell myself this. I have been swamped with prior and competing obligations, some professional, some personal. I have been traveling a lot. I have been learning how to teach large, undergraduate courses again, after several years of not teaching such demanding courses. I have been helping to develop a new academic program on campus. The reasons go on and on.

What does my failure to write up until now say about my "will" to write, if anything? Are we to take my reasons for not writing at face value? To presume that the will does not always provide a way after all, when other people and things or duties and responsibilities intervene? Or is my failure

to write up until now prima facie evidence of my *lack* of will, perhaps even
of a pathology of will, the kind that might have caught the attention of the
pioneering German psychiatrist, Emil Kraepelin (Good, Chapter 8)? And if
this *is* a lack or failure of will, who is to blame (Garro, Mattingly, Groark,
Mageo, this volume)? Must I shoulder all the responsibility myself or do the
"chains of agency" (Stewart and Strathern, Chapter 7) extend beyond myself
to the people and community around me, perhaps even to the spirits, gods,
and ancestors around me, whom have either enabled or impeded my work?
Is it possible that other people not only share responsibility for my failure
to write, but have intervened actively, magically or otherwise, to *prevent* me
from writing (Garro, Chapter 4), so as to hurt or embarrass me?

Or is the whole line of thinking a form of self-deception (Fingarette
1969) and bad faith (Sartre 1974) on my part, which allows me to evade my
personal responsibility and lack of will? Perhaps I have other less conscious
or even unconscious motives and desires that have interfered with my will
to write (cf., Mageo, Groark, this volume). Perhaps I worry that I will disap-
point people and let them down. Or fear excessive and unfair criticism. Or
perhaps I harbor secret feelings of defiance toward anyone or anything that
appears to constrain my freedom, so that my apparent lack of will is actually
an indirect and disguised *assertion* of will, the willfulness of noncompliance.

But if the reasons for my failure to write are potentially so varied, complex, and multi-layered, how are we ever to decide which reasons are actually
at play, which descriptions of my will (or lack of will) most accurate and
convincing? What kinds of information would you need to know about me
to determine that? And how would you go about obtaining such information
in an ethical, nonjudgmental, "anthropological" way?

The chapters in this volume help us think through such puzzling issues
about the will and related phenomenal states. All of them make the will or
some aspect of willing the primary and explicit focus of analysis, which as
the editors note, is unusual in the anthropological literature, even within
the more specialized field of psychological anthropology. This alone makes
the volume an important contribution. But more significantly, these chapters
when taken collectively throw light on a paradox at the very heart of our
conception of the will: namely, that our sense of volition and control over
ourselves and other things, even when felt most strongly, is always embed-

ded in and influenced by biological, social, and cultural processes of which we are usually unaware or that extend far beyond ourselves. Acknowledging this does not necessarily mean conscious will is a complete illusion, as Daniel Wegner (2002) has argued recently. But it does mean that the will is more complex and over-determined that we often have taken it to be, and that grand old debates about free will versus determinism will need to be recast more in terms of free will *and* determinism (cf. Mitchell 1988, Groark, Chapter 5). Indeed, cross-cultural perspectives such as these enable us to recognize the extent to which many of these grand old debates are themselves rooted in cultural traditions that valorize, morally and pragmatically, individual initiative and autonomy over other types of human action and behavior. I will have more to say about this later.

I will not comment at length on all the contributions here, even though all are worthy of extended comment. Rather, I will discuss several issues that interweave among the chapters. I separate these themes out and highlight them for purposes of analysis, but as we shall see, almost all of them entail one another, both logically and ethnographically. My points of departure are the central organizing questions that all of the authors address, either directly or indirectly: What is the will? Where it is located (in both space and time)? What is its moral valence? Does it imply conscious awareness and choice?

WHAT IS THE WILL?

The editors note that one of their goals here is to encourage anthropologists and others to be more explicit in their description and analysis of "willing" and related phenomena. They note that the term is often used interchangeably and in a confusing way with such related concepts as volition, purpose, wish, desire, intention, agency, and so on (cf. Throop, Garro, Mattingly, all this volume). Throop (Chapter 2) in particular is intent on cutting through some of these conceptual tangles. Drawing on a phenomenological framework, he attempts to identify three core aspects of willing that could be found anywhere and that clearly distinguish it from other phenomenological and psychological states. These being the sense that one is the author of one's own thoughts, ideas, and actions ("own-ness"), that one anticipates an outcome as it unfolds into the future ("anticipation/goal directedness"), and that one's intended act or behavior requires effort or energy ("effortful-ness"). While Throop contends that all three of these aspects must be present for an act of willing to be identified, he suggests as well that the three may vary independently of one another, as cultures either underscore and exag-gerate their significance or underplay and elide them (cf. Levy 1973, 1984). For example, willing will be experienced differently in a place where a sense of own-ness is culturally highlighted but effortful-ness downplayed than in a place where the reverse is true. Given this analytical framework—three aspects of willing all varying independently of one another from nearly (but not completely) absent to clearly present in an exaggerated way—one read-ily apprehends the multi-dimensionality of the willing process, its experien-tial richness and potentialities, and its dependence on cultural processes that may vary widely from one time and place to another.

This call for anthropologists to be more explicit and systematic in their cross-cultural analyses of basic psychological and phenomenological states is reminiscent of the one Hallowell (1955) made for the study of "self" and other emotional states and processes more than fifty years ago, and it follows in the wake of those like White and Kirkpatrick (1985) whom more recently have encouraged the study of "ethnopsychologies." But despite the familiarity of the call, it is a difficult, challenging one, and one that none of the contribu-tors here answers in quite the way that Throop proposes. Of course this is partly because the authors have had little time to incorporate Throop's sug-gestions into their contributions. But I think it is also because the messiness of the willing process and its investigation in fieldwork settings resist the conceptual explicitness and clarity that Throop envisions, however meritori-ous. For example, Stewart and Strathern (in New Guinea) and Mageo (in Sāmoa) report the difficulty of finding a word or concept that captures very precisely either the denotations or connotations of *will* or *willing* in English. And almost all the contributors note, in one way or another, how seemingly difficult it is for people to clearly and unambiguously identify willing-like processes in themselves or in other people, given how opaque such processes can be and how easily influenced and contested by other people, oneself, and even by ghosts, spirits, gods, ancestors, and other entities.

The diversity of willing-like processes reported here, including their ambiguities and fuzzy boundaries, may very well reflect cultural variations on an underlying phenomenological theme or state, the possibility that Throop suggests. But on their face, they suggest we should be cautious about drawing such conclusions. Part of the problem here is indeed one of translation. Even keeping in mind cultural variations on the three core aspects of willing that Throop proposes, is the Samoan term *loto*, with its conflation of "thinking," "feeling," and "willing" really referring to the same phenomenological state that the Melpa term *noman* does, with its references to "being" and action that is "straight" and "strong" or "crooked"? And what is the relation of these terms and the processes they reference to those of the "good" and "bad" medicine of the Anishinaabe reported by Garro and the Mayan concepts of dreaming and the "essential soul" reported by Groark? Are all of these groups using different terms to refer to the same core aspects of the willing process? Or does their very multiplicity and complexity—conflating phenomenological states English speakers take to be distinct, discriminating among those English speakers take to be whole—suggest that there are no willing processes apart from the social, cultural, linguistic, and psychological processes in which they are embedded and which they, in turn, co-constitute? In other words, when do cultural variations on a phenomenological theme become distinct themes in and of themselves, and how would we know?

Caution is also warranted because of the historical and conceptual baggage that come with our own English language terms for *the will*, especially when used unselfconsciously as a point of comparison with willing processes elsewhere. Herbert Fingarette exposes some of this bias in his exposition of Arjuna's "will" in the Bhagavad Gita (2004, 94–95):

> The Gita does not state clearly what the exact relationships are when it comes to the causal influences on Arjuna's purposes and the power of Arjuna genuinely to initiate. . . . It is more important at this point to appreciate that the Gita bypasses, and in an important sense undercuts, the traditional Western preoccupation with free will and determinism. It is not that the Gita declares one side or the other in the debate to be wrong. Instead the Gita's teaching implies that the very preoccupation with the question arises out of delusion.

> More specifically, the central delusion (*moha*) arises from erroneously adopting the perspective of action as of the ultimate significance, rather than adopting the truly ultimate perspective, which is that of suffering. It is the focus on action, on the

individual as actor, that leads naturally to the whole cluster of familiar ideas associated with the free will debate. These include the idea of the individual's moral responsibility, and the related ideas of personal guilt, remorse, retributive blame, punishment, and reward as a personal desert. These notions are designed to make sense of a world in which the actor's purposeful initiative is seen as centrally meaningful.

Fingarette's point is that in the "western" world, there is a tendency to valorize action that is self-initiated or "willful" and to disvalue that which is not, even though "it is both experientially and conceptually apparent that each and every action is also nonaction" (2004, 93) when viewed from the perspective of initial or more general purpose. Which is why, as Fingarette explains, Krishna says he is confused if he imagines himself the doer of some action since from another, more encompassing perspective, he is not the doer (2004, 93). The English language association between notions of action and personal ownership—one of the core vectors of willing, according to Throop—is also evident in the use of the same word *will* to refer not only to the sense of purposeful action but also to the act and documentation of bequeathing one's property to another.

None of this is meant to discourage us from answering the editors' call for a more explicit and systematic analysis of willing processes. But rather to say that the great value of the ethnographic and historical approaches taken here is that they demonstrate for us just how intimately connected to the outside world certain psychological and phenomenological states, such as the sense of self-initiated action, really are. As a result, they do help us ferret out unwitting biases, whether of perception or conception, in our comparative studies. And by embracing the complexity of willed action, rather than ignoring or downplaying it, they better position us to understand not an invariant core of willfulness, which probably does not exist, but rather *the range* of social and cultural variables and contexts that promote and maintain a sense that we are, at least some of the time, the masters of our own behavior.

WHERE IS THE WILL?

One of the difficulties in defining, measuring, or assessing willful action is in knowing where its boundaries are, in either space or time. From a spatial point of view, even some of our most "willful" actions clearly have been influenced by others' behaviors or by events either just prior to or contiguous with our own choices and decisions. Stewart and Strathern, for example, report how acts of suicide among the Duna of Papua New Guinea are so deeply embedded in networks of social actions and reactions, which they refer to as "chains of agency," that even the Duna themselves may have difficulty deciding just who or what drove a person to suicide, and who is to be held accountable. Mattingly makes a similar point by referring to the process whereby a woman named Sonya learns to be decisive and "strong" in the care of her disabled son as a "social project," "one in which [Sonya's] whole family becomes involved by supporting her and counseling her when difficult choices arise."

From an etic point of view, such "chains of agency" and "projects" of support and influence affect almost every allegedly willful act we can conceive of, no matter when or where (cf. Wegner 2002, Baumeister 2008). But if so, how does this square with the notion that an act must be "owned" by someone to be considered willful? What are the cultural values and conditions that support and promote the sense of ownership over one's action, and do they necessarily entail countervailing strategies of denying or eliding the extent to which one's behavior *is* influenced by other people and events? Is Krishna right when he says that he would be deluded to think that he could ever be the sole, true author of his actions?

Either explicitly or implicitly, all of the papers here raise this question about the boundary between one person's or being's will and another. Where is the boundary? How clear or fuzzy is it presumed to be? When people disagree over where the boundaries are, how are those disagreements settled? What are the rules of evidence (if any) people refer to in such disputes? And ultimately, and ironically, who gets to "decide" whose will is or is not at play? Garro gives a particularly clear example of how complicated all this can become in her analysis of attributions of "good" and "bad" medicine among the Anishinaabe in the Manitoba region of Canada. She reports how experiences of illness or misfortune may lead Anishinaabe to consider carefully why other people or "other than human" beings may wish to harm them or why perhaps their own behavior may be worthy of punishment or retribution, an analysis of motives and willfulness that may require the assistance and authority of a "medicine person" before being settled. Garro points out that attributions of willfulness to others or oneself are a function, in part, of the number of the culturally plausible ways (or schemas) one has for explaining ambiguous behavior or events; the more interpretative possibilities you have, the more potentially confusing, uncertain, and fleeting your conclusions about willfulness might be, thus her title, "By the Will of Others or by One's Own Action?"

Things are no less complicated from a temporal point of view. Throop reminds us (cf. Mattingly and Garro, this volume), citing William James, Henri Bergson, Alfred Schutz, Paul Ricoeur, and others, that acts of willing unfold over time. This is one of the reasons, he argues, why discussions about the will can become so confused and unproductive, because different researchers may describe and analyze the willing process quite differently, depending on which part of the process they focus on. For William James, the time dimension was important, in part, because he conceived of deliberative willing as the ongoing, highly dynamic interplay between the conscious forces and motives impelling a certain kind of action versus those inhibiting it. Such interplay and tension could stretch over long periods of time, according to James (1962, 427), perhaps even indefinitely:

The deliberation might last for weeks or months, occupying at intervals the mind. The motives which yesterday seemed full of urgency and blood and life to-day [sic] feel strangely weak and pale and dead. But as little to-day as to-morrow [sic] is the question finally resolved. Something tells us that all this is provisional; that the weakened reasons will wax strong again, and the stronger weaken; that equilibrium is unreached; that testing our reasons, not obeying them, is still the order of the day, and that we must wait awhile, patiently or impatiently, until our mind is made up "for good and all." This inclining first to one, then to another future, both of which we represent as possible, resembles the oscillation to and fro of a material body within the limits of its elasticity. There is inward strain, but no outward rupture. And this condition, plainly enough, is susceptible of indefinite continuance, as well in the physical mass as in the mind. . . .

Here is why post hoc explanations of decision making can be so misleading and unilluminating at times, because they often miss all the uncertainty and ambivalence that may proceed and lead up to the making of decisions.

Mattingly also emphasizes the temporal dimensions of willful acts, noting they often entail a reorientation of attention and self that may take much time, energy, and effort to achieve. Like James, but citing Iris Murdoch (1970), she is critical of the idea that decisions, especially morally significant ones, "just happen" or happen quickly and easily. In a compelling illustration of this based on extensive longitudinal data, she discusses the willing, decision-making processes of a young, African American mother as she learns, over a number of years, how to respond to and care for a severely burned son. After listing several of the moral and medical dilemmas that the mother she calls Sonya faces, Mattingly (80–81) writes:

While some of these practical and moral problems require clear decisions that result in action, befitting the dominant notion of willing, these decisions came only after significant reorientation of her emotions (Sonya does decide to have the surgeries after the initial accident and when he got older, she did decide to send him to burn camp). She had to struggle internally in order to be able to make these decisions from a place of strength. (There is no resonance, in any of her accounts, with the existentialist picture of a free will acting in an otherwise determined world.) Further, many of the moral dilemmas she has named over the years (and listed above), like the ones that have to do with whether she should be angry or not—have no obvious action consequences at all but speak, just as Murdoch insists, to an internal struggle to envision her world in what she deems the right (most moral) way. Notably, discussions of patient choice in the clinical literature often portray these situations as *moments* of choice. But this is not how she experienced such situations. [emphasis added]

These temporal dimensions to willing implicate the spatial ones of course. The farther out we push the temporal dimensions, the larger the networks of people and events that conceivably have some impact on what and how someone wills.

Here again, the boundary issue arises. If acts of willing unfold over time, sometimes over quite extended periods of time, how do we determine where they actually begin and end? If an act of willing sets the stage for, and is implicated in, subsequent willful actions, and if none of these are immune from the influence of other people and events, where and how are meaningful boundaries to be drawn among them? And how exactly do cultural influences affect both our perceptions of these boundaries and the boundaries

themselves? If a culture redundantly valorizes individual initiative and decisive action, might that actually tend to delimit the duration and experience
of the willing process in that culture, in looping fashion (cf. Hacking 1995),
so that the "wills" of people there really are significantly different from those
of others? Or does culture have more of an impact on our perception of the
willing process, in oneself and in others, rather than on its architecture per
se? Only many more studies of the kind we find here will allow us to answer
such questions definitively.

However, even the limited sample we do have available here suggests that
cultural influences on willful action will be partial, punctuated, and contingent, not uniform or determinative. Throop suggests that because willful
actions occur over time, not instantly, they can be affected by culture at any
number of points during their unfolding—not necessarily at all points or
in the same way at the points that are affected. Garro suggests that people
are differentially exposed to cultural schemas that may affect willful action,
from those with no exposure at all to those with who are exposed repeatedly
and with behavioral consequences. Mageo and Groark, on the other hand,
raise the possibility that creative, willful-like manipulation of symbols and
meanings in dreams may lead to behavior that either reinforces or under-
mines prevailing cultural schemas, depending on the needs and wishes of
individual dreamers. So if cultures shape willful action, it seems equally true
that willful actors and dreamers may reshape and innovate culture.

WHAT IS THE MORAL VALENCE OF THE WILL?

While it may be difficult for us to find agreement on precisely what willing
entails or precisely where it is to be located, there seems to be unanimous
agreement that whatever or wherever it is, it *matters*. All the people in the
case studies presented here and all those we can think of (I would wager),
presume themselves and others have willful control over their behavior at
least part of the time. Further, all people spend considerable time and energy assessing whether other people's behavior is willful or not and explaining or defending their own behavior as willful or not, though some societies
and people probably spend more time and energy doing this than others.
This would not surprise Irving Hallowell (1955), who long ago theorized that

group-oriented *human* societies could not have evolved or persisted without self-conscious, willful actors capable of assessing and managing their own behavior relative to normative standards of conduct. According to Hallowell, human societies are not only social orders but also moral orders. They are predicated upon actors capable of imagining alternative lines of conduct and their respective outcomes, in at least some contexts, and of willfully choosing among them (cf. Garro, Stewart and Strathern, this volume). For all people, it is important to know when and to what extent others should be held accountable for (i.e., responsible for) their behavior, whether that behavior conforms to community norms and values or not. Such capacities for self-control and evaluative behavior have given humans a unique evolutionary style, by enabling behavioral strategies that are highly flexible, adjustable, and context dependent (Baumeister 2005, 2008).

But if it is clear that all human societies are moral orders that presume willful behavior and the capacity to choose among alternatives, it is also quite clear that people may use vastly different norms and values to assess when and where and why it should be presumed (or not) that others have willful control over their behavior. This is another area where the ethnographic approach can be particularly helpful to us, and the case studies presented here illustrate nicely just how varied these assessments and evaluations can be. Among the Duna, for example, we see that the friends and relatives of a man who commits suicide may be held as accountable for that man's death as the deceased himself (Stewart and Strathern, Chapter 7). Garro demonstrates how complex and anxiety-provoking assessments of others' motives and willfulness can become in a community such as the Anishinaabe in which it is never certain who may be practicing harmful, "bad" medicine and who not. Groark and Mageo, in turn, provide interesting examples of how responsibility for willful-like behavior can be displaced or mitigated through the use of special cultural idioms such as dream analysis and interpretation.

Societies may also vary in the extent to which they value and promote willfulness as an end in itself, and this valuation may change over time (Mageo, Chapter 6), though as noted above, no culturally based group (i.e., no human group) could function on a day-to-day basis without self-conscious, willful people. The social and moral philosopher, Herbert Fingarette (2004), contends that many "western" cultures and societies valorize individuals as active actors who should purposely and willfully attempt to control their lives and behaviors. In particular he contrasts this attitude with that promoted in the Hindu text the Bhagavad Gita and in the teachings of Confucius, which, though not denying the willfulness of people, emphasize more the notion that people are not so much the controllers of their lives as their lives recipients, embedded in physical and cosmological forces that transcend them and which they are "enduring" or "undergoing" or "suffering" at all times (cf. Groark, Chapter 5). Of the Bhagavad Gita, he writes:

The gist of my analysis of the Gita . . . is that, whatever the sources of our purposes and action, it matters not. They may in some respects be entirely determined by the *gunas* [impersonal forces of nature]. The may be determined by our past *karma* or by anything else. They may in some respects be of genuinely de novo origin in the self. For in any case, no matter which one or combination of these assumptions be made, it would still be that the emergence of initial purpose is something I do not control. For initial purpose is not brought into being as the execution of some prior purpose. Thus it is my role as sufferer [one who undergoes], and not as actor, that is of deepest and widest significance. (Fingarette 2004, 95)

Fingarette's point is not that any culture fully eliminates either willfulness or determinism from human life, but that by valorizing "the actor" or "the sufferer" or any other image of human action, cultures may indeed influence the relative significance of willfulness in human life and the likelihood that it will be enacted (cf. Groark, Chapter 5).

Interestingly, the evolutionary psychologist, Roy Baumeister, hypothesizes that promotion of the belief in free will benefits a society by better enabling people to cooperate with one another, follow the rules (whatever those are), and avoid misbehavior. Supporting this contention, he claims, is experimental work by Vohs and Schooler (2008) who

found that participants who had been induced to disbelieve in free will were subsequently more likely than a control group to cheat on a test. Further studies by Baumeister, Masicampo, and DeWall (2006) using the Vohs-Schooler methods founds that inducing participants to disbelieve in free will made them more aggressive and less helpful toward others. If we combine the cheating, aggression, and helping findings, it seems reasonable to suggest that belief in free will is conducive to better, more harmonious social behavior. (Baumeister 2008, 18)

Putting aside for the moment the question of whether experimentally induced "disbelief" in free will is actually the equivalent of any kind of belief or motivation we could find in naturally occurring human behavior, is it the case that promotion of human willfulness is always as benign, if not advantageous, as Baumeister suggests? Byron Good's chapter (Chapter 8) offers us a cautionary tale in this regard. He reviews the work of the famous German psychiatrist, Emil Kraepelin, linking some of his contentions about how pathologies of will, especially its "weakness" and "degeneracy," underlie various forms of severe mental illness to his Bismarckian political views that only Germany's "noblest and fittest sons," with strength and steadfastness of will, were capable of defending the nation from both internal and external threat. Good credits Kraepelin for his astute descriptions and classifications of mental illness, many of which still inform the modern day *Diagnostic and Statistical Manuel of Mental Disorders* (1994). And he reminds us that Kraepelin, who died in 1926, cannot be held accountable for how some of his theories of social degeneracy were later taken up and used by the Nazis to justify their own willful "cleansing" of the German body politic during World War II. But he does use Kraepelin's life and legacy to suggest that research on "the will" never occurs in a political or moral vacuum and that anthropologists must be extremely cautious in their analyses and evaluations of others' willfulness, not only to avoid ethnocentric bias, but also because they have so little control over how their findings might be used (or abused) in the future.

But if willfulness can be deliberately used for nefarious purposes, its unintended consequences may be no less harmful at times. Contra Baumeister, Gregory Bateson has argued that because human conscious purpose or willfulness usually focuses attention on but a small part of the overall circuitry of the biological and ecological systems in which it is embedded, its dictates, reflecting this relatively limited, tunnel-like focus and perception, may sometimes lead to actions or behaviors that, in the long run, undermine those larger systems upon which it is so dependent.

On the one hand, we have the systematic nature of the individual human being, the systematic nature of the culture in which he lives, and the systematic nature of the biological, ecological system around him; and on the other hand, the curious twist in the systematic nature of the individual man whereby consciousness is, almost by necessity, blinded to the systematic nature of the man himself. Purposive consciousness pulls out, from the total mind, sequences which do not have the loop structure which is characteristic of the whole systemic structure. If you follow the "commonsense" dictates of consciousness you become, effectively, greedy and unwise—again I use "wisdom" as a word for recognition of and guidance by a knowledge of the total systemic creature. (Bateson 1972, 434)

For Bateson, then, the evolutionary scorecard on conscious purpose and willfulness has yet to be tallied.

MUST WILLFULNESS BE CONSCIOUS?

Most definitions and phenomenological descriptions of willing emphasize the fact that it involves attention, effort, awareness, deliberateness, and sense of personal ownership and responsibility, all of which imply that it is a relatively conscious process. William James ([1892] 1985) also implies this, reminding us how consciously uncomfortable and conflicted the deliberative process can be, as first one motive or reason for acting or inhibiting action comes to mind, and then another, and then another, and so on. But does this characterization hold up, especially given all the new evidence we have that consciousness of all kinds, including willing, are dependent upon a enormous number of cognitive and emotional processes that usually remain outside our conscious awareness (see for example, Mitchell 1988; Wegner 2002; Schacter 1996; LeDoux 1996, 2002; Damasio 1994, 1999; Edelman and Tononi 2000)?

Both Mageo and Groark challenge traditional characterizations of willing by examining what they regard as willful-like behavior in dreams, a state of mind and consciousness usually thought to reflect an *absence* of the kind of self-regulation and voluntary action so typical of willful (waking) behavior. Mageo reports that in traditional Sāmoa, morally approved willfulness was actually expressed through its curtailment and suppression, by conforming to the rules and expectations of authority in a hierarchically organized society. In colonial and postcolonial Sāmoa, however, with the introduction of Christianity and discourses of "sincerity" and free will, the moral valence of willful behavior becomes scrambled. People become more frustrated by and resentful of traditional forms of deference and respect, but they also resist, however indirectly, the seduction of alien, non-Samoan forms of individuality and morality. And all of this moral ambivalence, willfulness, and resistance gains expression in dreams, which according to Mageo, "are constantly personalizing cultural schemas and reacting to them in ways that clarify what is wish fulfillment and what is nightmare. These realizations, however nonverbal, cannot but subtly affect choices in waking cultural life. This imaginal deliberation, moreover, constitutes a form of agency, perhaps an originary form."

Groark, on the other hand, argues that "In the highland Maya model of a tripartite self, we find an explanatory construct that allows the experience of willfulness to be decentered away from the waking self of everyday social life, and located in one of several extensions of self, all understood—somewhat paradoxically—as lying outside of the volitional control of the waking self to which they are connected" (141). In particular, he examines how an idiom of dream investiture enables people to pursue "highly valued personal and social goals (such as becoming a curer) while simultaneously disavowing any authorial role in *having chosen* to pursue those goals," by converting the dreamer's own willful desire into an experience of the "essential" dream soul, whom the Catholic saints visit during dreaming and call or order to action. From the waking self's point of view, then, it is the saints who initiate action towards certain valued goals, not oneself.

But here we return to issues of definition yet again. One could take the view that Mageo and Groark are actually describing something other than willfulness, since their dreamers do not "own" their dream experiences in a completely self-conscious, effortful, truly willful way. And yet, as I have suggested repeatedly, we have much to learn from such cross-cultural examples, because they illustrate for us the *variety* of ways willful-like behavior can be constituted, culturally mediated, and expressed. Further, the notion that even willful behavior has its nonconscious and unconscious determinants or correlates is both an old and new idea. Freud ([1900] 1965) placed the concepts of repression and self-deception at the heart of his model of mind and consciousness, and argued that secondary process thinking (that is, rational, logical, willful thinking) is never completely free of its primary process antecedents. Contemporary psychoanalysts like Stephen Mitchell have gone further to claim that "agency and unconscious motives are not alternative explanations, but simultaneous properties of all mental events" (1988, 248).

As Groark notes, such a conceptualization "of the mutually-determining co-presence of willfulness and unconscious determinism encourages a focus on how, why, and in what contexts the individual either foregrounds a sense of 'owness' and authorship (emphasizing the self as a choosing and acting subject), or backgrounds this sense of volition or agency (emphasizing the self as passive object, as one who is acted upon)" (160). The highland Maya use dreams to background their conscious sense of willfulness and agency while contemporary Samoans, on the other hand, use them to sort through and express ambivalence about conscious willfulness, both foregrounding and back-grounding willfulness as the case may be.

As I noted above, the idea that willfulness exists in a dynamic interrelationship with many nonconscious sensory, cognitive, and emotional processes has been developing in the contemporary neuro- and cognitive sciences as well. Baumeister, for one, argues that "it is necessary to posit two systems for guiding behavior: a default one that mostly runs the show and an occasional one that sometimes intervenes to make changes. Free will should be understood not as the starter or motor of action but rather as a passenger who occasionally grabs the steering wheel or even as just a navigator who says to turn left up ahead (2008, 14)."[1] Interestingly, though, Baumeister does not dismiss or minimize the role or significance of willfulness in human affairs because of its immersion in other behavioral processes, but rather draws attention to it:

Shifts in the social distribution of causality and agency are important to people, and these correspond to social phenomena that people have encountered for millennia. Power, for example, confers on one person the right to make decisions that may affect others (e.g., Kelter, Gruenfeld, & Anderson, 2003), and the long history of power struggles can be viewed as being about who gets to choose. Studies by Brehm (1966) and his colleagues have also shown that people are very sensitive to having their freedom of choice restricted by others. When an option is taken away from them, they respond by desiring that option more, and even by aggressing against whomever restricted their freedom. Such patterns seem hard to reconcile with the view that all free will and choice (in every sense) are illusions: Why would people care so much about something that is entirely inconsequential? (Baumeister 2008, 16)

The idea that willfulness may be partially shaped, constrained, or qualified by behavioral processes operating outside of conscious awareness may eventually transform fairly radically how we conceptualize it and its moral implications, raising new questions about when and under what circumstances people can and cannot be held responsible for their actions. It also poses new challenges for ethnographers and anyone else wishing to study willfulness in context, for if willful-like behavior can be found in dreams, in what other shadows of mind, imagination, and cultural behavior might it be lurking?

CONCLUSION

This is an important contribution to the study of willfulness because it extends it beyond the disciplines of philosophy and psychology into the worlds of culture and history. Ethnographic and historical studies such as these challenge us to rethink our definitions of willfulness, expose our own biases in its conceptualization, demonstrate the myriad ways in which it both mediates and is mediated by a myriad of social and cultural processes, and remind us that our ideas about its meaning and moral valence are potentially dangerous, depending on how they get used.

Inevitably, volumes like this raise as many questions as they answer, which is appropriate, given how little we know about how willfulness manifests itself in the everyday lives of people around the world. Accordingly, it should not be seen as the endpoint of the anthropological investigation of willfulness, but as one of its starting points.

I mentioned at the outset that questions about willfulness bleed into one another, and we can see that clearly now. You cannot define willfulness without knowing what its boundaries are. But you cannot know its boundaries until you know how and in what ways it is shaped and mediated by nonconscious and unconscious processes, which are themselves embedded in specific social, cultural, and historical contexts. In turn, your ability to investigate any of these issues will be constrained by the way willfulness is culturally valuated, which will affect when and where and why it becomes more or less visible and accessible to you. And so on.

The Bhagavad Gita tells us those who willfully act are also acted upon. This volume brings some specificity to that basic insight, a specificity that only the ethnographic investigation of naturally occurring behavior can provide.

REFERENCE MATTER

NOTES

CHAPTER 1

We would like to thank Roger Ivar Lohmann and an anonymous reviewer, whose sharp insights and observations greatly improved our work. Thanks also to a number of supporters who have encouraged us in their own ways, including Niko Besnier, Alessandro Duranti, April Leininger, and Elinor Ochs. And many thanks to our editors, Jennifer Hele and Kate Wahl, who have patiently and compassionately guided us through the publication process.

1. In a very general sense there may be Durkheimian and Weberian schools of thought that emphasize will as a product of social collectives or motivating individual rational action respectively. However, while German idealism and British empiricism helped shape early social scientific investigations of the individual in society, the explicit attention to willing present in the work of Kant, Schopenhauer, Locke, and others never trickled down directly into a Durkheimian or Weberian worldview.

2. While we acknowledge the requisite caveats about etymological reductionism and the inherent biases that come along with focusing on one language and its lexicalized cultural concepts, we find it instructive to examine how *will* has shifted in English language contexts (semantically and syntactically), and what implications this might have for reconceptualizing the will anthropologically. This is by no means intended to restrict the discussion to an inherently Indo-European conceptualization of the will. Rather it allows us to choose a point of departure that aligns with the fact that a great deal of modern anthropological theorizing and analysis of subjective experience exists in the English language.

3. We have decided to restrict our overview more or less to the field of anthropology, though other social scientists, in particular in sociology, have attempted to grapple with similar conceptual material (see especially Parsons 1937; Mead 1934, 1977; Garfinkel 1967; Giddens 1983).

4. It is interesting to note in this regard that the psychological anthropologist Gananath Obeyesekere argues that Sahlins can be criticized for exaggerating the extent to which cultural

systems shape the "rational" functioning of a human mind that is constituted out of a "common human neurobiological nature" (1992, 16). Further, he asserts that Sahlins's focus on the unintentional transformation derived from the confluence of structures of conjunction is problematic from the standpoint that it leaves "little room for motivation, agency, or the significance of the subject in the molding of society and consciousness" (1992, 17), or, in other words, a space for volition. Obeyesekere sees this as an example of the pernicious and prevalent tendency in European thought to divest non-European populations of individuality, improvisational acumen, and creativity.

CHAPTER 2

I would like to thank Rachel Brezis, Alessandro Duranti, Julia Eksner, Linda Garro, Byron Good, Kevin Groark, Douglas Hollan, Jeanette Mageo, Cheryl Mattingly, Amira Mittermaier, Keith Murphy, Elinor Ochs, Andrew Strathern, Pamela Stewart, and the participants at UCLA's Meta-Epistemology seminar for insightful comments and contributions to this chapter.

1. Bourdieu's practice theory can be contrasted with Giddens's theory of structuration, which is grounded in an attempt to understand an agent's ongoing "reflexive monitoring of action" (Giddens 1984, 5–6, 191, 289, 376).

2. Intentionality as understood by Edmund Husserl ([1931] 1962) consists of the orientation of consciousness toward an intentional object (see also Brentano [1874] 1995; Duranti a1993a, 2001, 2006; Jacquette 2004).

3. Hannah Arendt ([1971] 1978, 4) suggests that "denunciation of the Will as a mere illusion of consciousness and the refutations of its very existence" are tied to the fact that "what aroused the philosopher's distrust of this faculty was its inevitable connection to Freedom" ([1971] 1978, 5).

4. Ricoeur seems, at times, to utilize the term *voluntary* as a synonym for *willing* ([1950] 1966, 6), while at other times he emphasizes how the "voluntary" and the "involuntary" can be understood as interrelated, but, distinct, aspects of "willing" ([1950] 1966, 7).

5. This three-fold distinction can be understood to coincide, at least partially, with Wegner's cognitive psychological distinctions between feeling of doing and anticipation and Paul Ricoeur's descriptive phenomenological discernment of the "most natural articulations of willing," which include: (1) "that which I decide"/"the direction of action" (i.e., the "project"); (2) voluntary movement/effective action; and (3) acquiescence to the involuntary (Ricoeur [1950] 1966, 7). Since first writing this chapter as a paper in the summer of 2003, I have recently come across yet another complementary perspective in Bayne and Levy's (2006) examination of the phenomenology of mental causation, the phenomenology of authorship and the phenomenology of effort as three core aspects to understanding the experience of agency.

6. Cf. Mead (1934, 177).

7. I should note that Ricoeur is also critical of Bergson's view that the spatialization of temporality is connected to the idea that one could have always acted otherwise. He asserts instead that "the impression of having been able to choose another alternative is not of a piece with the spatializing illusion—it is an immediate datum of consciousness" ([1950] 1966, 163).

8. As Sartre notes, "It is strange that philosophers have been able to argue endlessly about determinism and free will, to cite examples in favor of one or the other thesis without ever attempting first to make explicit the structures contained in the very idea of *action*" ([1943] 1984).

9. Cf. Mead (1934, 177–78).

10. Cf. Mead (1934, 176–77).

11. Cf. James ([1890] 1983).

12. The connection between attention and willing figures prominently in the writings of William James ([1890] 1983), Alexander Shand (1895, 1897), and F. H. Bradley (1902a, 1902b). Ricoeur draws from Shand and Bradley's insights throughout *Freedom and Nature*.

CHAPTER 3

I would like to thank members (past and present) of the "Boundary Crossing" research team: Erica Angert, Nancy Bagatell, Jeanine Blanchard, Jeannie Adams, Lanita Jacobs-Huey, Teresa Kuan, Stephanie Mielke, Ann Neville-Jan, Melissa Park, and Kim Wilkinson. I want to especially acknowledge Teresa Kuan for all her help in the preparation of this chapter. Particular heart-felt thanks goes to my long-time research partner, Mary Lawlor. Thanks also to the Narrative Study Group for comments on earlier versions of this chapter: Linda Garro, Elinor Ochs, Janet Hoskins, Marjorie Goodwin, Gelya Frank, Nancy Lutkehaus, and again, Mary Lawlor. I gratefully acknowledge support by the National Center for Medical Rehabilitation Research, The National Institute of Child Health and Human Development, the National Institutes of Health (no. 1RO1HD38878).

1. The argument presented here connects to my larger project of constructing a narrative theory of practice, and here my inspiration also comes from phenomenological and hermeneutic philosophical traditions, literary theory, and cultural psychology—as well as anthropological theories of practice, performance, and experience. The narrative theory I propose is both practice-oriented and phenomenological. It highlights the activities and experiences of particular agents in particular historical situations as these illuminate and help to construct complex social spaces and reveal the exigencies of practical reasoning and practical experience.

2. Charles Taylor argues that the link between will and morality (especially morality defined as transformation of the will) was introduced into western thought primarily through Christianity, but that this connection has gone through various secularizing transitions, and, in its secular guises, remains one of the most powerful ethical precepts in western thought (1989, 22).

3. MacIntyre gives the following example. "In answer to the question, 'What is he doing?' the answers may, with equal truth and appropriateness, be 'Digging', 'Gardening', 'Taking exercise', 'Preparing for winter' or 'Pleasing his wife'. Some of these answers will characterize the agent's intentions, others unintended consequences of his actions, and of these unintended consequences some may be such that the agent is aware of them and others not" (1981, 192). Some of these answers situate the episode within a narrative history of the cycle of domestic activities in a particular social place—gardening in Northern England, let's say. Others point toward a history of one marriage, and perhaps marriage as a social institution in some social place. To make it even more complicated, histories of domestic activities and histories of marriage are, obviously, interrelated.

4. Taylor builds from Heidegger's discussion of the temporal structure of being—especially Heidegger's essential argument that we know who we are as beings who become—to make a strong case for narrative identity that is, at base, a moral identity. "From my sense of where I am relative to [the good], and among different possibilities, I project the direction of my life in relation to it. My life always has this degree of narrative understanding, that I understand my present action in the form of an 'and then': there was A (what I am), and then I do B (what I project to become)" (1989, 47).

5. This case is based on interview data, fieldnotes, and videotapes of home and hospital interactions. However, for the sake of brevity, I rely heavily on several years of interviews with the mother, Sonya.

CHAPTER 4

I thank the volume editors, two anonymous reviewers, and Robert Whitmore for constructive feedback on earlier versions of this chapter.

CHAPTER 5

1. The fieldwork upon which this chapter is based took place between August 2002 and September 2003 in the Tzotzil township of San Juan Chamula, as well as the regional center of San

Cristóbal de Las Casas. Fieldwork was supported the National Science Foundation, Ford Founda-
tion-ISOP, the Center for Latin American Studies at UCLA, and the Department of Anthropology, UCLA.

2. See Jedrej and Shaw (1992a) and Ray (1992) on strikingly similar personal and social uses of
"success-dreaming" in Africa.

3. Among the highland Maya, there is no system of shamanic apprenticeship—all curing
knowledge is purportedly gained directly from dream experience. However, as Fabrega and Silver
(1973) have pointed out, shamanic vocation tends to run in families, providing ample opportunities
for indirect tuition.

4. The description I present here is based on extensive interviewing with Chamula informants.
The present description should be understood as a sort of minimal model with which most Mayan
Catholic "traditionalist" Chamulas would agree. For more detailed ethnographic treatments of
highland Maya soul beliefs, see Vogt (1965, 1970), Gossen (1975, 1999a, b), Rachun Linn (1989) and
Page Pliego (2005) on the Tzotzil, and Pitarch Ramón (1996, 2003) and Pitt-Rivers (1970) on the
Tzeltal.

5. See Lohmann (2003) for an extended discussion of the ubiquity of the "dream as soul
travel" trope throughout the Pacific. Although this framing of dreaming as soul-based travel is
quite common (see the essays in Tedlock [1992] and Mageo [2003] for similar dream beliefs in
diverse cultural settings), it can also occur alongside more complex constructions, in which certain
kinds of dreams are understood *not as travel to* another realm, but as *visitations from* this realm (see
Mittermaier 2006, 81).

6. Bollas (1987, 135–56) introduced the notion of the "normotic" as a counterbalance to the
psychotic. The normotic personality highlights the potentially pathological effects of an excessive
emphasis on secondary-process mentation, concerned primarily with reality-testing and adherence
to consensual reality. In the spirit of Winnicott, both the psychotic and normotic character orga-
nizations represent a failure of the dialectical movement between primary and secondary process
mentation, a process through which fantasy and imagination come to infuse everyday life (while
simultaneously reflecting and being tempered by actuality).

7. American relational psychoanalyst Stephen Mitchell has provided what is perhaps the most
thoughtful discussion of this topic (1988). He argues that the problem of will has been incorrectly
framed—rather than providing alternative explanations, "both agency and unconscious motivation
must be regarded as simultaneous properties of all mental events" (ibid., 248). The subjective experience of will or agency is always constrained and conditioned by deep intrapsychic and relational
commitments—usually unconscious—the violation of which threatens to disrupt the individual's
familiar experiential world, giving rise to anxiety. This conceptualization of the mutually determining co-presence of willfulness and unconscious determinism encourages a focus on how, why,
and in what contexts the individual either foregrounds a sense of "ownness" and authorship (emphasizing the self as a choosing and acting subject), or backgrounds this sense of volition or agency
(emphasizing the self as passive object, as one who is acted upon) (see Throop, this volume).

8. Many highland Maya are quite conscious of the legitimizing role of dreams, as well as the
potential for strategic manipulation through dream telling. There is a clear awareness that some individuals falsify "election" dreams in an attempt to legitimize their status as a curer. In such cases,
the skepticism is not about the validity of dream election as mode of experience—rather, it centers
on the truth of the call of any particular individual.

9. When viewed cross-culturally, the Western "scientific" or etic psychological models of
dream experience described here appears somewhat anomalous. The implicit folk models of dreaming and dream experience attested to by many Westerners—particularly among ethnic or racial

subgroups such as African Americans (see Shafton 2002)—are quite variable, and tend toward an "objectivist" framing quite like that of the Maya (although usually lacking the armature of supporting ethnotheories).

10. I owe the phrase "cultural psychodynamics" to April Leininger (2002), who coined it while participating in a psychoanalytic reading group at UCLA. I thank her for permission to use the term and elaborate it according to my own sensibilities.

CHAPTER 6

I thank the volume editors and Stanley P. Smith for their comments on earlier versions of this chapter.

CHAPTER 7

1. Articles about Dr. Kelly can be found on the Internet at media.guardian.co.uk and www .cnn.com.

CHAPTER 8

I express particular appreciation to Michelle Levine for help searching out relevant literature and assembling it as I was initially preparing the work in this chapter. I thank the volume editors and two anonymous reviewers for helpful comments on earlier versions of this chapter. And I dedicate it to the memory of Robert Barrett, whose writings on schizophrenia first introduced me to the link between theories of degeneracy and continued pessimism about the possibilities for recovery from schizophrenia.

1. See also Kraepelin's "self assessment," where he describes similar views (Kraepelin 2002). Compare Engstrom, Burmair and Weber (2002) with Shepherd (1995) for competing interpretations of how to read Kraepelin's obvious anti-semitism.

2. Michael Shepherd describes the apparent contradictions between Kraepelin's scientific accomplishments and his political views, calling them the "two faces of Emil Kraepelin" (Shepherd 1995). Engstrom questions this view, suggesting that Kraepelin had more than two "faces" and that understood in the Lamarkian context of his time, these are not as contradictory as they seem (Engstrom 2007; Engstrom, Burgmair and Weber 2002).

AFTERWORD

1. Compare this image of a passenger occasionally grabbing the steering wheel to Freud's (1923) characterization of the relationship between ego and id in which the ego is like a rider who tries to control and direct the energy and direction of the vastly larger and more powerful "horse" of the id.

REFERENCES

Aeschylus. 1960. Agamemnon. In *Greek Tragedies, vol. 1,* edited by David Grene and Richmond Lattimore. Chicago: University of Chicago Press.

Ahearn, Laura M. 2001. Language and Agency. *Annual Review of Anthropology* 30:109–37.

Aijmer, Göran. 2000. Introduction. In *Meanings of Violence: A Cross Cultural Perspective,* edited by Göran Aijmer and Jon Abbink, 1–22. Oxford: Berg.

Alexander, Jeffrey C. 1988. *Action and Its Environments: Toward a New Synthesis.* New York: Columbia University Press.

American Psychiatric Association (APA). 1994. *Diagnostic and Statistical Manual of Psychiatric Disorders.* 4th ed. Washington, DC: APA Press.

Appadurai, Arjun. 1996. *Modernity at Large: Cultural Dimensions of Globalization.* Minneapolis: University of Minnesota Press.

Archer, Margaret S. 2003. *Structure, Agency, and the Internal Conversation.* Cambridge: Cambridge University Press.

Arendt, Hannah. [1971] 1978. *The Life of the Mind.* New York: Harcourt Brace & Company.

Arias, Jacinto. 1975. *El Mundo Numinoso de los Mayas: Estructura y Cambios Contemporáneos.* México, D. F.: SepSetentas.

Bakhtin, Mikhail M. 1990. *Art and Answerability.* Austin: University of Texas Press.

Barrett, Rob. 1996. *The Psychiatric Team and the Social Definition of Schizophrenia.* Cambridge: Cambridge University Press.

Barsam, Richard Meran. 1975. *Film Guide to Triumph of the Will.* Bloomington: Indiana University Press.

Bartlett, Francis C. [1932] 1995. *Remembering: A Study in Experimental Social Psychology.* Cambridge: Cambridge University Press.

Basso, Keith. 1984. "Stalking with Stories": Names, Places, and Moral Narratives Among the Western Apache. In *Text, Play, and Story: The Construction and Reconstruction of Self and Society*, edited by Edward Bruner, 19–55. Prospect, IL: Waveland Press.

Baumeister, Roy F. 2005. *The Cultural Animal: Nature, Meaning, and Social Life*. New York: Oxford University Press.

———. 2008. Free Will in Scientific Psychology. *Perspectives on Psychological Science* 3:14–19.

Bayne, Tim, and Neil Levy. 2006. The Feeling of Doing: Deconstructing the Phenomenology of Agency. In *Disorders of Volition*, edited by Natalie Sebanz and Wolfgang Prinz, 49–68. Cambridge, MA: MIT Press.

Berger, Harris M. 1999. *Metal, Rock, and Jazz: Perception and the Phenomenology of Musical Experience*. Hanover, CT: Wesleyan University Press.

Berger, Harris M., and Giovanna P. Del Negro. 2002. Bauman's Verbal Art and the Social Organization of Attention: The Role of Reflexivity in the Aesthetics of Performance. *Journal of American Folklore* 115(455): 62–91.

Bergson, Henri. [1889] 2001. *Time and Free Will: An Essay on the Immediate Data of Consciousness*. Toronto: Dover.

Berrios, G. E., and M. Gili. 1995. Will and Its Disorders: A Conceptual History. *History of Psychiatry* 6:87–104.

Berrios, G. E., and R. Hauser. 1988. The Early Development of Kraepelin's Ideas on Classification: A Conceptual History. *Psychological Medicine* 18:813–21.

Biehl, João, Byron Good, and Arthur Kleinman. 2007. *Subjectivity: Ethnographic Investigations*. Berkeley: University of California Press.

Black, Mary. 1977. Ojibwa Power Belief System. In *The Anthropology of Power: Ethnographic Studies from Asia, Oceania, and the New World*, edited by Robert D. Fogelson and R. N. Adams, 141–51. New York: Academic Press.

Blashfield, Roger K. 1984. *The Classification of Psychopathology: Neo-Kraepelinian and Quantitative Approaches*. New York: Plenum Press.

Bleuler, Eugen. 1924. *Textbook of Psychiatry*. New York: Macmillan.

Bollas, Christopher. 1987. *The Shadow of the Object: Psychoanalysis of the Unthought Known*. New York: Columbia University Press.

———. 1992. *Being a Character: Psychoanalysis and Self Experience*. New York: Hill and Wang.

———. 1995. *Cracking Up: The Work of Unconscious Experience*. New York: Hill and Wang.

Bourdieu, Pierre. 1977. *Outline of a Theory of Practice*. Cambridge: Cambridge University Press.

———. 1990. *The Logic of Practice*. Palo Alto, CA: Stanford University Press.

———. 2000. *Pascalian Meditations*. Palo Alto, CA: Stanford University Press.

Bowles, John R. 1985. Suicide and Attempted Suicide in Contemporary Western Samoa. In *Culture, Youth and Suicide in the Pacific: Papers from an East-West Center Conference*, edited by Francis X. Hezel, Don H. Rubinstein, and Geoffey M. White. Honolulu: Center for Asian and Pacific Studies, University of Hawaii.

Bradley, F. H. 1901a. On Active Attention. *Mind* 8:1–30.

———. 1901b. The Definition of Will. *Mind* 8:29–144.

Braceland, Francis J. 1957. Kraepelin, His System and His Influence. *American Journal of Psychiatry* 113:871–76.

Brand, Myles. 1995. Volition. *The Cambridge Dictionary of Philosophy*. Cambridge: Cambridge University Press.

Brentano, Franz. [1874] 1995. *Psychology from an Empirical Standpoint*. London: Routledge.

Briggs, Jean L. 1998. *Inuit Morality Play: The Emotional Education of a Three-Year-Old*. New Haven: Yale University Press.

Brink, Louise, and Smith Ely Jelliffe. 1933. Emil Kraepelin, Psychiatrist and Poet. *Journal of Nervous and Mental Diseases* 87:134–52, 274–82.

Bruner, Jerome. 1986. *Actual Minds, Possible Worlds*. Cambridge, MA: Harvard University Press.

Butler, Judith. 1997. *The Psychic Life of Power*. Palo Alto, CA: Stanford University Press.

Cain, Carole. 1991. Personal Stories: Identity Acquisition and Self-Understanding in Alcoholics Anonymous. *Ethos*, 19:210–53.

Casey, Edward. 1976. *Imagining: A Phenomenological Study*. Bloomington: Indiana University Press.

Chodorow, Nancy. 1999. *The Power of Feelings*. New Haven, CT: Yale University Press.

Comaroff, Jean. 1985. *Body of Power, Spirit of Resistance*. Chicago: University of Chicago Press.

Comaroff, Jean, and John Comaroff. 1992. *Ethnography and Historical Imagination*. Boulder, CO: Westview Press.

Crapanzano, Vincent. 1980. *Tuhami: Portrait of a Moroccan*. Chicago: University of Chicago Press.

———. 2004. *Imaginative Horizons: An Essay in Literary Philosophical Anthropology*. Chicago: University of Chicago Press.

Csordas, Thomas. 1990. Embodiment as a Paradigm for Anthropology. *Ethos* 18:5:5–47.

———. 1993. Somatic Modes of Attention. *Cultural Anthropology* 8(1): 135–56.

———. 1994. *The Sacred Self: A Cultural Phenomenology of Charismatic Healing*. Berkeley: University of California Press.

D'Andrade, Roy. 1987. A Folk Model of the Mind. In *Cultural Models in Language and Thought*, edited by Dorothy Holland and Naomi Quinn, 112–48. Cambridge: Cambridge University Press.

D'Andrade, Roy, and Claudia Strauss, eds. 1992. *Human Motives and Cultural Models*. Cambridge: Cambridge University Press.

Damasio, Antonio R. 1994. *Descartes' Error: Emotion, Reason, and the Human Brain*. New York: Avon Books.

———. 1999. *The Feeling of What Happens: Body and Emotion in the Making of Consciousness*. New York: Harcourt Brace.

Davidoff, Leonore, and Catherine Hall. 1987. *Family Fortunes: Men and Women of the English Middle Class, 1780–1850*. Chicago: University of Chicago Press.

Dornan, Jennifer L. 2002. Agency and Archaeology: Past, Present, and Future Directions. *Journal of Archaeological Theory and Methods* 9(4): 303–29.

DuBois, John W. 1987. Meaning Without Intention: Lessons from Divination. *Papers in Pragmatics* 1:80–122.

Dumont, Louis. 1966. *Homo Hierarchicus*. Translated by Mark Sainsbury. Chicago: University of Chicago Press.

Duranti, Alessandro. 1984. Intentions, Self, and Local Theories of Meaning: Words and Social Action in a Samoan Context. *Center for Human Information Processing Report* 122. La Jolla, CA.

———. 1988. Intentions, Language, and Social Action in a Samoan Context. *Journal of Pragmatics* 12:13–33.

———. 1993a. Truth and Intentionality: An Ethnographic Critique. *Cultural Anthropology* 8(2): 214–25.

———. 1993b. Intentions, Self, and Responsibility: An Essay in Samoan Ethnopragmatics. In *Responsibility and Evidence in Oral Discourse*, edited by Jane Hill and Judith Irvine, 24–47. Cambridge: Cambridge University Press.

———. 1994. *From Grammar to Politics: Linguistic Anthropology in a Western Samoan Village*. Berkeley: University of California Press.

———. 2001. Intentionality. In *Key Terms in Language and Culture*, edited by Alessandro Duranti, 129–31. Oxford: Blackwell Publishers.

———. 2004. Agency in Language. In *Companion to Linguistic Anthropology*, edited by Alessandro Duranti, 451–73. Malden, MA: Blackwell.

———. 2006. The Social Ontology of Intentions. *Discourse Studies* 8(1): 31–40.

———. In press. The Relevance of Husserl's Theory to Language Socialization. *Journal of Linguistic Anthropology*.

Durkheim, Emile. 1979. *Suicide: A Study in Sociology*. New York: Free Press.

———. 1984. *The Division of Labor in Society*. New York: Free Press.

———. 1995. *The Elementary Forms of Religious Life*. New York: Free Press.

Edelman, Gerald M., and Giulio Tononi. 2000. *A Universe of Consciousness: How Matter Becomes Imagination*. New York: Basic Books.

Engstrom, Eric J. 1991. Emil Kraepelin: Psychiatry and Public Affairs in Wilhelmine Germany. *History of Psychiatry* 2:111–32.

———. 1992. Introduction to Emil Kraepelin, Psychiatric Observations on Contemporary Issues. *History of Psychiatry* 3:253–56.

———. 2007. "On the Question of Degeneration" by Emil Kraepelin (1908). *History of Psychiatry* 18:389–398.

Engstrom, Eric J., Wolfgang Burgmair, and Matthias M. Weber. 2002. Emil Kraepelin's 'Self-Assessment': Clinical Autography in Historical Context. *History of Psychiatry* 13:89–98.

Evans-Pritchard, E. E. 1937. *Witchcraft, Oracles and Magic Among the Azande*. Oxford: Clarendon Press.

Fabrega, Horacio Jr., and Daniel B. Silver. 1973. *Illness and Shamanistic Curing in Zinacantan: An Ethnomedical Analysis*. Palo Alto, CA: Stanford University Press.

Fingarette, Herbert. 1969. *Self-Deception*. London: Routledge and Kegan Paul.

———. 2004. *Mapping Responsibility: Explorations in Mind, Law, Myth, and Culture*. Chicago: Open Court.

Fortes, Meyer. 1987. *Religion, Morality and the Person: Essays on Tallensi Religion*, edited by Jack Goody. Cambridge: Cambridge University Press.

Foucault, Michel. 1980. *Power/Knowledge*. New York: Pantheon Books.

———. 1990. *The History of Sexuality, vol. 1: An Introduction*. Translated by Robert Hurley. New York: Random House.

Foulkes, David. 1985. *Dreaming: A Cognitive-Psychological Analysis*. Hillsdale, NJ: Lawrence Erlbaum.

Freeman, Derek. 1983. *Margaret Mead and Samoa: The Making and Unmaking of an Anthropological Myth*. Cambridge, MA: Harvard University Press.

Freud, Sigmund. 1900. The Interpretation of Dreams. *Standard Edition of the Complete Psychological Works of Sigmund Freud (SE)*, 4–5. London: Hogarth.

———. 1915. The Unconscious. SE, 14:159–204. London: Hogarth

———. 1923. The Ego and the Id. SE, 19:1–66. London: Hogarth

———. 1925. Some Additional Notes on Dream-Interpretation as a Whole. SE, 19:127–38. London: Hogarth

———. 1960. *The Ego and the Id*. New York: W.W. Norton & Company.

———. [1900] 1965. *The Interpretation of Dreams*. New York: Avon Books.

———. 1989. *Civilization and its Discontents*. New York: W.W. Norton & Company.

———. 2000. *Three Essays on the Theory of Sexuality*. New York: Basic Books.

Garfinkel, Harold. 1967. *Studies in Ethnomethodology*. Englewood Cliffs, NJ: Prentice-Hall.

Garro, Linda. 1990. Continuity and Change: The Interpretation of Illness in an Anishinaabe (Ojibway) Community. *Culture, Medicine and Psychiatry* 14:417–54.

———. 1998. On the Rationality of Decision Making Studies: Part 2: Divergent Rationalities. *Medical Anthropology Quarterly* 12:341–55.

———. 2000. Cultural Meaning, Explanations of Illness, and the Development of Comparative Frameworks. *Ethnology* 39:305–34.

———. 2001. The Remembered Past in a Culturally Meaningful Life: Remembering as Cultural, Social and Cognitive Process. In *The Psychology of Cultural Experience*, edited by Carmella C. Moore and Holly F. Mathews, 105–147. Cambridge: Cambridge University Press.

———. 2002. Hallowell's Challenge: Explanations of Illness and Cross-Cultural Research. *Anthropological Theory* 2:77–97.

———. n.d. By Whose Will? Unpublished Manuscript.

Garro, Linda, and Cheryl Mattingly. 2000. Narrative as Construct and Construction. In *Narrative and the Cultural Construction of Illness and Healing*, edited by Cheryl Mattingly and Linda Garro, 1–49. Berkeley: University of California Press.

Geertz, Clifford. 1968. *Islam Observed: Religious Development in Morocco and Indonesia*. New Haven: Yale University Press.

Geertz, Hildred. 1959. The Vocabulary of Emotion: A Study of Javanese Socialization Processes. *Psychiatry* 22:225–36.

Gerber, Eleanor R. 1975. *The Cultural Patterning of Emotions in Samoa*. Doctoral dissertation. University of California at San Diego.

———. 1985. Rage and Obligation: Samoan Emotion in Conflict. In *Person, Self and Experience: Exploring Pacific Ethnopsychologies*, edited by Geoffrey M. White and John Kirkpatrick, 121–67. Berkeley: University of California.

Giddens, Anthony. 1983. *Central Problems in Social Theory*. Berkeley: University of California Press.

———. 1984. *The Constitution of Society*. Berkeley: University of California Press.

Good, Byron J. 1992. Culture and Psychopathology: Directions for Psychiatric Anthropology. In *New Directions in Psychological Anthropology*, edited by Theodore Schwartz, Geoffrey M. White, and Catherine A. Lutz, 181–205. Cambridge: Cambridge University Press.

Goodwin, Charles. 1994. Professional Vision. *American Anthropologist* 96(3): 606–33.

Goodwin, Marjorie H. 1990. *He-Said-She-Said: Talk as Social Organization Among Black Children*. Bloomington: Indiana University Press.

Gossen, Gary H. 1975. Animal Souls and Human Destiny in Chamula. *Man* 10 (n.s.): 448–61.

———. 1976. The Other in Chamula Tzotzil Cosmology and History: Reflections of a Kansan in Chiapas. *Cultural Anthropology* 8(4): 443–75.

———. 1999. From Olmecs to Zapatistas: A Once and Future History of Maya Souls. In *Telling Maya Tales: Tzotzil Identities in Modern Mexico*, edited by Gary Gossen, 225–46. New York: Routledge.

Graves, Robert. 1960. *The Greek Myths*, vol. 2. New York: Penguin Books.

Greenberg, Jay R., and Stephen Mitchell. 1983. *Object Relations in Psychoanalytic Theory*. Cambridge, MA: Harvard University Press.

Groark, Kevin P. 2009. Discourses of the Soul: The Negotiation of Personal Agency in Tzotzil Maya Dream Narrative. *American Ethnologist* 36(4).

Grøn, Lone. 2005. Winds of Change, Bodies of Persistence: Health Promotion and Lifestyle Change in Institutional and Everyday Contexts. Ph.D. dissertation, Department of Anthropology and Ethnography, University of Aarhus.

Gunson, Niel. 1987. *Messengers of Grace: Evangelical Missionaries in the South Seas, 1797–1860.* New York: Oxford University Press.

Hacking, Ian. 1995. *Rewriting the Soul: Multiple Personality and the Sciences of Memory.* Princeton, NJ: Princeton University Press.

Haggard, Patrick. 2006. Conscious Intention and the Sense of Agency. In *Disorders of Volition*, edited by Natalie Sebanz and Wolfgang Prinz, 69–85. Cambridge, MA: MIT Press.

Hallowell, A. Irving. 1942. *The Role of Conjuring in Saulteaux Society.* Philadelphia: University of Pennsylvania Press.

———. 1955. *Culture and Experience.* Philadelphia: University of Pennsylvania Press.

———. 1958. Ojibwa Metaphysics of Being and the Perception of Persons. In *Person Perception and Interpersonal Behavior*, edited by Renato Tagiuri and Luigi Petrullo, 63–85. Palo Alto: Stanford University Press.

———. 1959. Behavioral Evolution and the Emergence of the Self. In *Evolution and Anthropology: A Centennial Appraisal*, edited by B. J. Meggers. Washington, DC: Anthropological Society of Washington.

———. 1960. Ojibwa Ontology, Behavior and World View. In *Culture in History: Essays in Honor of Paul Radin*, edited by Stanley Diamond, 19–52. New York: Columbia University Press. Reprinted in Hallowell 1976, 357–90.

———. 1976. *Contributions to Anthropology: Selected Papers of A. Irving Hallowell.* Chicago: University of Chicago Press.

———. 1992. *The Ojibwa of Berens River, Manitoba: Ethnography into History.* Jennifer S. H. Brown, ed. Fort Worth, TX: Harcourt Brace.

Hanks, William F. 1990. *Referential Practice: Language and Lived Space Among the Maya.* Chicago: University of Chicago Press.

Harris, W., M. Gowda, J. Kolb, C. Strychacz, J. Vacek, P. Jones, A. Forker, J. O'Keefe, and B. McCallister. 1999. A Randomized, Controlled Trial of the Effects of Remote, Intercessory Prayer on Outcomes in Patients Admitted to the Coronary Care Unit. *Archives of Internal Medicine* 159:2273–278.

Hollan, Douglas. 2000. Constructivist Models of Mind, Contemporary Psychoanalysis, and the Development of Culture Theory. *American Anthropologist* 102(3): 538–50.

Holland, Dorothy. 1992. How Cultural Systems Become Desire: A Case Study of American Romance. In *Human Motives and Cultural Models*, edited by Roy D'Andrade and Claudia Strauss. 61–89. Cambridge: Cambridge University Press.

Holland, Dorothy, William Lachicotte Jr., Debra Skinner, and Carole Cain. 1998. *Identity and Agency in Cultural Worlds.* Cambridge, MA: Harvard University Press.

Holmes, Lowell D. 1974. *Samoan Village.* Palo Alto, CA: Stanford University Press.

Howes, David, ed. 1991. *The Varieties of Sensory Experience.* Toronto: University of Toronto Press.

———. 2003. *Sensual Relations: Engaging the Senses in Culture and Social Theory.* Ann Arbor: The University of Michigan Press.

Huebner, Thom. 1986. Vernacular Literacy: English as a Language of Wider Communication and Language Shift in American Samoa. *Journal of Multi-Lingual and Multi-Cultural Development* 7(5): 393–411.

Hunt, Harry T. 1989. *Dreams.* New Haven, CT: Yale University Press.

Husserl, Edmund. [1931] 1962. *Ideas: General Introduction to Pure Phenomenology.* New York: Collier Books.

Iacoboni, Marco. 2008. *Mirroring People: The New Science of How We Connect with Others.* New York: Farrar, Straus & Giroux.

Jackson, Michael. 1989. *Paths Toward a Clearing: Radical Empiricism and Ethnographic Inquiry.* Bloomington: Indiana University Press.

———. 1995. *At Home in the World.* Durham, NC: Duke University Press.

Jacquette, Dale. 2004. Brentano's Concept of Intentionality. In *The Cambridge Companion to Brentano*, edited by Dale Jacquette, 98–131. Cambridge: Cambridge University Press.

James, William. [1890] 1983. *The Principles of Psychology.* Cambridge, MA, and London, England: Harvard University Press.

———. [1892] 1985. *Psychology: A Briefer Course.* New York: Collier Books.

Jedrej, M. C., and Rosalind Shaw, eds. 1992a. *Dreaming, Religion and Society in Africa.* Leiden: E. J. Brill.

Jedrej, M. C., and Rosalind Shaw. 1992b. "Introduction." In *Dreaming, Religion and Society in Africa,* edited by M. C. Jedrej and Rosalind Shaw, 1–20. Leiden: E. J. Brill.

Kahn, Eugen. 1956. Emil Kraepelin. February 15, 1856–October 7, 1926. *American Journal of Psychiatry* 112:289–94.

Khan, M., and R. Masud. 1974. The Use and Abuse of Dream in Psychic Experience. In *The Privacy of the Self: Papers on Psychoanalytic Theory and Technique,* edited by M. Masud and R. Khan, 306–15. New York: International Universities Press.

Kirmayer, Laurence J. 1984. Culture, Affect and Somatization (Part I). *Transcultural Psychiatric Research Review* 21:159–88.

Kleinman, Arthur. 1995. *Writing at the Margin: Discourse Between Anthropology and Medicine.* Berkeley: University of California Press.

Kleinman, Arthur, and Joan Kleinman. 1991. Suffering and Its Professional Transformation: Toward an Ethnography of Interpersonal Experience. *Culture, Medicine and Psychiatry,* 15:275–301.

Klerman, Gerald L. 1978. The Evolution of a Scientific Nosology. In *Schizophrenia: Science and Practice,* edited by John C. Shershow, 99–121. Cambridge, MA: Harvard University Press.

Kockelman, Paul. 2007. Agency: The Relation between Meaning, Power, and Knoweldge. *Current Anthropology* 48(3): 375–401.

Kracke, Waud. 1991. The Self and Kagwahiv Dreams. In *The Psychoanalytic Study of Society, Volume 16: Essays in Honor of A. Irving Hallowell,* edited by L. Bryce Boyer and Ruth M. Boyer, 43–53. Hillsdale, NJ: The Analytic Press.

Kraepelin, Emil. [1899] 1990. *Psychiatry: A Textbook for Students and Physicians.* Volume 1 General Psychiatry, Volume 2 Clinical Psychiatry, edited by Jacques M. Quen. Canton, MA: Science History Publications.

———. 1904a. *Psychiatrisches aus Java. Centralblatt fur Nervheilkunde und Psychiatrie* 27 (=N.F. 15): 468–469.

———. 1904b. *Vergleichende Psychiatrie. Centralblatt fur Nervheilkunde und Psychiatrie* 27 (=N.F. 15): 433–437.

———. [1908] 2007. On the Question of Degeneration. *History of Psychiatry* 18: 399–404.

———. 1913. *Lectures on Clinical Psychiatry.* 3rd Ed. Translated from the 2nd German Edition by Thomas Johnstone. New York: William Wood & Co.

———. [1919] 1992. Psychiatric Observations on Contemporary Issues. *History of Psychiatry* 3:253–69.

———. 2002. Emil Kraepelin's "Self-Assessment." *History of Psychiatry* 13:98–119.

Krämer, Augustin. [1902] 1994–1995. *The Samoan Islands: The Outline of a Monography Giving Special Consideration to German Samoa.* Translated by Theodore Verhaaren. 2 Volumes. Honolulu: University of Hawaii Press.

Lacan, Jacques. 1968. The Mirror Phase. *New Left Review* 51:70–79.

———. 1977a. *Écrits: A Selection*. New York: W. W. Norton.

———. 1977b. *The Four Fundamental Concepts of Psycho-Analysis*. New York: W. W. Norton.

Lambek, Michael. 1981. *Human Spirits: A Cultural Account of Trance in Mayotte*. Cambridge: Cambridge University Press.

———. 1993. *Knowledge and Practice in Mayotte: Local Discourses of Islam, Sorcery, and Spirit Possession*. Toronto: University of Toronto Press.

———. 2003. Rheumatic Irony: Questions of Agency and Self-Deception as Refracted through the Art of Living with Spirits. In *Illness and Irony: On the Ambiguity of Suffering in Culture*, edited by Michael Lambek and Paul Antze, 40–59. Oxford: Berghahn Books.

Landes, Ruth. 1968. *Ojibwa Religion and the Midewiwin*. Madison: University of Wisconsin Press.

Langacker, Ronald. 1985. Some Observations and Speculations on Subjectivity. In *Iconicity in Language*, edited by John Haiman, 109–50. Philadelphia: John Benjamins.

Laughlin, Robert M. 1975. *The Great Tzotzil Dictionary of San Lorenzo Zinacantán*. Washington, DC: Smithsonian Institution Press.

———. 1976. *Of Wonders Wild and New: Dreams from Zinacantán*. Washington, DC: Smithsonian Institution Press.

Leder, Drew. 1990. *The Absent Body*. Chicago: University of Chicago Press.

LeDoux, Joseph. 1996. *The Emotional Brain*. New York: Simon and Schuster.

———. 2002. *Synaptic Self: How Our Brains Become Who We Are*. New York: Penguin Books.

Leininger, April. 2002. Cultural Psychodynamics Among 1.5-Generation Vietnamese Americans. Paper presented at the Annual Meeting of the American Anthropological Association, New Orleans, November 20–24.

Levinson, Steven. 2003. *Space in Language and Cognition: Explorations in Cognitive Diversity*. Cambridge: Cambridge University Press.

Levy, Robert I. 1973. *Tahitians: Mind and Experience in the Society Islands*. Chicago: University of Chicago Press.

———. 1974. Tahiti, Sin, and the Question of Integration Between Personality and Sociocultural Systems. In *Culture and Personality*, edited by Robert A. LeVine, 287–306. New York: Aldine.

———. 1984. Emotion, Knowing, and Culture. In *Culture Theory: Essays on Mind, Self, and Emotion,* edited by Richard A. Shweder and Robert A. LeVine, 214–37. Cambridge: Cambridge University Press.

Loewald, Hans. [1978] 2000. Primary Process, Secondary Process, and Language. In *The Essential Loewald: Collected Papers and Monographs,* edited by Norman Quist, 178–206. Hagerstown, MD: University Publishing Group.

Lohmann, Roger I. 2003. Turning the Belly: Insights on Religious Conversion from New Guinea Gut Feelings. In *The Anthropology of Religious Conversion*, edited by Andrew Buchser and Stephen D. Glazier, 109–22. Boulder, CO: Rowman and Littefield.

———, ed. 2003. *Dream Travelers*. New York: Palgrave.

Luhrmann, Tanya. 1989. *Persuasions of the Witch's Craft: Ritual Magic in Contemporary England*. Cambridge, MA: Harvard University Press.

———. 2004. Metakinesis: How God Becomes Intimate in Contemporary U.S. Christianity. *American Anthropologist* 106:518–28.

Lutz, Catherine, and Geoffrey M. White. 1986. The Anthropology of Emotions. *Annual Review of Anthropology* 15:405–36.

MacIntyre, Alasdair. 1981. *After Virtue: A Study in Moral Theory*. Notre Dame: University of Notre Dame Press.

Macpherson, Cluny, and La'avasa Macpherson. 1985. Suicide in Western Samoa, A Sociological Perspective. In *Culture, Youth and Suicide in the Pacific: Papers from an East-West Center Conference*, edited by Francis K. Hezel, Donald H. Rubinstein, and Geoffrey M. White, 36–73. Honolulu: Center for Asian and Pacific Studies, University of Hawaii at Manoa.

———. 1987. Towards an Explanation of Recent Trends in Suicide in Western Samoa. *Man* (n.s.) 22:305–30.

Mageo, Jeannette. 1989. *Amio/Aga* and *Loto. Oceania* 59:181–99.

———. 1991. *Ma'i Aitu*: The Cultural Logic of Possession in Samoa. *Ethos* 19:352–83.

———. 1992. Male Transvestism and Culture Change in Samoa. *American Ethnologist* 19(3): 443–459.

———. 1994. Hairdos and Don'ts. *Man*, 29:407–32.

———. 1996. Spirit Girls and Marines. *American Ethnologist* 23:61–82.

———. 1998. *Theorizing Self in Samoa*. Ann Arbor: University of Michigan Press.

———. 2002. Towards a Multidimensional Model of the Self. *The Journal of Anthropological Research* 58:339–65.

———, ed. 2003. *Dreaming and the Self*. Albany: SUNY Press.

———. 2008. Zones of Ambiguity and Identity Politics in Samoa, *Journal of the Royal Anthropological Institute* 14:61–78.

Manning, P. K., and Horacio Fabrega, Jr. 1973. The Experience of Self and Body: Health and Illness in the Chiapas Highlands. In *Phenomenological Sociology*, edited by George Psathas, 251–301. New York: Wiley & Sons.

Markus, Hazel R., and Shinobu Kitayama. 1991. Culture and the Self: Implications for Cognition, Emotion and Motivation. *Psychological Review* 98:224–53.

Marx, Karl. 1990. *Capital*. New York: Penguin Classics.

Mattingly, Cheryl, and Linda Garro. 1994. Introduction: Narrative Representations of Illness and Healing. *Social Science and Medicine* 38:771–74.

Mauss, Marcel. [1938] 1985. A Category of the Human Mind: The Notion of Person; the Notion of Self. In *The Category of the Person*, edited by Michael Carrithers, Steven Collins, and Steven Lukes, 1–25. Cambridge: Cambridge University Press.

Mead, George. H. 1934. *Mind, Self, and Society*. Chicago: University of Chicago Press.

———. 1977. *On Social Psychology*. Chicago: University of Chicago Press.

Mead, Margaret. [1928] 1961. *Coming of Age in Samoa*. New York: Morrow Quill.

Milgram, Stanley. 1974. *Obedience to Authority: An Experimental View*. New York: Harper & Row.

Merleau-Ponty, Maurice. 1962. *Phenomenology of Perception*. London: Routledge & Kegan Paul Ltd.

Mills, W. 1844. March 19, letter to London Missionary Society Headquarters from Upolu, CWM (17/6/B). School of Oriental and African Studies, University of London.

Mitchell, Stephen A. 1988. *Relational Concepts in Psychoanalysis: An Integration*. Cambridge, MA: Harvard University Press.

———. 1993. *Hope and Dread in Psychoanalysis*. New York: Basic Books.

Mittermaier, Amira. 2006. Dreams That Matter: An Anthropology of the Imagination in Contemporary Egypt. Ph.D. Dissertation, Department of Anthropology, Columbia University.

Munn, Nancy. 1986. *The Fame of Gawa*. Durham, NC: Duke University Press.

Murdoch, Iris. 1970. *The Sovereignty of Good*. New York: Ark Paperbacks.

Murray, A. 1839. January 15 letter to London Missionary Society Headquarters from Tutuila, CWM Archives (12/6/A). School of Oriental and African Studies, University of London.

Noy, Pinchas. 1969. A Revision of the Psychoanalytic Theory of the Primary Process. *International Journal of Psychoanalysis* 50:155–78.

Nussbaum, Martha. 2001. *Upheavals of Thought: The Intelligence of Emotions*. Cambridge: Cambridge University Press.

Obeyesekere, Gananath. 1992. *The Apotheosis of Captain Cook: European Mythmaking in the Pacific*. Princeton, NJ: Princeton University Press.

Ochs, Elinor. 1984. Angry Words. Paper presented at the 83rd Annual Meeting of the American Anthropological Association, Denver, CO.

Ochs, Elinor, and Lisa Capps. 2001. *Living Narrative: Creating Lives in Everyday Storytelling*. Cambridge, MA: Harvard University Press.

Ochs, Elinor, R. Smith, and C. Taylor. 1989. Dinner Narratives as Detective Stories. *Cultural Dynamics* 2:238–57.

Ochs, Elinor, and Bambi B. Schieffelin 1984. Language Acquisition and Socialization: Three Developmental Stories and Their Implications. In *Culture Theory: Essays on Mind, Self and Emotion*, edited by Richard A. Shweder and Robert A. LeVine, 276–320. Cambridge: Cambridge University Press.

Ogden, Thomas H. 1986. *The Matrix of the Mind: Object Relations and the Psychoanalytic Dialogue*. Northvale, NJ: Jason Aronson.

O'Meara, Tim. 1990. *Samoan Planters*. Fort Worth: Holt, Rinehart and Winston.

Ortner, Sherry B. 1984. Theory in Anthropology Since the Sixties. *Comparative Studies in Society and History* 26(1): 126–66.

———. 1996. *Making Gender: The Politics and Erotics of Culture*. Boston: Beacon Press.

———. 2006. *Anthropology and Social Theory: Culture, Power, and the Acting Subject*. Durham, NC: Duke University Press.

Oxford English Dictionary. 1989. 2nd ed. Oxford: Clarendon Press.

Palombo, Stanley R. 1978. *Dreaming and Memory*. New York: Basic Books.

Page, Pliego, and Jaime Tomás. 2005. *El Mandato de los Dioses: Etnomedicina entre los Tzotziles de Chamula y Chenalhó, Chiapas*. San Cristóbal de Las Casas, Mexico: Programa de Investigaciones Multidisciplinarias Sobre Mesoamérica y el Sureste/UNAM.

Parsons, Talcott. 1937. *The Structure of Social Action*, 2 Vols. New York: The Free Press.

Pick, Daniel. 1989. *Faces of Degeneration: A European Disorder, c. 1848–c.1918*. Cambridge: Cambridge University Press.

Pitarch Ramón, Pedro. 1996. *Ch'ulel: Una Etnografía de los Almas Tzeltales*. México, D.F.: Fondo de Cultura Económica.

———. 2003. Dos Puntos de Vista, Una Sola Persona: El Espacio en Una Montaña de Almas. In *Espacios Mayas: Representaciones, Usos, Creencias*, edited by Alain Breton, Aurore Monod Becquelin, and Mario Humberto Ruz, 603–17. México D.F.: Centro de Estudios Mayas, IIFL, UNAM / Centro Francés de Estudios Mexicanos y Centroamericanos.

Pitt-Rivers, Julian. 1970. Spiritual Power in Central America: The Naguals of Chiapas. In *Witchcraft, Confessions and Accusations*, edited by Mary Douglas, 183–206. London: Tavistock.

Pratt, George. 1977. *Pratt's Grammar and Dictionary of the Samoan Language*. Apia, Samoa: Malua. Reprint. Originally published in 1862 and 1911.

Preston, J., and Daniel Wegner. 2005. Ideal Agency: On Perceiving the Self as an Origin of Action. In *On Building, Defending, and Regulating the Self*, edited by Abraham Tesser, Joanne Wood, and Diederik Stapel, 103–25. Philadelphia: Psychology Press.

Pritchard, William T. 1866. *Polynesian Reminiscences; or, Life in the South Pacific Islands*. London: Chapman and Hall.

Pronin, Emily, Daniel Wegner, Kimberly McCarthy, and Sylvia Rodriguez. 2006. Everyday Magical Powers: The Role of Apparent Mental Causation in the Overestimation of Personal Influence. *Journal of Personality and Social Psychology* 91:218–31.

Rachun Linn, Priscilla. 1989. Souls and Selves in Chamula: A Thought on Individuals, Fatalism and Denial. In *Ethnographic Encounters in Southern Mesoamerica: Essays in Honor of Evon Zartman Vogt, Jr.*, edited by Victoria R. Bricker and Gary H. Gossen, 251–62. Albany: Institute for Mesoamerican Studies, State University of New York, Albany.

Ray, Keith. 1992. Dreams of Grandeur: The Call to Office in Northcentral Igbo Religious Leadership. In *Dreaming, Religion and Society in Africa*, edited by M. C. Jedrej and Rosalind Shaw, 55–70. Leiden, Netherlands: E. J. Brill.

Reddy, William. 1999. Emotional Liberty: Politics and History in the Anthropology of Emotions. *Cultural Anthropology* 14(2): 256–88.

Ribot, Theodule. 1894. *The Diseases of the Will*. Translated from the 8th French edition of *Les Maladies de la Volonte* by Merwin-Marie Snell. Chicago: Open Court.

Ricoeur, Paul. [1950] 1966. *Freedom and Nature*. Evanston, IL: Northwestern University Press.

———. 1970. *Freud and Philosophy: An Essay on Interpretation*. New Haven, CT: Yale University Press.

———. 1984. *Time and Narrative*. Vol 2. Chicago: The University of Chicago Press.

Robbins, Joel. 2004. *Becoming Sinners*. Berkeley: University of California Press.

Roelcke, Volker. 1997. Biologizing Social Facts: An Early 20th Century Debate on Kraepellin's Concepts of Culture, Neurasthenia, and Degeneration. *Culture, Medicine and Psychiatry* 21: 383–403.

Rosaldo, Renato. 1984. Grief and a Headhunter's Rage: On the Cultural Force of Emotions. In *Text, Play, and Story: The Construction and Reconstruction of Self and Society*, edited by Edward Bruner. Prospect, IL.: Waveland Press.

Rosen, Lawrence. 1995. *Other Intentions: Cultural Contexts and the Attribution of Inner States*. Santa Fe, NM: School of American Research Press.

Sahlins, Marshall. 1981. *Historical Metaphors and Mythical Realities*. Ann Arbor: University of Michigan Press.

———. 1985. *Islands of History*. Chicago: University of Chicago Press.

———. 1995. *How "Natives" Think: About Captain Cook, For Example*. Chicago: University of Chicago Press.

Sartre, Jean-Paul. 1984. *Being and Nothingness*. New York: First Washington Square Press.

Schachtel, Ernest G. 1959. *Metamorphosis*. New York: Basic Books.

Schacter, Daniel L. 1996. *Searching for Memory: The Brain, the Mind, and the Past*. New York: Basic Books.

Schafer, Roy. 1973. Action: Its Place in Psychoanalytic Interpretation and Theory. *The Annual of Psychoanalysis* 1:159–96.

———. 1976. *A New Language for Psychoanalysis*. New Haven, CT: Yale University Press.

Schopenhauer, Arthur. 1958. *The World as Will and Representation*. Mineola, NY: Courier Dover Publications.

Schutz, Alfred. [1932] 1967. *The Phenomenology of the Social World*. Evanston, IL: Northwestern University Press.

Shafton, Anthony. 2002. *Dream-Singers: The African American Way with Dreams*. New York: John Wiley & Sons.

Shand, Alexander F. 1895. Attention and Will: A Study in Involuntary Action. *Mind* 4:450–71.

———. 1897. Types of Will. *Mind* 6:289–325.

Shweder, Richard A. 1984. Anthropology's Romantic Rebellion Against the Enlightenment, or There's More to Thinking than Reason and Evidence. In *Culture Theory: Essays on Mind, Self, and Emotion*, edited by Richard A. Shweder and Robert A. LeVine, 27–66. Cambridge: Cambridge University Press.

Shweder, Richard A., and Edmund J. Bourne. 1984. Does the Concept of the Person Vary Cross-Culturally? In *Cultural Conceptions of Mental Health and Therapy*, edited by Anthony J. Marsella and Geoffrey M. White, 97–137. Dordrecht, Netherlands: D. Reidel.

Sontag, Susan. 1980. Fascinating Fascism. In *Under the Sign of Saturn*, 73–103. New York: Farrar, Straus, Giroux.

Spiro, Melford. 1997. *Gender Ideology and Psychological Reality*. Princeton, NJ: Princeton University Press.

Stephen, Michele. 2003. Memory, Emotion and the Imaginal Mind. In *Dreaming and the Self*, edited by Jeannette Mageo, 97–132. Albany: SUNY Press.

Stewart, Pamela J., and Andrew Strathern. 2000. Fragmented Selfhood: Contradiction, Anomaly, and Violence in Female Life Histories. In *Identity Work: Constructing Pacific Lives*, edited by Pamela J. Stewart and Andrew Strathern, 58–77. Pittsburgh: University of Pittsburgh Press.

———. 2001. *Humors and Substances: Ideas of the Body in New Guinea*. London: Bergin and Garvey.

———. 2002a. *Remaking the World: Myth, Mining, and Ritual Change among the Duna of Papua New Guinea*. Washington, DC: Smithsonian Institution Press.

———. 2002b. *Violence: Theory and Ethnography*. New York: Continuum Press.

———. 2003. Dreaming and Ghosts Among the Hagen and Duna of the Southern Highlands, Papua New Guinea. In *Dream Travelers: Sleep Experiences and Culture in the Western Pacific*, edited by Roger I. Lohmann, 43–60. New York: Palgrave Macmillan.

Stoker, Bram. [1897] 1997. *Dracula*. Harmondsworth, UK: Signet Classics.

Strathern, Andrew. 1981. *Noman*: Representations of Identity in Mt. Hagen. In *The Structure of Folk Models*, edited by Ladislav Holy and Milan Stuchlik, 281–303. London: Academic Press.

Strathern, Andrew, and Pamela J. Stewart. 2004. *Empowering the Past, Confronting the Future: The Duna People of Papua New Guinea*. New York: Palgrave Macmillan.

———. 2005. The Ulster-Scots: A Cross-Border and Trans-National Concept. *Journal of Ritual Studies* 19 (2): 1–16.

———. 2006a. Introduction: Terror, the Imagination and Cosmology. In *Terror and Violence: Imagination and the Unimaginable*, edited by Andrew Strathern, Pamela J. Stewart, and Neil L. Whitehead, 1–39. London: Pluto Press.

———. 2006b. Narratives of Violence: And Perils of Peace-Making in North-South Cross-Border Contexts, Ireland. In *Terror and Violence: Imagination and the Unimaginable*, edited by Andrew Strathern, Pamela J. Stewart, and Neil L. Whitehead, 142–70. London: Pluto Press.

———. 2008. Introduction: Aligning Words, Aligning Worlds. In *Exchange and Sacrifice*, edited by Pamela J. Stewart and Andrew Strathern, xi–xxxvi. Durham, NC: Carolina Academic Press.

———. 2009. Introduction: A Complexity of Contexts, a Multiplicity of Changes. In *Religious and Ritual Change: Cosmologies and Histories*, edited by Pamela J. Stewart and Andrew Strathern, 3–68. Durham, NC: Carolina Academic Press.

Strathern, Marilyn. 1988. *The Gender of the Gift*. Berkeley: University of California Press.

Strauss, Hermann, and Herbert Tischner. 1962. *Die Mi-Kultur der Hagenberg Stämme im Östlichen Zentral-Neuguinea*. Hamburg, Germany: Cram de Gruyter.

Sutter, Frederic K. 1980. Communal Versus Individual Socialization at Home and in School in Rural and Urban Samoa. Doctoral Dissertation. University of Hawaii.

Taylor, Charles. 1989. *Sources of the Self: The Making of Modern Identity*. Cambridge, MA: Harvard University Press.

Tedlock, Barbara, ed. 1987. *Dreaming*. Cambridge: Cambridge University Press.

————, ed. 1992. *Dreaming: Anthropological and Psychological Interpretations.* Santa Fe, NM: School of American Research Press.

Throop, C. Jason. 2003a. On Crafting a Cultural Mind: A Comparative Assessment of Some Recent Theories of "Internalization" in Psychological Anthropology. *Transcultural Psychiatry* 40(1): 109–39.

————. 2003b. Articulating Experience. *Anthropological Theory* 3(2): 219–41.

————. 2005. Hypocognition, a "Sense of the Uncanny," and the Anthropology of Ambiguity: Reflections on Robert I. Levy's Contribution to Theories of "Experience" in Anthropology. *Ethos* 33(4): 499–511.

————. 2008. From Pain to Virtue: Dysphoric Sensation and Moral Sensibilities in Yap (Waqab), Federated States of Micronesia. *Transcultural Psychiatry* 45(2): 253–86.

————. Forthcoming. *Suffering and Sentiment: Exploring the Vicissitudes of Pain and Experience in Yap.* Berkeley: University of California Press.

Throop, C. Jason, and Keith. M. Murphy. 2002. Bourdieu and Phenomenology: A Critical Assessment. *Anthropological Theory* 2 (2): 185–207.

Tomberlin, James, ed. 2001. *Action and Freedom.* London: Blackwell Press.

Turner, George. [1861] 1984. *Nineteen Years in Polynesia.* Papakura, New Zealand: R. McMillan.

Van Inwagen, Peter. 1983. *An Essay on Free Will.* Oxford: Oxford University Press.

Vogt, Evon Z. 1965. Zinacanteco Souls. *Man* 29:33–35.

————. 1970. Human Souls and Animal Spirits in Zinacantán. In *Echanges et Communications, Mélanges Offerts à la Occasion de son 60ème Anniversaire,* edited by Pierre Maranda and Jean Pouillon, 1148–1167. The Hague: Mouton.

Wegner, Daniel. 2002. *The Illusion of Conscious Will.* Cambridge, MA: MIT Press.

————. 2004. Precis of *The Illusion of Conscious Will. Behavioral and Brain Sciences* 27:649–92.

————. 2005. Who Is the Controller of Controlled Processes? In *The New Unconscious,* edited by R. Hassin, J. S. Uleman, and J. A. Bargh, 19–36. New York: Oxford University Press.

Weissman, Myrna M., and Gerald L. Klerman. 1978. Epidemiology of Mental disorders: Emerging Trends in the Unite States. *Archives of General Psychiatry* 35:705–712.

Whorf, Benjamin Lee. 1956. *Language, Thought, and Reality.* Cambridge, MA: MIT Press.

White, Geoffrey M., and John Kirkpatrick. 1985, eds. *Person, Self, and Experience: Exploring Pacific Ethnopsychologies.* Berkeley: University of California Press.

Wikan, Unni. 1989. Beyond the Words: The Power of Resonance. *American Ethnologist* 19:460–82.

————. 1990 *Managing Turbulent Hearts: A Balinese Formula for Living.* Chicago: University of Chicago Press.

————. 1991. *Behind the Veil in Arabia.* Chicago: University of Chicago Press.

Wilson, Mitchell. 1993. DSM-III and the Transformation of American Psychiatry: A History. *American Journal of Psychiatry* 150:399–410.

Williams, Raymond. 1977. *Marxism and Literature.* London: Oxford University.

Winnicott, Donald W. 1951. Transitional Objects and Transitional Phenomena. In *Through Paediatrics to Psycho-Analysis.* London: Hogarth Press.

————. 1959. The Fate of the Transitional Object. In *Psychoanalytic Explorations,* edited by Clare Winnicott, Ray Shepherd, and Madeleine Davis, 53–58. Cambridge, MA: Harvard University Press.

————. 1971. *Playing and Reality.* London: Tavistock.

Zubin, J., G. Oppenheimer, and G. Neugebauer. 1985. Degeneration Theory and the Stigma of Schizophrenia. *Biological Psychiatry* 20:1145–48.

CONTRIBUTORS

Linda C. Garro holds doctorates in Social Sciences–Anthropology (1983, University of California, Irvine) and Cognitive Psychology (1982, Duke University) and is Professor of Anthropology at the University of California, Los Angeles. Her research activities are in the areas of medical and psychological anthropology and include representing cultural knowledge about illness; variability in cultural knowledge; health care decision making; health concerns in everyday life; illness narratives; and remembering as a social, cultural, and cognitive process. Along with numerous articles, she is coauthor, with James Young, of *Medical Choice in a Mexican Village* and coeditor, with Cheryl Mattingly, of *Narrative and the Cultural Construction of Illness and Healing*. In 1999 she received the Stirling Award from the Society for Psychological Anthropology.

Byron J. Good is Professor of Medical Anthropology in the Department of Global Health and Social Medicine, Harvard Medical School. Prof. Good has a long interest in theorizing illness experience and medical care across cultures. His current research is investigating early experiences of psychotic illness in Indonesia and the development of mental health interventions in post-conflict Aceh. He has special interests in the role of historical understandings of schizophrenia in promoting hopelessness and stigma. Prof. Good's broader concerns focus on the relations between madness and violence in Indonesia, on theorization of subjectivity in contemporary societies, on "post-colonial disorders," and on the relations among political, cultural and psychological renderings of language and the subject.

Kevin Groark is an anthropologist specializing in the medical culture and ethnopsychology of the highland Maya of Chiapas, Mexico. Since 1991 he has worked in both Tzeltal- and Tzotzil-speaking communities throughout the region, developing a body of research focusing on the dynamics of the folk medical system and its relation to broader questions of personhood, emotion, and sociality. He is currently an Assistant Professor at the University of Southern California, and is pursuing clinical psychoanalytic training at the New Center for Psychoanalysis in Los Angeles, California.

Douglas W. Hollan is Professor of Anthropology and Luckman Distinguished Teacher at UCLA and a senior instructor at the New Center for Psychoanalysis in Los Angeles. He is the author of numerous articles examining the relationships between cultural and psychological processes and co-author of *Contentment and Suffering: Culture and Experience in Toraja* and *The Thread of Life: Toraja Reflections on the Life Cycle.*

Jeannette Mageo is Professor of Anthropology at Washington State University. Her current work focuses on dreaming and the self and on how subjectivity, identity, and emotion evolve out of cultural and historical experiences. She has also researched and published on child development, sexuality, transvestism, prehistory and spirit possession. Mageo is the author of *Theorizing Self in Sāmoa: Emotions, Genders, Sexualities* (1998). She has also edited and coedited the following volumes: *Spirits in Culture, History, and Mind* (1996); *Cultural Memory: Reconfiguring History and Identity in the Postcolonial Pacific* (2001); *Power and the Self* (2002); and *Dreaming and the Self: New Perspectives on Subjectivity, Identity, and Emotion* (2003).

Cheryl Mattingly is Professor in the Department of Anthropology and the Division of Occupational Science at the University of Southern California. The constant themes in her research are narrative, moral reasoning, the phenomenology of chronic suffering, the culture of biomedicine and health disparities in the United States. For the past fifteen years she has explored clinical practices in a variety of inner-city health care settings in the United States. She is currently conducting ethnographic research among African-American families caring for children with severe disabilities and chronic illness in Los Angeles. She received the Victor Turner Prize in 2000 for *Healing Dramas and Clinical Plots* (1998). She also coedited (with Linda Garro) *Narrative and the Cultural Construction of Illness and Healing* (2000).

Keith M. Murphy is Assistant Professor of Anthropology at the University of California, Irvine. Much of his work explores the relationship between language, material culture, and sociopolitical processes, with a particular emphasis on how these domains intersect with human experience. As a linguistic anthropologist, his core research interests sit at the intersection of design—as both a cultural category and a social process—and the study of face-to-face interaction, including both verbal and non-verbal language. He has worked closely with architects in Los Angeles and product designers in Stockholm, Sweden.

Pamela J. Stewart and Andrew Strathern are a wife and husband research team with a long history of joint publications and research. They have published more than 35 books and 175 articles on their research in the Pacific region, Europe (Scotland and Ireland), and in Asia (Taiwan and China). They are the editors of the Ritual Studies Monograph Series and the Ethnographic Studies in Medical Anthropology Series with Carolina Academic Press. Their coauthored and coedited books include *Witchcraft, Sorcery, Rumors and Gossip* (Cambridge University Press, 2004); *Asian Ritual Systems: Syncretisms and Ruptures* (Carolina Academic Press, 2007); *Exchange and Sacrifice* (Carolina Academic Press, 2008) and *Religious and Ritual Change: Cosmologies and Histories* (Carolina Academic Press, 2009).

C. Jason Throop is an Assistant Professor in the Department of Anthropology at UCLA. He is the author of the forthcoming book *Suffering and Sentiment: Exploring the Vicissitudes of Experience and Pain in Yap* (University of California Press), which is based upon extensive research on subjectivity, morality, and pain in Yap, Federated States of Micronesia. Broadly speaking, his research interests are aligned with medical and psychocultural approaches to understanding how cultural, interpersonal, and personal processes of meaning-making differentially structure the dynamics of subjective experience and social action.

INDEX

actors: moral, 87–91; perspective of, 42–44,
  59–60; primary intentions of, 59, 91–94;
  psychology of, 52–53, 59–60; willful, 19,
  22–23, 30–31, 186–87; what is "at stake"
  for, 59, 60

act-phases (Casey), 43–44

affective action (Weber), 11

African Americans: focus on family/commu-
  nity support, 64–67; focus on strength
  and will power, 54, 60, 61–64

Agamemnon, 143–45

agency: anthropology and theories of, 12–18,
  29, 51; chains of, 148, 152, 178, 183; dual
  models of, 121, 135–36; experience of,
  198n5; increased by death, 151–53; Maya
  soul beliefs and, 108–9, 117–21; negotiation of, 117–20; not same as will, 136–37;
  and unconscious motives simultaneous,
  191; vs. autonomy, 77, 84

agentic shift, 75, 77–78, 87, 98, 99. *See also*
  direct willing/supernormal effects

Alcoholics Anonymous (AA), 58

American Psychiatric Association, 158, 161

ancestors, actions/knowledge imputed to,
  145–47, 156

Anishinaabe. *See* Ojibwa/Anishinaabe

anthropology, psychological: and agency,
  12–18, 29, 51; literature on will in, 2–4,
  9–12, 50, 69–73; study of emotions, 51, 57;
  work of, 1–2

anticipation/goal directedness: defined, 34–36;
  and gradient of willing, 44–45; imagination and, 43–44; and other correlates of
  willing, 36, 180; toward completed act,
  39, 42

Appadurai, Arjun, 155

Arendt, Hannah, 35, 198n3

Arjuna, 142–44, 181–82

attention: cultural organization of, 46–48;
  defined, 41; somatic modes of, 56; will as
  reorientation of, 55–60, 185

authorship: ascribed to others, 75–81; of
  dreams, 117; emotion of (Wegner), 75,
  79–80; and moral responsibility, 94,
  96, 117; own-ness and, 192, 200n7;
  past and future, 76. *See also* agentic
  shift

autonomy: bad medicine and loss of, 85–86,
  100; Maya skepticism regarding, 120–21;
  vs. personal agency, 77, 84